ASTROLOG II:

FAMILY, RELATIONSHIPS AND HEALTH

Louise Huber et al

HopeWell
Knutsford, England

A selection of articles first published in German
in the magazine *Astrolog* over the period 1990-2007

This first English translation published by HopeWell 2009

HopeWell,
PO Box 118, Knutsford
Cheshire WA16 8TG, U.K.

Copyright © 2009 Astrological Psychology Association Ltd.

All rights reserved. No part of this publication may be reproduced, sorted in a retrieval system, or transmitted in any form or by any means, electronic or otherwise, without the prior permission of the publisher. Reviewers may quote brief passages.

Translated by Heather Ross
Edited by Barry Hopewell

Jacket design by Barry Hopewell

ISBN 978-0-9558339-0-8

In memory of Agnes Shellens

1921 – 2005

*Her generous bequest made possible
the publication of this book.*

Symbols of the Planets

Sun	☉	♂	Mars
Moon	☽	♃	Jupiter
Saturn	♄	♅	Uranus
Mercury	☿	♆	Neptune
Venus	♀	♇	Pluto
ascending Moon Node	☊		

Symbols of the Signs

Aries	♈	♎	Libra
Taurus	♉	♏	Scorpio
Gemini	♊	♐	Sagittarius
Cancer	♋	♑	Capricorn
Leo	♌	♒	Aquarius
Virgo	♍	♓	Pisces

Abbreviations

AC = Ascendant   HC = House Cusp
IC = Imum Coeli   LP = Low Point
DC = Descendant   BP = Balance Point
MC = Medium Coeli   GM = Golden Mean

Aspects

Green	Semi-sextile	Angle of 30°	⚺
	Quincunx	Angle of 150°	⚻
Blue	Sextile	Angle of 60°	✶
	Trine	Angle of 120°	△
Red	Square	Angle of 90°	□
	Opposition	Angle of 180°	☍
Orange	Conjunction	Angle of 0°	☌

Contents

Introduction	**1**
Part 1: The Family	**3**
The Family Model – New Perspectives Wolfhard H. König	5
Family Secrets Harald Zittlau	17
Family Counselling Angelika Kraft-Boehm	27
The Family Reflected in the Horoscope Birgit Braun	43
Part 2: Children and Upbringing	**65**
The Child's Horoscope as an Aid to Upbringing Louise Huber	67
The Child's Horoscope Holger Oehmichen	87
Children's Horoscopes Rainer Bauer	97
The Horoscope as an Aid in the Teaching of Gifted Children Karin Goebel	139
Part 3: Relationships	**149**
Some Thoughts on Relationships Harald Zittlau	151
Relationship as a Developmental Process Louise Huber	169
A Life Not Worth Living Verena Bieri	187

The Transformation of the Heroine Dr. Reinhard Müller	195
Snow White Ruth Schmidhauser	205

Part 4: Health and Therapies — 217

The Language of the Body Bruno Huber	219
I am My Own Doctor Louise Huber	225
When the Psyche makes the Body Ill Agnes Hauser	251
When the Sweet Things in Life make us Ill Birgit Braun	259
The Tarot and Astrological Psychology Ruth Schmidhauser	267
Images of Man Christian U. Vogel	275

Contacts and Resources   307

Introduction

Along with the development of psychology, the 20th century saw the emergence of psychological approaches to astrology, through pioneers such as Fankhauser, Ring and Rudhyar. In the 1950s the young Bruno and Louise Huber developed their own system of astrological psychology after extensive research done in collaboration with Roberto Assagioli at his Institute of Psychosynthesis. In what became known as the 'Huber Method' they aimed to combine the best of astrology, depth psychology and the discoveries coming from their own research.

In 1964 Bruno and Louise founded the Astrological Psychology Institute (API) in Zurich, and devoted their lives to counselling, teaching and further research into this approach. Since then over ten thousand students have been trained with API, many achieving the Institute's professional Diploma.

In 1981 the German-language magazine *Astrolog* was established, and has been published bi-monthly since then. Each of the now-over-150 issues of *Astrolog* contains articles by contributors who include the Hubers, API teachers, students and Diploma holders, many of whom are professionals in other disciplines. Subjects have included amplification of aspects of the Huber Method, new ideas and research, practical experience, including relating to other disciplines, case studies etc. There is thus a large volume of experience and knowledge embedded in the past issues of *Astrolog*.

In 1983 an English-language school, API(UK), was established by Richard Llewellyn and Pam Tyler. API(UK) has since enrolled over 1000 students, many of whom have gained their own Diplomas and continue to use astrological psychology, either on its own or in conjunction with other disciplines. In the meantime, the Hubers' eight books on astrological psychology have become available in English and are sold across the world. There are thus now many people interested in this practical and proven approach.

Agnes Shellens was supportive of API(UK) from the early days, and helped its development, translating a number of articles from *Astrolog* into English, plus Bruno Huber's book *Astrological Psychosynthesis*. Agnes was unfortunately unable to continue this work in her later years, and it was with sadness that we learned of her death in 2005.

It was a pleasant surprise, some time later, to learn that Agnes had left a sum of money as a bequest to API(UK). It was deemed appropriate that this money should be used to make available in the English language more of that treasury of information in the back issues of *Astrolog*. This is the second of two books representing the fruit of Agnes's final generous demonstration of her support.

The set of articles selected for both books was chosen with a view to including material which would be of most value and interest, in the context of what is already available in the Hubers' books and the various publications produced by API(UK). We also aimed to include a reasonably wide selection of different authors.

All the articles have been translated by Heather Ross, who will be familiar to many as the translator of the books *Aspect Pattern Astrology* and *The Planets and their Psychological Meaning*.

Special thanks are due to Joyce Hopewell and Jane Ritson for their efforts in checking through the results of Heather's excellent translations plus my editorial adjustments.

This book has been structured into four parts, each containing articles related to a specific theme:

    Part 1: The Family
    Part 2: Children and Upbringing
    Part 3: Relationships
    Part 4: Health and Therapies

At the beginning of each part you will find a brief introduction to the articles contained therein.

We hope that you will find this book, and the previous volume *Astrolog I: Life and Meaning*, a valuable resource and a fitting memorial to the generosity of spirit of Agnes Shellens.

Barry Hopewell

Editor

Part 1: The Family

The family is perhaps the most important influence on the lives of most people. Here we group a selection of articles showing the power of astrological psychology and the Family Model in helping to uncover these formative influences and thus enable change in our lives and even those of succeeding generations.

The first two articles take a more theoretical view of the development and use of the Family Model and other astrological features in the light of modern psychological understanding.

The Family Model – New Perspectives, by Wolfhard H. König
 Considers the implications of the evolution of social roles and new insights of developmental psychology for the Family Model of astrological psychollogy.

Family Secrets, by Harald Zittlau
 Considers the subject of cross-generational influences and family secrets and suggests approaches of astrological psychology that can help.

The second two articles report on real life examples of use of astrological psychology in the counselling of a family.

Family Counselling, by Angelika Kraft-Boehm
 Gives an example of counselling a nuclear family using radix and moon node charts and the Family Model.

The Family reflected in the Horoscope, by Birgit Braun
 Assesses significant factors in the charts of five members of a nuclear family, concentrating on features of the radix charts and various relationship 'click' charts.

Readers who are unfamiliar with the use of astrological psychology in a family context, and particularly the Family Model, are recommended in the first instance to read the following introductory works:

The Cosmic Egg Timer, by Joyce Hopewell and Richard Llewellyn
A basic introduction suitable for beginners.

The Living Birth Chart, by Joyce Hopewell
A deeper and more practical workbook taking it to the next stage.

The Family Model and personality integration are covered in more depth in:

Astrological Psychosynthesis, by Bruno Huber
A psychological introduction to astrological psychology.

The Family Model – New Perspectives

Wolfhard H. König

First published in AstroLog Issues 104-106, June-October 1998

In the modern Western world the traditional model of the nuclear family (i.e. father, mother and an average of two children), with strict division of labour and roles for mother and father, is increasingly being replaced by new domestic arrangements. I include the USA when I talk about the West, as there we are dealing with similar psychological changes against a similar cultural background. The development of the nuclear family model took place mainly after the Renaissance and during the Industrial Revolution.

Before this, the 'extended family' model dominated, usually among peasant folk. This involved several generations and often also several degrees of kinship living on one farm, which was communally run and was the common source of economic survival. There was not such a division between life and work as there is today. Even among the middle classes in the towns and cities, several generations usually lived together (and carried out a trade).

This family model was even more prevalent in earlier clan societies, and it still dominates in the third world. A clan is usually formed of several large families, which not only ensures economic survival but also achieves political influence and is therefore a powerful force (witness the infamous military confrontations of the different clans in the Lebanon). The clan controls and determines each member's individual development, from choosing a career to a marriage partner; these are life choices that individuals are not allowed to make for themselves. It was initially the freedom of thought that developed in the Renaissance and later in the French Revolution that led to the breakup of clan ties. More and more people wanted to make their own life choices. Although this involved renouncing the security and protection of the clan, the economic importance of the clans decreased as more people moved to towns and cities to work in factories. The nuclear family arose with the father/husband as the sole breadwinner. Previously children had been raised in large families, where the grandparents were around to care for the children so that the women too could work on the farm. Now though, women were increasingly responsible for looking after the home and children by themselves. (Schiller: *"The husband must go out into the hostile world, while the woman rules virtuously at home..."*) This 'nuclear family' model was dominant in the 20th century.

The parents' emotional roles are clearly defined. The mother, who is also usually the biological mother, looks after spiritual and emotional care. She must be available more or less round the clock, especially in the all-important early years of childhood (1st and 2nd years of life). The mother is responsible for intuitively knowing and  meeting the baby's needs, a role that Winnicott has called "holding". In older developmental psychology textbooks, it is obvious that by allocating this task to the mother, the father has been left out.

The father's role is equally one-sided. While hardly involved at all in the child's early years, he is later responsible for leading the child "out into the world" (the domain where he is already active). The emphasis is now on independence, toughness and perseverance and should be acquired by identifying with the father. It is seen as the father's role to begin the child's individuation process (is it thought that mothers cannot do this because women are not supposed to be individualised at all…)

These clear role divisions are misleading right from the start as they arise from the confusion of roles and archetypal tasks on the one hand and the real people, the father and the mother on the other. When we consider the changes in family structure from the 1960s onwards, it is vital to distinguish between archetypal roles (paternal or maternal) and the people who perform these roles, whether they are biological parents or not.

The increasing frequency of separation and divorce and the subsequent founding of new families means that family structures are changing; children are increasing likely to form close relationships with people to whom they are not related. This leads to some important consequences from the point of view of family dynamics.

The number of single parent families, usually mothers but increasingly fathers too, is rising rapidly. These children grow up in a household with only one adult. Two things can happen: firstly, they live with the mother and often have little or no contact with the father. Secondly, the mother finds a new partner and the child becomes close to this stepfather. This relationship with a stepfather can happen at a very early age, for example in the first or second year of life, which is a defining life phase. The same scenario can also occur when a single father finds a new partner, who then becomes the child's stepmother. According to recent statistics (see Rauchfleisch), in Western countries, almost half of children now grow up in stepfamilies (where a stepfather or stepmother is present). In addition, there are increasingly stepfamilies in which children of several different marriages of their parents live together, so that stepbrothers and sisters also become important attachment figures.

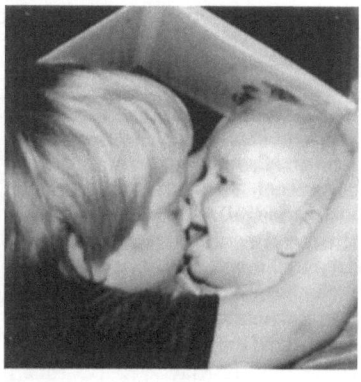

Modern depth psychologists reacted quickly to these changed circumstances and soon began to deal with the issue of how these circumstances affect the child's identification with father and mother with reference to the formation of inner representatives (imagos) of the father and mother, which are crucial for psychological stability and development.

The first was Winnicott, who researched this issue with regard to the experience of mothering that is internalised by the child. He talks about "good-enough mothering" (1961) as a requirement for the child's development of basic trust and a stable self. The term "good-enough mothering" means that the child receives good maternal attention, i.e. has a good experience of the maternal archetype. It may be the biological mother who is the primary provider of this experience. It can also be the biological mother and the grandmother. Good enough mothering can also be provided by a foster mother or nanny. Bruno Bettelheim's research in Israeli kibbutzim went one step further. There the baby lives with the biological mother for just the first three months and is then cared for in the daytime in the nursery by the metapelet (usually more than one). These children therefore have a "mother group" and often do not develop a close relationship with one person or the biological mother. It seems that the protection of the larger group can be particularly important (Jung/Neumann had already referred to the fact that groups can provide important archetypal maternal functions.)

And finally, men/fathers can possess better maternal archetype qualities than women/mothers. Some men can be very good at mothering and building empathetic relationships. In the case of patients with "early dysfunction" (i.e. dysfunction in the basic trust relationship in the early years of life) male therapists must perform holding, i.e. forming good basic trust relationships and be able to provide a "correcting emotional experience". Otherwise, all therapies with early dysfunction patients would fail when the therapist is a man, which is not the case. The male therapist can therefore provide a maternal archetypal experience. It can therefore happen that in a family the father is better able to provide a sensitive, empathetic holding experience than the mother. For stable psychological development of the child it appears to be of fundamental importance that the child has good enough mothering irrespective of who provides it, whether biological mother, foster mother, childminder, father or a combination of these. It appears that the child ultimately accumulates the total of "good enough mothering" which allows him to have a positive experience of himself and the world (OK reaction).

This experience can naturally also be provided by a single mother or father. It may well be that men still usually react more nervously and insecurely to babies or small children due to their own upbringing and lack of experience. But we are increasingly seeing the type of "new father" who gets involved with his child from the start and forms a holding relationship, i.e. participates in "good enough mothering."

What is the Modern Paternal Archetype?

Independence, individuation in the sense of "finding and going one's own way" (even in the face of criticisms from the collective) and the ability to handle conflict, to conquer a "piece of the world", to be a "centre of personal initiative" (Kohut) summarise the paternal experiences the child needs. If the father is capable of providing this, he will give the child a triangular experience – a different kind of relationship from the holding experience. Here the father is the "third party", who stands outside the close symbiotic mother-child relationship. His role is to provide an alternative relationship, outside the maternal bond, thereby increasing the potential scope of the child's freedom and development. Modern developmental psychology calls this process triangulation, as the father is the third party who complements the mother-child relationship.

Two Important Issues

Firstly: what happens to the triangular experience in the case of single mothers?

Single mothers or women need to muster great courage to manage alone. The child becomes aware of the mother's individualisation, which actually corresponds to the paternal archetypal qualities that every woman possesses, and can use them as a role model. The mother must then provide the child with both archetypal models, the holding experience and the triangular experience, which is very demanding and challenging, but certainly not impossible. Likewise, the single father also has no alternative but to act as mother and father to the child. Actually, everyone has both archetypes within them and can therefore put them into practice. Both parents can take on the maternal role, i.e. provide a sensitive holding experience for their child when required, and both can set goals for themselves that they work towards, thereby providing a role model for individuation.

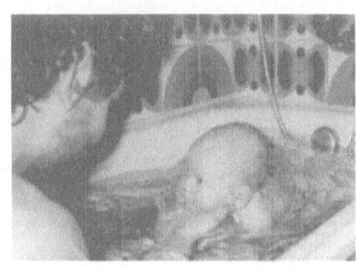

Additionally, children of single parents will get as much triangular experience with people (men and women) outside the family as they can. While I was studying, one of my fellow students was a single mother who enjoyed going to coffee shops to study and read books, etc. She took her five-year-old daughter with her, who kept an eye on the door and approached men who entered the shop. She went up and spoke to them and asked when they would be coming back again. This led to many friendships and eventually even one for her mother. The important thing was that the mother allowed her daughter to have these experiences and to explore her environment.

Children therefore seek out their own "paternal" experiences: be it with teachers, neighbours or older pupils at school. They all help to provide an alternative to the child's exclusive relationship with the mother (or father).

Incidentally, the search for further, complementary maternal or paternal attachment figures is important in the latency phase (ages 6-12) for every child, even if there are good role models within their own family. And such experiences pave the way for successful separation from the parents in adolescence.

Secondly, the father may be physically present in the family but not emotionally accessible to his children.

We recently had many such cases at our psychological institute in Munich: the fathers went to work in the morning, came home in the evening, ate quickly and then went off to practise their hobbies where nobody, not even their sons, could reach them. We call them "absent fathers". They played no role in the family dynamics; they never constituted a "third force" in the family, an alternative to the power of the mother. And the children had to put up with it. "I didn't have a father" said one of these patients. He had no real paternal experience, although a "father" was constantly (physically) present, and counted among the official family numbers.

To sum up: paternal archetype experience is possible even if there is no father physically present and it is (unfortunately) not necessarily provided if the biological father is present, or lives with the family.

Conversely, a single father may provide good mothering while at the same time also setting boundaries and providing a model of individuation. But in this case, the child will look for other good maternal experiences, for protection in groups, for example. For this reason, peer groups can be particularly important in early adolescence.

Now the opportunities and problems created by step families should be mentioned. If for example the holding or triangular experiences are not sufficiently present in the primary family, in the step family, with the entry of a new partner, there is another opportunity for good maternal or paternal experience. However, loyalty problems always arise between the primary and the step family. The child often feels guilty if they become attached to a new mother or father figure in a good relationship. Is it not a "betrayal" of the biological parents? After all, they will still be the child's biological parents for their lifetime. However, if they have failed as psychological parents, it is a great opportunity to deal with it as a step parent.

Modern depth psychology has recognised that it is necessary to differentiate between two things:

firstly, the paternal or maternal archetypal experience, the child's holding or triangular experiences, which enables the child to construct a stable inner mother or father representative, and

secondly the people who contribute to these internalised experiences. They may be the biological mother, nanny, grandmother, childminder, biological father, stepfather etc. A whole group of people can therefore contribute towards the provision of a good maternal or paternal experience.

In future we must therefore make this distinction between the roles or relationship experiences and the people who provide them. In the case of psychosomatic illnesses (like neurodermatitis), modern psychoanalytical literature refers not to "dysfunctional mother-child relationship" but to "lack of good mothering" or more precisely: "dysfunction in the basic trust relationship on the one hand and lack of delimitation and detachment on the other – i.e. the existence of an ambivalent bond". It is therefore no longer the responsibility, or even the fault, of individual people or certain genders. There is no longer any truth in the saying "everything is the mother's fault" – or even the father's, if the child experiences problems with separation and independence. Here too, Winnicott was quick to understand that it is a question of a failure of the "social environment". What a child needs, according to Winnicott, is a "good enough social environment".

The social environment is provided by many people: the biological mother and father, grandparents, schools, social culture, etc. However, the people and circumstances responsible for the child's early care (until age 2) are particularly important, as during this phase the child is so dependent on those around it and is extremely open to the relationship experiences that it undergoes and internalises.

Winnicott's term "mothering" should also be supplemented by an analogous term "fathering" (which tellingly does not yet exist). Then the Jungian terms for the maternal archetypal or paternal archetypal experience would be most clearly distinguishable from the people or groups who provide them.

Consequences for Astrology

I assume that developments that are currently taking place in depth psychology will sooner or later also be adopted by serious astrological psychology. After all, both areas have important common features: the consultation process and the contact (or therapy) with clients (or patients), who come to the consultation with questions and needs on the issues mentioned above.

In the family model of astrological psychology, the Moon represents the archetypal child's experiences, Saturn the archetypal maternal experiences and the Sun the archetypal paternal experiences. On the astrological scene there is universal acceptance of the Sun as a reflection of paternal experiences. It is not surprising that the attribution of maternal experiences is more problematic. Modern depth psychology even distinguishes between the "symbiotic mother" and the "separation mother" or "reality mother".

The symbiosis mother (Moon experience) provides the early experiences of basic trust relationship; if this goes wrong it leads to early dysfunction (which makes psychoses or borderline and narcissistic disorders more likely). A symbiotic–merging experience is however only experienced by the child (Moon position); the individuated mother is not completely involved in the symbiotic bond, she just makes this Moon experience available to her child.

The mother who provides both bonding and stability, which quite crucially includes the setting of boundaries, is the Saturn mother.

It sometimes seems that astrology does not take into account modern developmental psychology from Mahler to Stern. But nearly all significant impulses to further development in modern depth psychology come from this developmental psychology research, e.g. the development of new therapeutic techniques for borderline or narcissistic disorders, or self disorders, as they are now called.

However, based on the above findings concerning changes in family structure, hardly any universal conclusions can be reached from the planetary positions related to individual people.

If a child grows up in a nuclear family with "traditional" mother and father, without significant role division, then it may still be possible to attribute a planet to each person to a certain extent.

For example, the Moon may reflect symbiotic and basic trust experiences from the child's perspective (as described in Daniel Stern's latest developmental psychology). Saturn may reflect the concrete experiences of delimitation and separation, but also bonding and protection (see Margaret Mahler on the 'second birth'), and the Sun may reflect the triangular experience with the father.

In the complex examples described above though, it is much more difficult to make a planet/person attribution (e.g. Sun as father-role, even as biological father). It would mean that the Sun in the horoscope represents all paternal archetypal, triangular experiences, irrespective of who provides them, that Saturn represents all experiences with boundaries, stability and being held, irrespective of who provides them, and that the Moon represents all good, basic trust forming, symbiotic experiences, no matter who provides them.

The planets in the horoscope therefore indicate the type of archetypal experiences a child can undergo and internalise, and which representatives of parental and child roles they may reflect. These representatives fundamentally affect the type of parental experience the future parents can give to their children.

It is therefore possible that in the horoscope of a child of a single mother, the Sun is in a strong position because all-important triangular influences were provided by the mother herself or by people other than the father. Likewise, the horoscope of a child with a single father may contain a well-placed Moon because the father was very empathetic and other carers have provided a sensitive upbringing.

So how do we astrologers deal with complex family circumstances?

1st Example: Female Patient

A patient was put into a home by her mother as soon as she was born, and lived the first 18 months of her life there. Her "mother" was the nurses in the orphanage. She is no longer in touch with any of them. There was no father figure. According to modern developmental psychology, at least by the end of the first year of development, the patient will have developed its first close personal relationship, have internalised a real mother figure, but today she cannot remember it. That is not surprising, as we very rarely remember anything before the fourth year of life, apart from a few exceptions. But she was suddenly separated from this "good mothering experience" when she left the home, which constitutes a rupture in the relationship experience.

Afterwards she went to good foster parents who cared for her until age 6. The foster mother must have been a caring woman, but the foster father in particular appears to have formed a very loving relationship with the patient, an experience she had not known before. Memories of how she trustingly held his hand and spent her days in his workshop are still among her most valued inner possessions.

Then her biological mother married and her stepfather wanted to take the children back into the family (the mother had four children by four different fathers.) The patient was legally and violently separated from the care of the foster parents (her main trauma is that no good relationship can last.) At first, she fell into the role of the family scapegoat and was often beaten by mother and stepfather. From age 11 the stepfather sexually abused her and the mother beat her for being a "rival" and a bad child.

This patient has internalised three different layers of parental experience. The "primary mothering" in the orphanage, the good foster father and the stepfamily in which she lived between the ages of 6 and 18, which she suddenly left and later confronted her stepfather with his actions in a therapeutic context. There are three different layers of both maternal and paternal experience: how is this reflected by the positions of Moon, Saturn and Sun in the horoscope?

In the paternal experience, the good relationship with her foster father must have been deeply influential, but also the abuse at the hands of her stepfather. The latter was "very kind" to the patient, and "worshipped" her, but also abused her sexually. All these paternal experiences necessarily affect the patient's father image.

As for the mother image; first there was mothering in the orphanage, which we know little about. It cannot have been so bad though, as at this time the research of R. Spitz had already made an impact. At the end of the 1950s, Spitz researched orphanages in the USA and found significantly higher death rates of infants and young children than in normal families, despite the provision of perfect medical care and good nutrition. The children died from inadequate attention, from the lack of love.

Too few carers looked after too many babies and small children. Sooner or later, the children fell into the state of "anaclitic depression", and then died of some illness (virus, etc.) So now we know that there must be good enough mothering, i.e. a good enough ratio of carers per small child to stop this happening. Modern orphanages have taken on board these important findings. For this reason, during the time when the patient was in the orphanage, she should have been able to form a relatively successful basic trust relationship.

She then went into a basically positive relationship experience with foster parents, in which the mother apparently provided stability and order (Saturn experience), but the father in particular was able to provide her with a sensitive, warm and close relationship. There is no doubt that this constituted a holding relationship experience for the patient. Then came the forced separation. In the face of great resistance, the mother and stepfather removed the daughter from the positive situation with the foster parents: she was snatched and taken away in a car. The modern way, i.e. allowing the child to make the decision in court, was obviously not considered, as she would have stayed in the good relationship with the foster parents.

Now followed the hostile relationship with the biological mother and the sexual abuse by the stepfather, which continued until the patient was 18.

2nd Example: S

S's mother became pregnant at 17, when she lived in one room with her mother. She would have liked to keep her child, but did not see how she could as an apprentice. She gave the child to an orphanage. S. lived in three different homes before the age of 2½.

Then she went to live with foster parents. Why the homes changed is not known. They were all run by nuns. Was there a father there? "Yes" said the client "there was God the Father, and everyone worshipped him." God the Father as the only man? "And there was the devil – he was also a man." An illustrious choice of father imagos!

With the foster parents there was bickering and fighting. The relationship never worked as child and foster mother did not get on; the foster father liked the child but was only there at weekends. After two years she was "given away" again to a children's clinic in Munich. After 6 months she was fortuitously brought to an SOS Children's Village in Ammersee. She stayed there in stable conditions until age 17. There was a village mother, who the client considered as her own (psychological) mother and still sees today. There was also a big group of village siblings, and the patient is still in touch with many of them. Here at least she found good maternal protection and affection. Was there a father? There was a children's village leader and a village foreman/handyman (both traditionally men). The patient had quite a good relationship with the village leader as she was a close friend of his daughter. At age 17, S. left the village and became independent.

Here again we are dealing with several layers of parental experiences. There are firstly the experiences in orphanages. It is unusual to change orphanages twice, and the client had to get used to new forms of mothering. This could have been a big problem in her second year, when a child needs a stable mother image.

Then came the unsuccessful years with foster parents, despite which she has good memories of the foster father.

It was not until she entered the children's village that S. found the protection of a family and a stable lifestyle. The fact that her subsequent development has been positive and stable shows that she must have experienced "good enough mothering" in the village. Hermann Gmeiner, founder of the children's villages, stated: "I wanted nothing more than to provide the uprooted child a world of protection that it needs in order to thrive." This certainly seems to have been achieved for this client.

Can we not also assume that Moon, Saturn and Sun reflect all these parental experiences? But to what extent are these levels involved in the positions of these planets?

These are two examples where a simple linear application of the Family Model is impossible. There are many more such examples.

It is therefore not only depth psychology but also modern astrological psychology that must also carry out research and find convincing answers. This is only possible in the consulting room, by analysing people's real lives, and the findings must do them justice.

Both horoscopes are provided for your consideration.

Looking to the Future

We have discussed the consequences of changes in the way families are structured and people relate to each other. Here I would also like to bring up man's modern questioning of even the biological pre-conditions for childhood and parenthood, taking it into unknown territory. There is the case of a Californian woman who, before dying of cancer, had twelve fertilisable eggs removed and frozen. Her parents found a surrogate mother to carry the embryos for a fee.

Such a child will have to live with the fact that its biological mother died when it was a deep-frozen embryo, that its father is an anonymous sperm donor and that it exists because of the wishes of its grandparents. How long will they be there for the child? Who will replace them then? And what can it mean for a person's soul, his identity, his self-image to have such a background? And what would his horoscope look like? And last but not least, what implications does this have for us all?

Bibliography:

1) Rauchfleisch, Udo: *Alternative Familienformen*
2) Buchheim, P. et al: *Neue Lebensformen – Zeitkrankheiten – und Psychotherapie*
3) Kaplan, Louise: *Die zweite Geburt. Die ersten Lebensjahre des Kindes.*
4) Mertens, Wolfgang: *Psychoanalytische Entwicklung der Psychosexualitaet und der Geschlechtsidentität*
5) Visher und Visher: *Stiefeltern, Stiefkinder und ihre Familien*

◻ ◻ ◻ ◻ ◻

Family Secrets

The Phenomenon of Cross-Generational Influence

Harald Zittlau

First published in AstroLog Issue 127, April 2002

We are fascinated by stories that our parents or grandparents tell about their parents and relatives. We may find such anecdotes amusing, shocking or thought-provoking. They are particularly interesting if we can recognise ourselves in them, and similarities in terms of personal qualities or even a similar destiny. Often structures that we have inherited are inappropriate for our own lives, or they may support us or help us to find ourselves.

"Like father, like son" as the old saying goes. From a genetic point of view, this seems to be completely accurate and many people seem to blindly follow their genetic programming on their life journey. This used to mean that the son followed in the father's professional footsteps, and the daughters married as well as possible. In other cultures many people are still unable to leave their own caste. But there are also many examples of people from the poorest circumstances who had very successful careers or we hear of children of rich or famous parents who "end up in the gutter".

The following thoughts should encourage us as practising or future counsellors to take an objective look at our ancestors. Many problems that people have to overcome during their lives have a connection with their family environment, and in consultations, we deal with questions of how upbringing, social milieu or genes affect the here and now. ("What is the cause of my depression, why didn't my father love me, etc.?")

It is often very difficult to see such connections. The effects of the physical, emotional and mental legacy unfold subversively and may not be perceived as significant in our lives for some time.

To my mind, inheritance is not a one-off act of the transmission of qualities at birth. It is rather a very complex, dynamic process of transferring all elements of being.

It is possible to distinguish between three different areas of this transfer, as follows.

1. Genetic Inheritance

Research into the transfer of genetic information lies in the domain of the natural sciences (biology, chemistry, medicine, genetic engineering, etc.) For a while now, high tech laboratories have been working on the "mapping" of the human genome. The enormous complexity of the creation is indicated by the modern biomedical knowledge, that a person possesses about 30,000 – 40,000 genes, which correspond to 400,000 to several million proteins, the so-called proteome.

The relatively "simple" genetic code is composed of 4 bases and forms the "hardware" or the "database" of human biology. This genetic information remains the same throughout our lives. Only about 3 per cent of a person's illnesses are rooted in their genetic structure or result from so-called genetic defects. The code of the proteome is composed – much more complicatedly – of 20 amino acids and corresponds to the "software" in human biology. It guides the majority of biochemical processes (hormone, messengers, signals, energy, disposal of waste, etc.) The composition of the proteins in the cells is constantly changing, as is also therefore the information about the overall condition of the biological system. Well over 90% of all illnesses are caused by these metabolic processes and nearly all medical manipulation takes place on this level (with medicines).

The proteome constructs and regenerates itself according to information provided by the genome. However, how the user (person concerned) uses their software (proteome) does appear to be significant, i.e. how he treats his body during his life.

Still largely unexplained are the interactions between the existing genetic basis (biological basic configuration) and proteomic processes (living and environmental conditions, moral conduct/way of life) of one or more generations, which lead to a modification of the genetic code.

2. Socio-Cultural Inheritance

This refers to social, economic and societal conditions on the one hand and cultural, political and religious orientations on the other. Over thousands of years, these two worlds formed a naturally continuous structure, which it was difficult if not impossible for individuals to break out of. With the awakening of individual awareness after the discovery of new spiritual dimensions (Uranus, Neptune, Pluto), the firmly established relationship between individual and society started to change: people increasingly had to learn to take responsibility for shaping their own lives. All historical models of society are undergoing huge upheavals and even the apparently stable forms of world religions are affected. The forces of evolution are driving people to expand their consciousness in order to achieve an optimal balance between the self-determination of the individual and the interests of the collective. In this respect, mankind is still involved in unrestrained confrontation over living space, supremacy, exploitation of resources and political or religious convictions. The fundamental survival of man as a species is dependent on the outcome of this struggle.

3. Psychological-Spiritual Inheritance

This encompasses the developmental state of qualities within the family in terms of problem solving strategies, inward and outward communication, role assignment, etc. This area is vital for the psychological development of individual family members, and is where take place the reinforcing and challenging of autonomous interests and needs, social skills and the capacity to love, and feelings of self-esteem.

It is also the area of "inherited waste", traumas, unresolved or potential conflicts with previous generations that have already influenced grandparents and parents, sometimes even psychologically "damaged" them and is otherwise know as the "family secret".

The three areas mentioned above are in a state of complex interaction. For example, emotional-psychological achievements within the family group can protect it from unconsciously adapting to political, cultural or religious demands from the social environment. However, the social environment can help an individual family member to free themselves from rigid, internal structures and pressures (break away).

The student movements at the end of the 1960s and the growth in religious extremism at the turn of the century are examples of social processes that exercise a certain pressure on the socio-cultural genetic condition of the people concerned.

The conditions, factors and chronological aspects of the modification of the genetic potential through environmental influences or upheavals in the family milieu are still insufficiently researched. A scientific definition of the breakdown or attribution of parts or features of the genetic code that originate from individuals in the chain of generations will only be possible in the very distant future, if at all.

Astrological psychology and counselling are primarily concerned with the generational issue from the perspective of developmental psychology, although genetic and socio-cultural considerations in the individual horoscope will receive more attention in the future.

Family Secrets

Family secrets in general encapsulate social-psychological, neurotic or psychotic syndromes or complexes, which are passed on from generation to generation within a family group. These may be dealt with consciously by some family members and suffered unconsciously by others. Their effects may be positive or negative.

There are secrets that are worth preserving, which are part of the family identity and provide social or cultural stability. There are also darker secrets that are destructive and which attack the living conditions of the family and individual members or can even destroy lives. Then they act like a curse, which can extend through generations in certain patterns of destiny.

Family secrets range from simple rituals or traditional customs to serious burdens of guilt, like incest, abuse or death. From a positive point of view, they can be deliberately embedded in the family tradition and are often carried by individuals within the family and passed on. They serve as a way of sealing the family off from the outside, if for example particular abilities or special knowledge are involved (secret recipe) or, for self-protection in "hostile" environments or to protect assets.

In the most serious cases though, the people concerned are usually unaware of these family secrets. They revolve around family and social taboo subjects like addictions, betrayal, sexuality (incest, abuse) or death and can lead to long-term chain reactions in more and more new forms.

Dark family secrets reoccur when the social and communication skills in the family unit are not sufficient to take conflicts out into the open and find adequate solutions. If the family is too weak to regulate taboo transgressions and there is no strong integration figure present to reveal the problem, events must be repressed and denied.

If the reality is repressed, those repressed feelings soon generate compensative mechanisms that have a depressing effect on the environment. The greater the traumatic power, the greater the danger that it will carry on devouring generation after generation like a festering sore, until it eventually explodes and takes its toll.

In many cases, the creator of a trauma puts enormous psychic pressure on the (usually weaker) members of the family unit (codes of honour, pledges of secrecy, fear, humiliation, withdrawal of affection, etc.) This behaviour reinforces the taboo atmosphere, which in turn passes on corresponding messages in the form of energetic ballast.

At some point, the cause of the guilt and fear disappears behind a wall of repression and silence. Such a burden can overshadow all social interactions and in the long term diminish the quality of life of the family members, although the individual people concerned have not had any conscious relationship with the source of the problem for a long time.

A grandfather can cover up his gambling addiction to some degree, but his uncle may not be able to shake off his addiction to drugs. What started as a secret affair can today end with an inability to commit to relationships.

The contagious atmosphere of family secrets can work like a "morphogenetic field", which structures and restricts psychic development. In this way, betrayal, suicide or unatoned-for murders that occurred long before the birth of a certain family member, can give this person feelings of self-abnegation, paranoia or deep depression.

In extreme cases, family secrets cause almost "paranormal" compulsive behaviour or lead to unconscious identification with another destiny.

An infamous example of the effects of a tragic family secret is provided by the acting family the Fondas. At the ages of 10 and 13, the siblings Jane and Peter had to cope with the sudden death of their mother. Their father explained to them that their mother had had a heart attack. They were not allowed to attend the funeral, but they found out that their father had returned to show business the very same day. He seemed to have forgotten his wife very quickly.

Years later, the Fondas suffered a series of mysterious "strokes of fate". Two of Henry Fonda's best friends committed suicide. Peter Fonda had an accident in which he was shot in the stomach and nearly bled to death. The following year, Peter also lost a girlfriend who committed suicide. It appeared as though the Fondas were unconsciously seeking out people who no longer wanted to live.

Jane then discovered the true background of her mother's death. Following a nervous breakdown, she was sent to a mental hospital where she took her own life. The father did not want to tell the children the truth, possibly because he himself could not cope with it and kept it a secret. The children found it hard to cope with this discovery. Peter withdrew from public life for a long time and Jane suffered from bulimia for years.

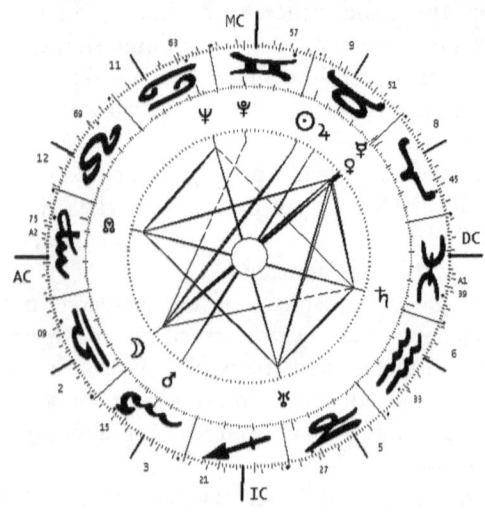

Henry Fonda
16.05.1905, 14:00. Grand Island, Nebraska, USA

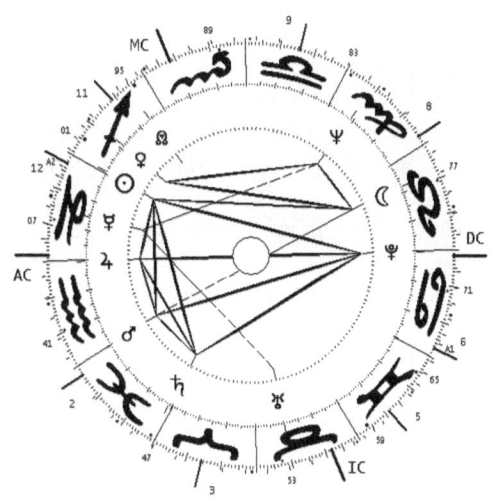

Jane Fonda
21.12.1937, 09:14, Manhattan, New York, USA

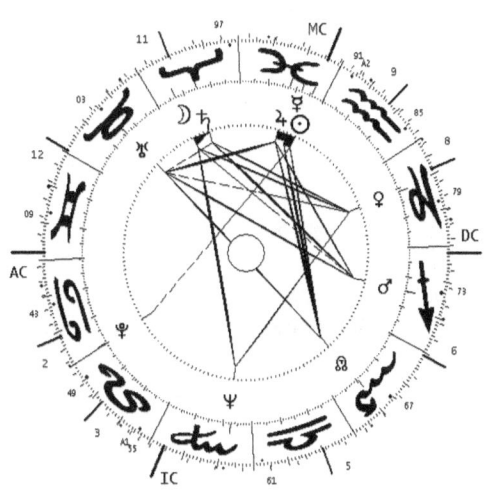

Peter Fonda
23.02.1939, 12:09, Manhattan, New York, USA

Those affected are, consciously or unconsciously, the bearers of secrets. Their task is to discover the family secret, if necessary to interpret it according to the circumstances of the time, to defend the positive and to pass it on in a suitable way to the following generations. In negative cases, the challenge is to gather the strength and responsibility to break the secret, to become aware of the conflicts or offences involved to enable a healing process to begin. Many family secrets in Europe are related to the human catastrophes of the First and Second World Wars.

The discussion of topics of family history in counselling entails a certain risk of opening up a can of worms. If this happens, the counsellor should behave suitably defensively, with care and sensitivity. They should pick up the consultee's conscious and unconscious messages and support him as he independently voices his fears and his point of view. As every individual's genetic factors and family influences are represented as a personal, dynamic universe, the astrological psychology approach requires a very careful examination of the connections presented.

In general, family secrets like secret biological parents or siblings, an adoption or a grandfather's criminal past, should be revealed to the children. Such a confrontation with truths can teach a person how to be strong. In later life, coming to terms with them usually means a slow healing process that uses up a lot of energy.

In the case of other secret complexes, disclosure can turn children into confidants, although they may not be able to deal with or shake off the effects. This includes relationship or sexual problems of the parents. A husband throws himself into his work, or he has left his wife and she projects her needs for closeness and love onto her son. Another setting is that of the father whose wife has left him, who uses the daughter as an ersatz partner. In such cases, family secrets arise out of an atmosphere of exploitation, the emotional variants of which represent the most common form of parent-child complex, of which sexual abuse is the most devastating.

Naturally, there are no universal concepts that can be satisfactorily applied in such areas. The interpretation of the horoscope must aim for the development of awareness of the challenges and opportunities that exist in the family background. At first, it is worth ascertaining whether the consultee has sufficient decision-making ability with regard to his autonomy and integration in family, cultural, political and religious systems. In many cases, this is the key to overcoming development-limiting factors. At the same time, the horoscope reveals individual routes to emancipation. Astrological psychology offers a few starting points for the characterisation of family settings:

* On the level of the zodiac signs, we can describe the quality of the energies that surround the inherited theme, which may involve genetic dispositions or emotional bonds. For example, planetary oppositions in sign axes can indicate defensive behaviour or restricting family traditions.

* The aspect structure reveals directions in which consciousness and learning strategies are most likely to move. Linear (cardinal) figures tend to (consciously or unconsciously) act out family secrets. Unconsciously, modified victim roles can be adapted, thus reinforcing or expanding the secret. If awareness of the secret is developed, there is the chance to break the "spell", leading to the coordination of interests, reconciliation and healing. Symmetrical aspect figures (fixed) have a corresponding tendency to preserve or to negate. If one's personal security identity is involved, it can take a very long time to face up to family secrets. Triangular figures look for insights in connections. Here, problems can be overcome by clarification or ignored due to repression. Incoherent structures constitute projection areas for family secrets and should be the subject of particularly careful discussion.

* The house positions of the planets allow the nature of early childhood influences to be discovered and personal development tasks to be identified. Worthy of attention are so-called compensation [stressed] positions of planets just before house axes and their contribution to role behaviour, adaptation to guiding norms or ersatz identities. The relative positions of the spiritual planets (Uranus, Neptune, Pluto) to the ego planets (Saturn, Moon, Sun) in the houses provide indications to leitmotifs, superego functions or unconscious dependencies, and/or links to role models or ideologies.

* The Age Point allows crises of socialisation and development phases to be discovered in advance so that the awareness exists for appropriate tasks to be set. Often during the period of the intersection of AP and Moon Node, AP offers intensive access to causes and consequences of family secrets. The AP enables the forms of influences to be ordered chronologically.

* The Family Model describes the quality of the bonds between the child self and maternal and paternal figures in the family environment and background and possible role adaptations resulting from this. It is particularly suited to overcoming unconscious expectations of relationships in later life and for developing a confident "I-You management".

* The moon node horoscope allows insights into, and a beginning to the spiritual transformation of, "inherited burdens", enabling overcoming of development-limiting burdens coming from acquired karma or the shadow of previous generations.

Not all problems, emotional disturbances or diffuse anxieties are caused by an unrecognised family secret. However, there are observable signals which it is worth investigating further if they are present. If no tangible causes can be seen in the examination of the person's life story that can explain existing conflicts and problems, attention should be turned to the family history. Primarily of interest here are the frequency of accidents, unusual illnesses, suicides in previous generations and all themes over which a cloak of secrecy lies or to which there are unnatural reactions in the family environment. Often, so-called "black sheep" or "eccentrics" who show an excessive desire for freedom or extreme living habits are bearers of a family secret.

Ultimately all that matters is to encourage such people never to give up, but to discover and develop their own potential. In this respect, making the best out of life means acknowledging the family inheritance, freeing oneself from restrictions and integrating the available substance into one's own life structure.

Bibliography

S. Tisseron: *Die verbotene Tür. Familiengeheimnisse und wie man nit ihnen umgeht.*
J. Bradshaw. *Family Secrets.*

❑ ❑ ❑ ❑ ❑

Family Counselling

Angelika Kraft-Boehm

First published in AstroLog Issues 114-115, February-April 2000

Introduction

There is a complex system of interactions between the members within a family. In order to retain some perspective, it is helpful to use the aspect patterns as a starting point. I do not think that a comparison of the radix horoscopes alone is sufficient. Some children still live strongly from their moon node horoscope, even though the process of immersion into the radix horoscope begins at birth. This process, and the reactions of the child to its new environment, is revealed in the house horoscope. Here I show comparisons of the radix horoscope with the family model. The aims of this consultation were to gain a better understanding of the "problem child", to establish the parents' responsibility for this problem and to examine the family dynamics more closely to see how they could be improved.

A Family Consultation

The mother of a family of four had made an appointment for herself, her husband and their two children to go for counselling. The parents were having problems with their daughter. She did not want to learn anything, or when she had learnt something such as how to ride a bike she had no interest in putting it into practice. They wanted her to be more responsible. The parents' loving and spontaneous devotion was immediately evident when the discussion turned to their son, their firstborn who was two years older than his sister.

The Aspect Patterns *[See charts on next two pages.]*

The parents are both triangular types, which indicates a flexible, adaptable consciousness. They want to understand the world and are motivated by contact and love.

There are also some linear figures to be seen, mainly in the son's horoscope, but also in the mother's and daughter's. They indicate a desire to move on, to be constantly on the go. So far, so good.

The daughter is basically a quadrangular type: life for her is a state. If internal or external influences cause trouble in one part of her life, if there is something wrong with one corner, she immediately wants to put it right. Inner stability, security and harmony are what

28 Part 1 – The Family

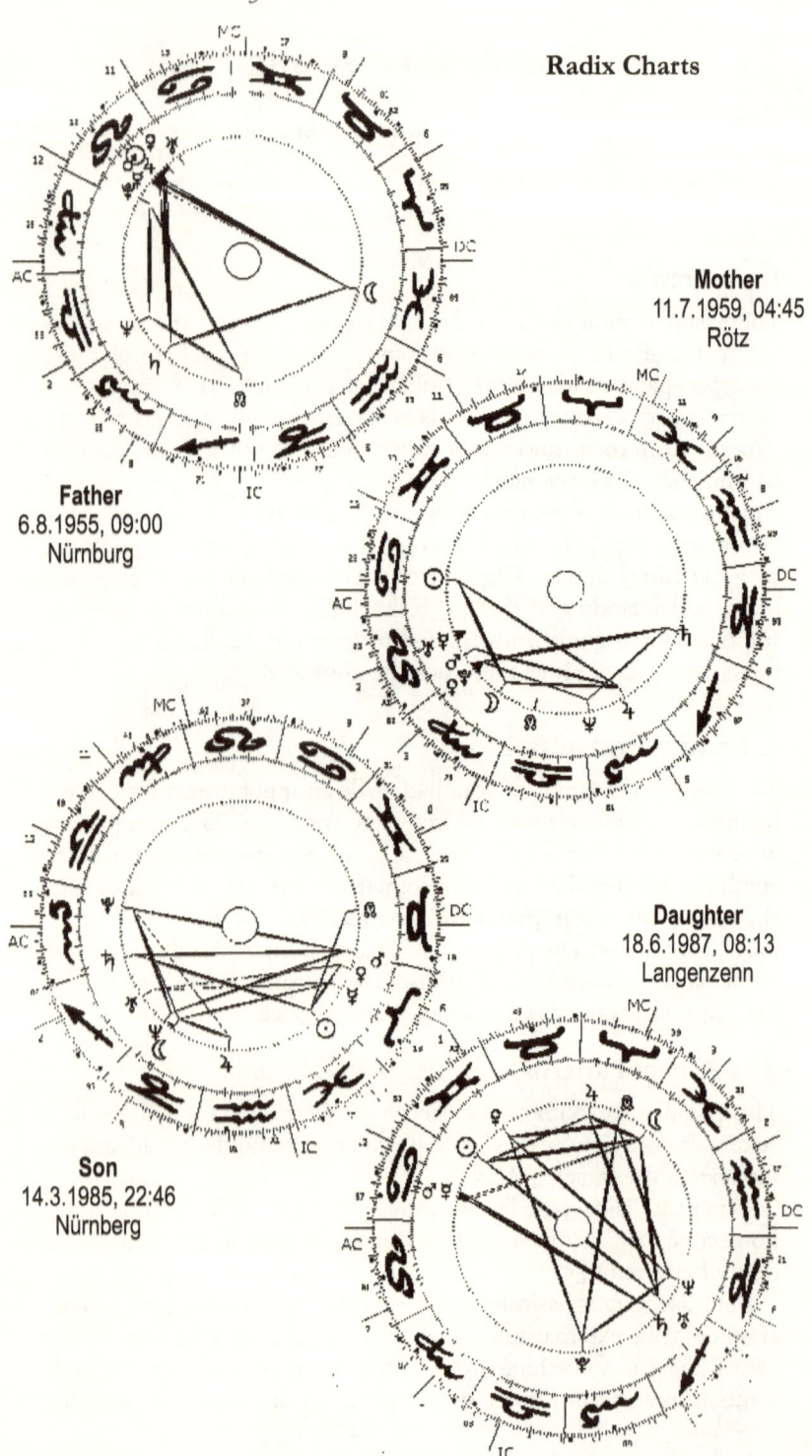

Radix Charts

Mother
11.7.1959, 04:45
Rötz

Father
6.8.1955, 09:00
Nürnburg

Daughter
18.6.1987, 08:13
Langenzenn

Son
14.3.1985, 22:46
Nürnberg

she needs. For the other family members, life is a dynamic process, while the daughter prefers just to "be" and to maintain her status quo. Her dynamic component consists of a Saturn quincunx Mars-Mercury conjunction, which is connected to the Moon by a trine. It is possible that she projects this element onto her mother and brother.

The girl's horoscope also shows an emphasis on the relationship axis 5/11 as a basis for development to the MC, to individuation. The top-heaviness of her horoscope gives her a theoretical approach to life's tasks. She is a self-confident personality who wants to lead and organise her own life. The horoscopes of the mother and brother are distinctly bottom-heavy. They experience themselves by doing; they learn from experience and enjoy feeling the protection of the collective. Both are sociable. It is important for them to meet other people, to relate to You, to compare themselves and even to compete with them. They are not so aware of their strengths, prefer to be led and are adaptable.

The father forms a kind of bridge between these two and the daughter. There is a You-orientation present in the dominant triangle with the Moon on the far right. In addition, there is strong emphasis on the 11th house, which is concerned with conscious perception of the self and conscious implementation of strengths. He would like to go against the flow, upwards but towards the self. This provides a space where he can encounter his daughter and also compete with her (both have 11th house Sun and Venus) and which balances out their striving for individuation. She is the only member of the family to have a roughly equal balance of individuation and contact aspects. Her consciousness strives upwards and seems to be hanging from Jupiter, Moon and Moon Node, almost like a bell. It fills the empty space of the three other family members in the 9th and 10th houses.

His aspect pattern also has something that looks like a harp whose strings have been plucked by the unconscious I space, where most of the mother's (7 plus Moon Node) and son's (6) planets are situated. The father is also anchored here by two of the triangle's corners and the Moon Node.

The main difference between the horoscopes of mother and daughter is in their colour. With four long green aspects, the girl probably feels great insecurity and has wishes, longings and hopes. There may also be a tendency to project parts of herself and she could have a strong imagination. She can develop her intellectual capacity, learn to differentiate and finally make decisions that then also set her willpower free. These processes require a lot of time and thought, introspection and perceptiveness. She has the ability to differentiate, while the mother is more prone to "black and white thinking". The mother's predominantly blue aspect pattern enables her to give her daughter stability and reassurance, but she does not understand her hesitancy, doubt and questioning. For her, things are either black or white; she sees things more simplistically. Her experience is characterised by harmony. Everything is in flux and can be integrated except for conflict, which is therefore particularly painful, while the daughter feels so much, is so alert and contains many more conflicts and contradictions within her (red/green aspects predominate.)

To sum up, I can say that the daughter's life motivation is opposite to that of the rest of the family. She brings a certain tension into the unity of the family existence as she asks for greater awareness.

The striving direction of the aspect patterns in the moon node charts show that the daughter and parents have already dealt with the issue of individuation. All three are familiar with this theme and they each have a different ego planet in the 10th house. The girl's Sun is in the strongest position. She has an autonomous, dominating, strong-willed personality and dominates the father, whose Moon is in the 10th house and is therefore dependent on sympathy and contact. He has found himself through love and relationships, and can now put this potential into practice. The mother's Saturn at the MC represents reliability and order. At the same time, she may have experienced fears and limitations on her path to the self and has a tendency to cling to established roles, forms and traditions. The whole family is gathered in the unconscious, and the roles of the father and daughter are reversed.

The son's moon node horoscope is also bottom-heavy. His horoscope turns on the individuation axis: the planets situated on the You side are now on the I-side and vice versa.

The Moon Node

The different developmental directions are also revealed in the position of the Moon Node. Both parents can evolve by becoming more and more rooted, experiencing themselves as people among people, expressing their feelings and also accepting feelings (Moon Node in 4th house). They have started their own family and built their nest in which they feel comfortable and have a sense of belonging together.

This sense of belonging together is obviously questioned by the daughter. She needs to develop her individuality and self-image, particularly with regard to her femininity, her ideal of love and her image of the perfect person. She favours self-reflection, going her own way and setting her own goals. She would like to belong emotionally to the collective and also allows herself to be influenced by collective opinions. This gives rise to an intense bond. The "first step" lies on

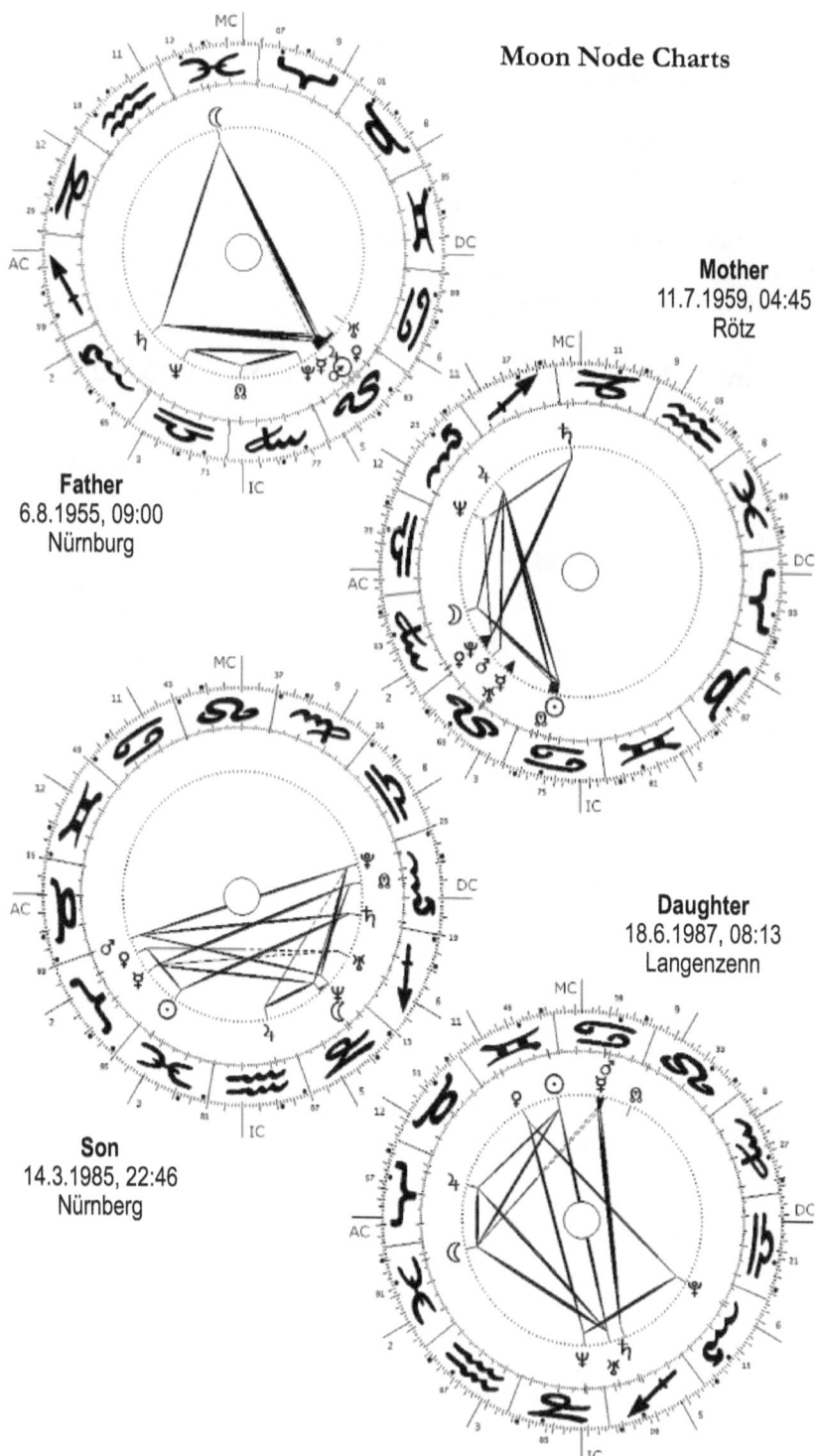

the same axis. Here there is a danger of projecting her own shadow onto other people. Both sides attach importance to knowing where they come from and accepting their own roots, both in order to connect with them and to free themselves from them.

The brother represents the possibility of synthesis on the corresponding cardinal axis. His developmental potential lies in the encounter with others. He needs to relate to others and find a balance between himself and other people. It is all about arrangements that suit both sides and finding a balance between giving and taking.

Family Members compared with the Family Model
Sonja, the Mother

Loving and sociable, and oriented towards the collective and relationships, Sonja would like to live in harmony. She would also like to grow out of the collective space. The sensitive planets at the Low Points have made her feel inhibited, misunderstood and even repressed and she wants to go out into the world. Both ego planets Sun and Saturn are on the top left and right, oriented towards the encounter axis. At the AC, she wants to assert her ego in the world; at the DC she wants to take responsibility for survival and for others. Her image is of someone who cares sensitively and maternally for others. She has a talent for nurturing relationships and for seeing exactly what is going on, and this allows her to fulfil her desire for harmonious togetherness in the collective space (e.g. with her siblings and their children). The Sun before the AC sometimes puts her in strongly competitive situations and makes her want to be the best, the first or the only one and her self-confidence is particularly affected by the thought that somebody does not feel comfortable with her, possibly even her own daughter! However, such setbacks enable her to learn to let go of the will of the small ego and to open herself up to the greater will of the higher self.

Mars square Jupiter is the only red aspect, which she uses productively and creatively in her hobby of restoring antique furniture. She is also professionally independent/self-employed and gets contracts from her firm. This balances her strong orientation towards other people. She has a lot of energy and works hard to gain resources (3 planets in the 2nd house).

In the other talent triangle, the feminine ability to accumulate education and collective knowledge is combined with her job and the ideal of serving and helping in a social context. She is involved with alternative healing methods and has learnt a little about herbs and Bach flowers, but does not know how to put this knowledge into practice. She works as a foreign language correspondent for a company. The relevant conjunction lies before the 3rd house cusp. The masculine model is still connected to her own essential resources and wants to implement them. However, in the stress area she definitely wants to belong to and to be in control of the collective knowledge. That is also why the academic success and education of her children is so important to her.

The Mercury-Uranus conjunction is unaspected. She could develop her linguistic abilities, her ideas and creative thought for her own enjoyment and use later for a transpersonal task.

The unaspected Moon Node, intercepted in Libra, is hard to find.

Sonja says:

She is the fifth child of a family of seven: six girls and one boy. She wanted to run away from home. Her brother often came home drunk and caused fights and confrontations. Her father also drank but never hurt her. The bad thing was that achievement was everything (Sun sextile Moon). She was actually considered stupid (Moon LP 3, unaspected Mercury-Uranus conjunction) and had to repeat her first year at school. She worked until she was the best in the class (Venus-Pluto conjunction, stress area at cusp 3, Sun in 3 in moon node horoscope). She thought that it was possible for things to be different. (In both talent triangles there is also self-satisfaction, but it receives great stimulus to perform from the stress planets and the square to Mars) As soon as she started to be successful, she became the "favourite". Her father in particular was very proud of her (Sun in Cancer).

Her family model shows that as a child she opened herself trustingly to her father and expected a harmonious, even osmotic relationship with him. She accepted his requirement for her to succeed, adapted to the way of thinking of the collective and was good and clever. He himself worked as an excavator driver; he always went to the pub after work and was therefore not accessible (Sun still in 12). The mother was never there for Sonja, for she worked hard on her farm to ensure the family's survival (Saturn in Capricorn, 6th house, not connected with Moon and Sun). She is a daddy's girl, like her daughter, and received neither the security nor the grounding for her emotional needs. Her sisters sometimes made her feel cared for and protected though. They could talk about their problems together, which she liked (Moon LP 3).

Sonja was not loved for her own sake, but for her achievements, and was neglected by both parents. She did not fight this, but overcame challenges as best she could and showed what she could do. It is this experience and structure that she now brings to her relationships with her own children.

Laura the Daughter

Laura's horoscope contains two quadrilaterals one inside the other. The Bathtub is formed by the projection triangle: Venus, Pluto and Neptune, the latter being square to the Moon Node. She would like to learn to take control of her life as a woman. Her mother had told her that she wanted to be a princess. She probably was one (in the moon node horoscope Venus lies in the same place in the 11th house.) Now she wants to understand clearly who she is as a woman in terms of her ideals and her sensitivity. In the Moon Node-Neptune square, there is a conflict between the ideal of serving and helping and her individuation and self-assertion as a woman. By consciously confronting this she can gain strength and stability. The two sextiles allow her to approach the processes of self-evolution and self-testing joyfully and light-heartedly and she would like the processes to be harmonious. In line with the character of the quadrilateral, everything should soon be in order again. She may resist change and further growth here. This order is again and again affected by other people's reactions to her self-image, which may make her want to learn from them.

The Animated quadrilateral makes her want to reconcile contact and love with self-actualisation. For her, the latter means being knowledgeable, well-informed, belonging in the 11th house to the elite or to a group of people who understand the world from a distance and possibly also work to improve it. This contrasts with her ideal of thinking creatively in direct contact with people and finding new solutions for herself and for others. With the Pisces Moon at the red apex of the triangle, she is under strong emotional pressure. She is interested in other people, wants to experience and give real human love and understanding in relationships. In the 9th house, she is very open to the world, feels everything that affects others and tries to be fair with everyone. There is achievement through empathy, understanding and adaptation and with the aspiration to be completely free and spontaneous. Her self-confidence will certainly lead her to experience frustrations and try to make up for them by placing high demands upon herself. The small green aspect that lies behind the Moon Node and the MC enables her to learn how to gain knowledge and how to reach compromises. She either appears indifferent or uses this opportunity to communicate intensively with those in authority, which allows her to develop her own identity and her own authority. It is a matter of achieving a genuine self-image in the sense of the AC: I am that and that am I.

Her experience of this theme is inwardly ambivalent. Her tender and oceanic feelings bring her into conflict with her own theories and thought structures, as well as with her father. Her perceptual capacity and creative ideas are connected to a talent from which inner serenity and even confidence can develop.

Saturn is loosely attached. The quincunx works like a sensitive guide and can sometimes be suppressed by the opposition of the Animated quadrilateral. She lacks direct contact with her body and its limitations. She would like to learn to test herself physically, in sport and in relationships. The better she can control her behaviour and physical abilities, the more secure she feels. However, the long green aspect causes her to experience uncertainty, searching, longing and questioning: she asks herself: how can I combine body, limitations and actions? She must always make a decision to do, say or learn something. She must use her emotions to develop and nurture the connection with her motor skills and linguistic abilities. One danger could be that the emotional pressure could cause her to direct aggression towards herself. In this aspect there is also the relationship to the brother, which can be open and perceptive.

What the Parents Say

Laura cannot handle pressure. They say there is no way around it. If the parents threaten to forbid her from doing something, she takes the wind out of their sails by saying that she does not want to do it anyway. She does not admit that it hurts her or put up a fight (Sun square Moon, which is square Uranus). On the other hand, she is good at asserting her wishes and the brother gets her to ask if both children want something from their parents. She does that out of love for her brother. When playing with him or also with a friend, although she may cry if something does not suit her, she then relents and is almost submissively acquiescent to the others so that they will still like her.

One evening, the mother had read a second good night story on condition that afterwards, the children did not start chatting again as they usually did. The children did not obey, and the mother was disappointed and cross. The son reacted guiltily and said to the sister:

"Now she is really cross, we must stop talking." But not Laura. She shrugged off responsibility and blame. The message to the mother was that she was responsible for her own feelings. For the daughter, this means that she can indeed assert herself, but this means that her own need to be loved and accepted is not met. She asserts her own wishes and does not want to be tied down by conditions, limits or rules. On the other hand, she is looking for boundaries and defies her mother. The Pisces Moon makes her very sensitive and open to her environment. She thrives in big groups, is open to the world but rather distant in close relationships. She learns to perceive and process her feelings and relationships consciously (9th house Moon, intersected square to the You space). This makes the parents feel rejected. They would like a greater sense of duty, obedience, closeness and belonging.

For the sake of Laura's own development, it is important that she detaches herself from what everyone else thinks, reflects upon herself and makes her own decisions. She must face this alone, as befits her abilities and her learning task.

In the family model she is a daddy's girl. She expects her father to accept her, and to be able to test herself against him and confront him. She will often experience this negatively as criticism, rejection, refusal and punishment. In her childhood search for understanding and love, in her emotional idealism, she felt misunderstood and pressurised by him. I will go into this theme later in more detail in the section on the father himself.

When she is in a relaxed state, she has a functional access to the mother. Through actions and/or communication, she tries and hopes to reach her mother, to find security and protection with her and to find her own limitations. When something is important to her, then she is willing to listen to her mother's explanations, who is then able to provide her with definite rules. She accepts them only when she understands their meaning and they are therefore accessible by rational and clear thinking (the ego planets in mutable signs, the top-heaviness, Moon Node in Aries before the MC). Her bond with her mother is sensitive (green-blue) and she does not feel dependent upon her, on the contrary. She is out of touch with her physical self and sense of reality. If the family wants to go hiking, she spends hours looking for the right shoes and needs a lot of persuading even to join in. Or she rides her bike when she is too tired, falls off and cuts her arm but does not cry.

Ewald, the Father

The Dominant triangle, a Learning triangle, conditions Ewald's personality, his whole life and indicates an ongoing learning process.

All three ego planets receive a lot of energy from their sign and are situated in the fixed area or Low Point of their respective houses. Each one lies in the area of the horoscope where it is most at home: Saturn at the bottom, the Moon in the centre and the Sun at the top.

He has a great fear of loss and he tends to build walls around himself for protection, which can make him very defensive.

Once he possesses something, he never wants to let it go, whatever it may be: money, knowledge or even the people he loves. He wants to protect himself with societal structures, but is also aware of the transience of material things. It is likely that he can find real autonomy and self-esteem in letting go of external securities and trusting his inner self.

At this corner of the triangle there is always a conflict: he has found security by serving and helping (Moon), but comes under pressure to perform and would like to realise his full potential. The Sun in the 11th house makes him want to belong to an elite, to create a group of like-minded friends with whom he can reflect on the world and on humanity. He needs to be free and to be a unique personality. As a Leo, he wants to prove himself in relationships. He wants to experience lively and creative relationships with others, and to find his own area of competence in which he can apply himself heart and soul. He can only believe in an ethic if it contains living, genuine human values.

All the mental functions of his thinking self are available simultaneously and they are controlled by his will. He listens to, sees, smells and tastes what is beneficial for his self-esteem and this determines his mentality. As the cusp of the 11th house still lies in Cancer, the whole conjunction is probably ultimately related to the 12th house. By turning inwards, much reflection and finding out what suits him, he finds real self-confidence and true love. That is why the second, Talent triangle is important, as Pluto at the cusp of the 12th house challenges him to turn inwards, to experience himself in the depths of his soul and to align himself with the Great Whole.

For the self, the question for the time being is how contact, serving and helping can all be consistent with his desire to fulfil his potential. A longing for contact, a search for how to understand and really help others is indicated. Then he feels a new sense of security and the process starts anew.

Ewald is a civil servant in the tax authority and when his Age Point transited the Moon, he had to break up his whole department and completely rebuild it in another place, because the old building was about to collapse! This is an image for his planets in the Dominant triangle.

It is hard for him to control or access the small Talent triangle. He also said he could very easily live without ideals. He can therefore also delegate to the Moon Node and not try to belong emotionally to the family or any other collective. His family model is contained in the retrograde Dominant triangle.

Ewald's Story

His parents were always fighting: his mother often worried about material security. His father had his own carpentry business and dealt with all business and money matters himself, never letting her get involved. She never knew how much money there was in it and was afraid that the business would suffer if he bought a new car for the company, for example.

They struggled to survive: in summer there was money, in winter there was not. After lunch, his mother went to work in another farm and was extremely frugal. His father had two opportunities to take a job in another company, which would have pleased his mother, as she thought it would be more secure than working for himself. She was unable to convince him though (square Saturn in Scorpio, LP 2 to the Sun in Leo in the 11th house fixed area).

After the war, his father was more and more a man-about-town. He drank and played cards. He belonged to quite a few clubs and was respected there. He was not a great believer in putting on airs and graces, but showed himself as he was, even with his crazy, childlike ideas: he was a colourful character, as Ewald described him. His father had no ambition. His basic approach to life was: to build on what is available, hold onto it and apart from that, live your life. He may have thought that his father had lost his ideals because of the war (the detached spiritual planets).

As a child, he was not put under any pressure to achieve. School was always relaxed and his father also sometimes helped with the chores at home. When Ewald was older, his father often came to have a talk with him and to tell him about his wartime experiences. His father's decadent lifestyle was always getting him into trouble with his family. His mother was always worried. The fifteen-year-old son took on the role of moralist, telling him: but we are better than this and must set an example. He worked with his father in the business and did not want to condone his selfish escapades. The father turned to Ewald in an attempt to restore family peace. He was to help his father, bond with him and understand him (Leo Sun in quincunx to Pisces Moon in the 6th house). Once he even promised not to reveal one of the father's mistakes and was rewarded with a bicycle. Playing this role cemented his involvement between his father and mother and gave him existential importance. He had to smooth over conflicts and restore harmony. At the same time, he experienced great distance, particularly from the two older siblings. Eventually, the father could reconcile "originality and freedom" only through the cooperativeness and love of the child, with the needs for the security of the mother and the family. The father abused his son's need for love and their roles reversed to a certain extent: the son became the father's protector.

Ewald received affection when he was needed and had to help. Otherwise he was left to his own devices. His daughter did not get involved at all. In any case she did not need him as an ally, on the contrary, she does not listen to reason, knows better and is autonomous.

Even today he dislikes the strong need for security. He was open to it, sensed his mother's worries and hardships and in order to relieve them, allied himself with his father in order to restore security and order, which are indeed demands of Saturn and the fixed cross.

As befits this personality structure, he established himself as a civil servant in a secure status. In his future family, security was experienced in a Saturnine sense. There was no room for a higher concept or having ideals. This situation is clearly indicated in his radix and house charts: the spiritual planets are and remain detached from the personality. He does indeed see standards in the system, human and economic, but adapts to them and exercises patience until new conditions arise. He sees no opportunity for reformatory activity, to work for higher ideals over and above normal functioning. He also tends to quickly put up barriers against his wife's interest in things that transcend the normal reality (like Bach flowers and alternative medicine), above all always asking: what does that do for us?

In the daughter's horoscope, this theme is found again in the Sun-Uranus opposition. She experiences her father in a defensive tension with respect to creative thought, a new world view or even the exploration of direct relationships. Even though she has a conservative material attitude he defends himself against the overstepping of boundaries. Laura must find a way out of the tension. In addition, the house causes the Moon's motivation to be mutable/cardinal, while the sign makes the Sun and Uranus mutable but the house makes their motivation doubly fixed. The father insists on security-oriented principles. He asks about profit, thinks economically, wants to hold on, possess and structure, while his daughter above all wants to love. She wants to change constantly through spontaneous, complete openness and expand her emotional awareness. She is idealistic (strong presence in the mutable cross and the loosely detached Saturn) and is also therefore just as much a challenge to her father as he is to her.

In addition, Uranus as maternal role model and also represents the grandmother. It is possible that Laura senses how her father represses this, fights against the subliminal dominance of his mother (who is, indeed, her grandmother). Like her father, she tries to bridge the contradiction. The difference is that she is in conflict with her emotions, fights and obviously/apparently suffers, struggles and must process and understand everything consciously. As a child and with her emotional world she can neither simply adapt nor avoid the opposites. That means that Laura's emotional structure is also opposite to that of the rest of her family. Both parents have internalised the demands as children (Moon blue and blue-green). For them, being personally loved is connected with the fulfilment of certain tasks. The mother had to be the best in the class, the father helped to defend the survival of the family. Laura too must fulfil certain tasks in order to be loved, but she is just looking for the solution in another way. She insists on her individuality, does not obey any orders that she cannot understand. She defends herself against having to be loved and prefers to look for contacts that expand her consciousness and stimulate her own ideas.

The difference with the brother is indicated among other things by Moon-Uranus trine in the 9th house, which corresponds to the rebellious child, while his Moon-Neptune cusp 3 makes him want to be loved at any cost.

Ferdinand, the Son

As mentioned above, the parents have no problem with Ferdinand and feel a bond with him. He is very approachable and takes school very seriously, so that when sometimes at night things cross his mind that he may have forgotten he must then check it up (Capricorn Moon cusp 3). His mother sometimes checks his schoolbag, which he does not like at all. Sometimes she sticks a cuddly toy in his school bag as an encouragement. His father does not take school so seriously and occasionally misses mistakes in his homework. Vis a vis the mother an emergency association again arises; they collaborate so that no mistakes will be discovered. With this attitude, the boy fits effortlessly into the relationship model of the parents. He accepts the performance requirements of his mother, needs the father and bonds with him and is open to both wishes and emotions.

Ferdinand's Family Model

Ferdinand's Moon has no direct aspect to either Sun or Saturn, and so perceives no dependency on either parent. He would like to belong to them, to be loved by the collective that surrounds him, to participate in the culture and education. He is prepared/willing to accept and empathise with emotional commitments and accepts performance requirements (cardinal earth element). He is the little angel of the family (Moon conjunction Neptune). Personal  emotions and desires are always combined with the demands of selflessness/altruism, devotion and empathy, in giving as in taking. Neptune stands at the blue corner of the ambivalence triangle. In the opposition, the energy of two masculine planets is combined. Pluto promotes internal spiritual growth, Mars the application of energies to the daily struggle for survival. On the one hand, the retreat from the world, doing absolutely nothing, but contemplatively experiencing himself transcendentally, on the other hand, working hard, implementing energy, being completely present in everyday life. The challenge is to cope with this tension, to clarify and master the survival question internally and externally, and then to make it useful in his encounters. With Neptune, he can sidestep the issue and adapt one-sidedly to the collective thought pattern in accordance with the saying: if I am good, always kind and ready to help, I also have the right to exist.

The Sun/Saturn trine lies between this opposition and the Moon/Neptune conjunction. It crosses all aspects between these planets, as though the parents were protecting the child from this tension and see him as detached from it. Ferdinand expects a harmonious, loving and substantial bond between his father and mother.

There are two ways to the parents: one via Neptune. Helping and collaborating with others out of love and understanding creates the bond with the mother. The other way goes via the square to Mercury. Here he must first overcome the language barrier. From his basic structure, he definitely finds easier access to the mother and via her to the father. Like his father, he has Saturn in Scorpio, here in the 1st house. The child is exactly confronted with the ego crisis with boundaries/limitations, with reality and thrown back onto himself and his own resources. This can also lead to feelings of guilt. A mother who was frustrated, who perhaps had to renounce her ego assertion for the family, might have transferred this onto her son.

Further Consideration

Laura's development goes from a loosely connected Saturn to a Saturn/Moon trine, to a substantial and direct maternal bond. Sonja has always missed the closeness with her mother and can now experience this with her daughter. Ewald seeks closeness with his son and can build a loving, harmonious and close relationship with him. Both children have decided to give up a lot of possibilities/opportunities and structure in order to develop a new personality pattern/model. As soon as they become aware of this, they can take control of their development and fill the offered, learnt structures with their own contents (dynamic calculations). Both parents could better understand themselves and their "problem child". Each person was able to see the others in a new light from the point of view of their family history.

Later, the mother called me again and said that things were now going very well with Laura.

▫ ▫ ▫ ▫ ▫

The Family Reflected in the Horoscope

Birgit Braun

First published in AstroLog Issue 141-142, August-October 2004

"Experiences are not inherited, we must make our own."

Kurt Tucholsky

The family into which we are born and in which we grow up has great implications for our physical, mental and spiritual development. We inherit our physical bodies from our parents and we are profoundly shaped by the upbringing and influences of our parents and siblings.

At the start of life, we cannot make decisions for ourselves but are dependent on our families, on our relationship to our father and mother, on the physical, emotional and mental preconditions and possibilities that our families offer us.

It is interesting and informative to examine our family relationships from an astrological perspective. We can see important influences in our childhood and our own psychological, mental and spiritual development in the context of the whole family dynamic. This can also enrich our understanding of so-called karmic family problems.

The Family Model – Sun, Moon and Saturn

Bruno Huber developed the Family Model, which is used to see a person's early childhood family situation in their horoscope. The Sun corresponds to the paternal model, Saturn to the maternal model and the Moon reflects the role and experiences of the child. The Sun need not necessarily always represent the real father; a single mother or an uncle can also provide a solar role function for the child. Similarly with Saturn and mother, the mothering function can be taken over by the father or an aunt.

The Sun and Saturn symbolise the parental roles as they are subjectively experienced by the child. The maternal model, Saturn, has the task of giving the child security and teaching it how to behave so that it is protected from danger, teaching it how to survive. The Sun as paternal model has the task of developing the child's creativity, developing its self-confidence and helping it to become autonomous. These abilities are important for the child to have a positive idea of itself as well as for the experience of being strong, powerful and independent and being able to make things happen. The Moon as child-model perceives everything, is open and in touch with the environment, particularly with the mother and father. It has the task of communicating to the child intense contact experiences, experiences of being loved or unloved, being adaptable and living spontaneously.

Aspects between Moon and Sun or Saturn are indicative of a close father or mother relationship whose quality depends on the type of aspect involved. It indicates to what extent the child identifies with its parents. Aspects between Sun and Saturn tell us about the type of relationship between the parents themselves, which the child perceives, assimilates and repeats in later life in its own relationships.

The positions of Sun, Moon and Saturn in the horoscope therefore reflect the child's experience of their early family situation. They also tell us about the personality structure, as Sun, Moon and Saturn are also the three ego planets, forming the threefold personality of Mental self (Sun), Contact self (Moon) and Physical self (Saturn). We can assume that the early childhood family situation has a crucial influence on our personality development.

In this article I examine the birth charts of the members of a family using the Family Model, comparing the individuals and their charts and picking up and analysing recurring themes. I also explore the psychology of their early childhood development, and consider family themes against this background. Finally, I look at the bonds between different family members using the click horoscope and the moon node horoscope.

The Father Heinz

Heinz was born out of wedlock. His mother was only 18, not much more than a child, and was overwhelmed by the upbringing of her son. Too involved with her own wishes and ideas, she was unable to adequately meet her child's needs. There were hardly any other caring adults around, so Heinz was very much left to his own devices. As his parents were not married, little Heinz was at the mercy of the environment and had few friends or playmates.

Father radix chart, born 1928

However, later the parents married and had two more children. As the eldest, Heinz was mainly responsible for looking after them.

The mother did not bother much about her children, and preferred to pursue her own interests. This caring role was naturally overwhelming for Heinz, especially as he himself had not received adequate care and upbringing during his own early childhood.

Heinz's father offered few alternative possibilities for development. In the first years of Heinz's life he was not present at all, as the parents were initially not married. Later his influence was minimal as he had a stressful job. When Heinz was about 13 years old, his father died in the war so was then completely out of reach.

Even as an adult Heinz can neither defend himself against nor distance himself from his mother's apparently unloving and selfish behaviour. During the course of his life, he has developed a pronounced addiction to alcohol and drugs. He also suffers from bronchial asthma, which is known to be caused by psychological factors, especially in the mother-child relationship. These connections were partly discovered in psychotherapeutic treatment but Heinz unfortunately stopped the therapy after a few months.

Heinz's aspect pattern is dynamic, three-coloured and concentrated in two quadrants. There is a preponderance of green aspects. The shape of the aspect pattern does not give an impression of stability. It consists of several triangles and linear figures that look to the observer as though they are drifting apart. The aspect pattern is held together by the conjunction between Venus and Mars and the one-way opposition from Sun/Mercury to Neptune. Saturn, Pluto and Moon Node are only attached to the rest of the aspect pattern by single aspects. The Moon is the strongest ego planet, at the descendant in fire sign Aries, indicating spontaneous, direct, sometimes unreflecting behaviour in social situations.

With Neptune at the 11th house cusp, there is a strong striving for ideal love and a high, idealistic wishful thinking in friendships and relationships. The Moon, the feeling and contact self, tries to contact this via the trine. The idealistic desires for love of Neptune can flow directly at the DC in encounters with the You. Here, the trine could mean that the You is approached with partly unadapted or excessive desires and claims for love. The trine does not just mean that a harmonious ability is involved. In my opinion, here it indicates that the energy flow between Moon and Neptune is not called into question, either by the horoscope owner himself or by the associated life experiences. The energy flows smoothly and harmoniously, but also uncriticised. The Moon/Neptune connection generally corresponds to the topic of personal and ideal love. The desire for love and belonging is great and seems to be obvious with the blue substance aspect. The Aries Moon also sometimes demands this impatiently and insensitively.

The Moon is also trine Saturn. Here too, energies flow unhindered between the physical and feeling selves. In the Family Model, this corresponds to a close bond between mother (Saturn) and child (Moon). Heinz accepts his mother's influence relatively easily, which does not reveal anything about the nature of the influence. In a positive case, the relationship with the mother could be harmonious, in which the basic trust could easily be passed on to the child. In a less positive case, "negative" influences from the mother could make a particularly strong and lasting impression, which seems rather likely in this case. At the same time, Heinz does not critically question why his mother behaved so coldly. He does not even perceive that her egocentric behaviour is not good for him and means that his fundamental needs are not met. Instead, with the trine he tries to establish a harmonious relationship with his mother, even at the cost of his own self-destruction, as his desire for love does not seem to be realisable. Perhaps Heinz also feels responsible for his mother or even "guilty" for his difficult relationship with her. Children often experience such situations irrationally and develop feelings of guilt, again a topic that fits with the Moon/Saturn aspect.

Saturn lies on the 3rd house cusp conjunct the south Moon Node, a clue that the chart owner falls back into old ways of reacting and behaving again and again, clinging to old habits. As far as the mother is concerned, this could indicate a karmic mother relationship that limits and restricts her own further development. The Sun lies on the balance point of the 5th house. At the green tip of the Eye figure it suggests an important ability for assimilating information. In opposition to Neptune, the ability for autonomy is not unconditionally encouraged. In Pisces and linked to Mercury, Jupiter, Venus and Neptune, this is an aesthetically oriented, musical and gentle self-confidence, which is rather uncomfortable with self-assertion and powerful expansion. The Sun/Neptune opposition also reflects Heinz's relationship with his father, who was absent for most of his childhood, and eventually became completely inaccessible due to his early death.

In crisis situations, one-way aspects tend to disappear completely; the Moon here would only be aspected to Saturn in an extreme life situation, the aspects to Neptune and Mars disappearing. The Sun would then be out of reach for the feeling self. In this connection, it is interesting that Heinz's bronchial asthma had its origin in a traumatic experience when he was 17: shortly before the end of the second World War, he was trapped in the cellar of a house during a bombing raid and only rescued after 24 hours. He must have been profoundly shaken by this experience of being buried alive. At the time his age point formed a square to the Moon. A few weeks later Heinz met and fell in love with Ingrid, his future wife.

The Mother Ingrid

Ingrid is the youngest of five children and grew up in the countryside. Her parents placed no value on further education or professional training for their daughter, and expected her to marry and have children. Ingrid has a difficult relationship with her mother, who was very cold towards her children. She was mainly interested in material things, allowing herself to be guided by what the neighbours, the church or other authorities thought. There was little emotional contact. As a child, Ingrid often felt alone and neglected.

Mother radix chart, born 1927

Ingrid's father found it hard to accept his profession of farmer. He felt he could do better. He would certainly have been able to pursue an academic career. His parents – themselves farmers – did not understand this and circumstances at that time did not permit this kind of education. Unfortunately, he did not make any effort to ensure a better education for his own children.

As an adult, Ingrid's experience of family life is insecure, particularly from a financial point of view. She constantly feels called upon to contribute actively to the family livelihood, as Heinz is not always able to "feed" his family due to his psychological problems. She suffers greatly due to her lack of education, which means that she can only do menial tasks. In addition, she must also bring up three children and take care of the household.

The Sun on the 4th house cusp is her strongest ego planet. At the 3rd house Low Point, Saturn is only attached to the aspect pattern by conjunction to Mercury/Mars. The Moon at the balance point of the 1st house has a sextile to Mars and a one-way opposition to Uranus. Interestingly, the Moon in a crisis situation would also be in a figure by itself, as the one-way opposition to Uranus would then disappear.

Saturn in the 3rd house can therefore be seen as a clue to the mother, who is strongly rooted in the thought norms of the collective, and cares about what people think, how one does things and what the neighbours might think, etc.

Ingrid's aspect pattern, like her husband's, is not very stable; at least the four planets in the collective area can provide an anchor. For the

Moon in the 1st house, although contacts are important, in opposition to Uranus, which is conjunct Jupiter on the DC, her contact with others is not always easy. Her behaviour sometimes seems abrupt, hard and erratic, irritating those around her. The feeling self does not understand this and reacts with huffiness or sulking.

The Sun at the IC is so-to-speak trapped in the collective, a good way of describing Ingrid's father. The striving for autonomy and individualisation naturally does not go down well in an environment in which one has to conform to the laws of the collective. Sun opposite Moon Node could indicate that the Moon Node's requirement for mental autonomy was ignored, perhaps because Ingrid – or her father – did not consider this necessary or important. Perhaps her relationship with her father was also structured in such a way that he restricted her development. In this respect, it is interesting that in her husband's chart Saturn lies at the south node, and that his relationship with his mother was equally restricting. In their moon node horoscopes, this corresponds to a Sun/Saturn conjunction click at the DC. Perhaps an indication of a karmic relationship that as a developmental task is intended to force a confrontation with each other's restricting parent?

The First Child, Daughter Anna

The first child, Anna, was born after nearly four years of marriage. Due to the accommodation crisis in the 1950s, Heinz and Ingrid lived with Heinz's mother and father. The relationship between Ingrid and her stepmother is tense, but without open confrontation.

The child Anna was at the centre of family life, the first of a new generation. Accordingly they tried to influence her, particularly her paternal grandmother. Anna is rather shy and introverted, always trying to be good and kind and to comply with her family's wishes. During her youth Anna was a conventional, obedient and quiet girl. She complied with her mother's desire for a good professional education with a secure future

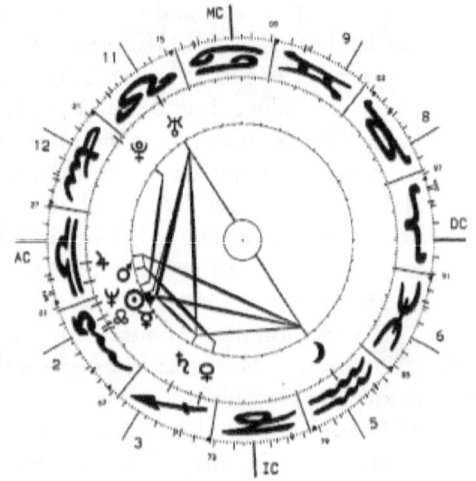

Anna radix chart, born 1957

and entered the Civil Service. The aspect pattern in Anna's radix chart consists of a static quadrilateral with three linear figures attached. The emphasis is in the first quadrant, especially the 1st and 2nd houses, and the left side of the chart. The colouring is predominantly red-blue, with just one green semi-sextile out of twelve aspects. Both Moon and Saturn are relatively strong ego planets, Saturn enjoying the benefit of the collective space, while the Moon suffers instead from its sandwich position. The Sun lies exactly on the 2nd house cusp conjunct Neptune/Mercury/Moon Node and square Uranus.

Saturn at the 3rd house cusp could tell us something about the mother, who during the early years of Anna's life was closely influenced by the ideas and approval of the collective – doing just what "people" expect or think is right and pursuing petty, personal goals.

In the conjunction Sun/Neptune in Scorpio, the father's addiction problem could suggest that it leads to him being in some respects insufficiently available for his daughter or at least periodically absent. In the 2nd house, he is concerned with the search for self-esteem, or quite generally with the acquisition of financial means.

A secure "job for life" in the civil service is very attractive for the Scorpio Sun at the 2nd house cusp, also satisfying Saturn on the 3rd house cusp in its solidarity with the collective, but also encouraging the Moon's compulsion to adapt in the fixed sign and house.

The "good daughter", especially in relationship to the mother, can be seen in the position of Moon and Saturn. They form a sextile, a harmony aspect, which can mean that anger is repressed instead of being expressed for the sake of harmony and peace. In spite of this, the aspect does show a close bond with the mother, as does the Moon-Saturn trine with the father.

The Second Child, Son Daniel

Daniel was born three years after Anna. The family financial situation had become more stable in the meantime, but they still lived with Heinz's mother. Ingrid had a trouble-free pregnancy, and the birth went smoothly. Ingrid developed a deep affection for Daniel, who was also very attached to his mother. He was an easy child, the prototype "boy next door": helpful, friendly and well-behaved. Even during puberty he is always kind and friendly. He met his future wife at the age of 18. A few years later they married and started a family.

Daniel has a close relationship with his mother. Outsiders soon notice that he is "mother's pet". Ingrid and Daniel themselves do not appear to be so aware of this and always deny it. The mother also asserts her influence over Daniel and encourages him, as she did his older sister, to find a stable job. He became a civil servant.

The relationship with his father is vague. Heinz has little opportunity to have a decisive role in the close relationship between mother and son. Daniel and his father have therefore always remained rather distant.

The focus of Daniel's chart is the right side, You-oriented. At first sight the aspect pattern looks like a cradle; on closer examination it only consists of triangles and linear figures. Blue aspects are in a majority – a quality of consciousness oriented towards harmony.

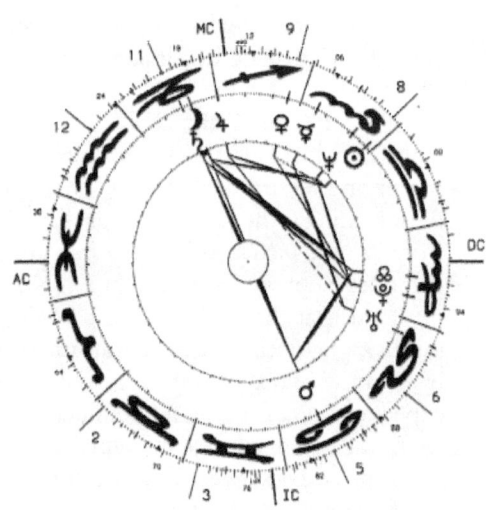

Daniel radix chart, born 1960

The aspect pattern is red-blue. Only a single green one-way semi-sextile is present, as with sister Anna. The Sun lies on the 8th house cusp, in conjunction to Neptune. The theme of the "Neptunian father" crops up here again, one who seems to be "far away". On the 8th house cusp in Scorpio, the important thing is to conform to social norms, to be "someone" in society, to have a position. The green-blue aspected Sun indicates that Daniel has not experienced his father as active, assertive, practical or inspiring, but weak, striving for harmony, possibly also lazy and shiftless.

The Moon and Saturn in Daniel's chart are in conjunction in the shadow of the 11th house cusp, which immediately evokes the close maternal bond. In the 10th house, Saturn provides little inner security, and cannot provide inner rootedness as it would down in the collective space of the 3rd or 4th houses. Saturn at the top of the chart is often a "worrying Saturn", and the close relationship with the mother also receives something existentially necessary, which seems to provide security. We can also infer that the mother "wears the trousers" in the family, as Saturn is clearly higher than the Sun. The opposition between Moon/Saturn and Mars on the 5th house cusp shows tensions and conflicts between his own masculinity (Mars) and the close mother/son bond. The subjective, close relationship with the mother could in this context also have led to feelings of guilt, if Daniel also tried to give more expression to his own masculine libido and aggression.

The Third Child, Daughter Laura

Laura was a late arrival, born 7 years after Daniel. The parents had moved to another town years earlier. The family appeared to be happy. The father had a well-paid managerial job in a large company. The mother took care of the household and brought up the three children, who were friendly and helpful.

However, in reality the father was finding it more and more difficult to cope with his job. His alcohol addiction became more and more threatening, until one day he lost his job in unfortunate circumstances. He was unemployed for several years, lost his professional connections, let himself go more and more and finally gave up. After this, he was drunk nearly every day. Family life suffered greatly.

Laura radix chart, born 1967

At first, in early childhood, Laura was not yet very consciously involved in this family background. She was a more restless child than her siblings, and not quite as good. On some occasions, she stubbornly tried to assert her will with her parents. It was hard for her to accept her mother's orders or rules: she wanted to know exactly why something was not allowed and was not satisfied with just being told "don't do that". The mother often compared Laura to the older siblings and wondered why they were so good and obedient, and Laura always caused problems.

Laura's relationship with her mother was tense. She wanted to do what mother said, but this was hard for her because it caused conflicts and problems. Often what her mother wanted conflicted with what she wanted. There were in frequent confrontations. Ingrid was anxious to support her family and at least outwardly maintain the appearance of a united family. She therefore had little time for Laura. Above all, she tried to teach her daughter to be independent and to have a good career, so that later she would not have to be dependent on a man – as she herself was.

During puberty, Laura did not understand why her mother did not get divorced. Family circumstances were extremely bad and Laura's greatest wish at this time was to leave home as soon as possible. At the age of 16, the opportunity presented itself to go to another town to start a training course, and she left her parents' house. She defied her mother's wish that she enter the civil service like her brother and sister.

The static aspect pattern, consisting of two large quadrilateral figures, gives a very stable impression. The Moon Node is unaspected, and Mercury is attached via two oppositions to Uranus and Pluto. The aspect pattern is red-blue, apart from a one-way semi-sextile, like her two siblings. The overall impression is of symmety and harmony, which can easily draw attention away from the inner tensions, with five separate oppositions. The direction of the pattern is vertically oriented towards the 10th house, where there is an accumulation of planets. Here the life theme is individual development, in a sense outgrowing the family and discovering one's own independence and autonomy.

Uranus and Pluto in conjunction in the 4th house indicate a parental home where the atmosphere was not really conducive to developing a feeling of rootedness and security. On the contrary, since earliest childhood Laura felt like a stranger in her own family, like a fifth wheel. As the third child and fifth member of the family, she found it hard to establish a close bond with parents or siblings, to find her place in the family. The large age difference between herself and her siblings made this even more difficult.

The semi-sextile between Sun and Saturn shows that already in Laura's earliest childhood, father and mother had little to say to each other. The Moon and Saturn form a one-way square, Sun and Moon a trine and Sun/Saturn a one-way semi-sextile. The 'I Am' archetype [of the three ego planets] forms a Learning triangle, to which Mars is connected in a large Talent triangle.

Laura's relationship with her mother is correspondingly burdened by the Moon/Saturn square; each has limited access to the other and usually thinks differently and has differing or even opposing wishes and needs. Sometimes Laura openly rebels against her; at other times she thinks she is a bad girl, especially compared to her conventional siblings. She then tends to have a bad conscience and feel guilty with regard to her mother. But the differences between mother and daughter are so deep that Laura, although she herself denies it, must look for confrontation. However, confrontation not only means unproductive fighting and conflict, but also presents the chance to develop awareness and self-knowledge. The square is appropriately in a vertical position in the conscious area of the chart.

Saturn lies after the Low Point of the 10th house in the intercepted sign of Pisces near the 'zero point'. This position indicates insecurity and anxieties. Mother Ingrid experienced great existential anxiety when she was pregnant with Laura and was very worried about the future. The trine to Neptune softens Saturn, and hence physical awareness and the ability to set boundaries. The mother has really tried to achieve security and autonomy. However, Saturn provides the image of Sisyphus, who has to roll the rock up to the 11th house cusp, but which falls back again and again into intercepted Pisces and the Low Point there. In Daniel's case, Saturn = mother is very close to the 11th house cusp: the mother thinks she is very close to achieving her goal, is ready to touch it and mobilises all her strength. However, in Laura's case, Saturn, or the mother, has fallen back powerlessly into the Low Point and the intercepted sign: she has not managed it and is in danger of giving up.

Laura is emotionally closer to her father than to her mother. They both understand each other well, even without words; they are "on the same wavelength". Both have Sun in Pisces, and they speak the same language. Laura probably suffers more from her father's troubles, which he seems to be trying to drown more and more in alcohol and drug abuse. This is expressed in the trine between Moon and Sun, which indicates a smooth relationship, albeit without including an evaluation as to whether the bond is positive or negative. Here it can also suggest an identification with the father that hinders her own development. In fact, Laura often worries about "ending up like her father".

The Sun is high up in the cardinal area of the 10th house, but in intercepted Pisces. It is aspected in blue and green. In the house horoscope, the Sun only has a one-way trine to Neptune and is otherwise unaspected. In her childhood fantasies, Laura imagined that her father had a special and unusual profession, e.g. policeman or fireman, etc. She admired him for it. But later she realised that this did not correspond to reality. On the contrary, her father was really not so great and wonderful; he was actually weak, unstable and not capable of asserting himself and ensuring his survival. He escaped into alcohol and drug addition, an analogy to the planet Neptune and the sign of Pisces. For Laura, this was a great disappointment, which is also fittingly Neptunian.

Comparing Horoscopes

The Family Models of the family members are now compared.

Moon/Saturn – The Mother-Child Relationship

In the basic horoscope of father Heinz, there is a Moon-Saturn trine, indicating a strong maternal bond with a certain coercion towards good conduct. This complicates any deliberate confrontation with his mother, as it might evoke conflicts that the trine may not like to experience.

His wife Ingrid's ego planets are only connected indirectly via a third planet. Saturn is only attached to the aspect pattern by conjunction to Mercury/Mars. The Moon stands in opposition to Uranus and sextile to Mars. Her parents' influence was only experienced indirectly, so Ingrid was able to distance herself from them more easily.

The older daughter Anna has Moon and Saturn connected by sextile. This reveals that, like her father, she has a strong bond with her mother and probably the mother's demands of Anna to adapt and to behave well. The sextile wants to adapt and avoid conflict in order to be able to live in a harmonious and peaceful world. This can result in Anna neglecting or even repressing any of her own wishes and needs which would conflict with a harmonious relationship.

Both parents have Saturn in the 3rd house, as does Anna. Saturn in the 3rd house suggests that security and protection is sought in a way of thinking that takes into account and conforms to collective norms and attitudes. Here I feel secure if I know how I should behave in certain situations and what I should say when. There is a desire to adapt to 'groupthink', perhaps also in the case of Moon/Saturn aspects in the form of the commandment "Thou shalt honour thy father and mother."

Anna's Moon stands in opposition to Uranus, a tension aspect to a spiritual principle and feminine planet. In the 5th house, the Moon would like to play, be carefree and have direct contact with others.

However, the aspects to it give the impression of inculcations from the environment such as: Pull yourself together! Don't be so open! Behave according to the rules! The Moon's contact behaviour is manipulated; it cannot move freely. Anna has the impression that she cannot express her feelings as freely as she would like, she feels controlled and guided by demands and (moral) claims. Interestingly, her mother also has this aspect in her chart, on the encounter axis 1/7. It suggests that the mother has passed her own Moon/Uranus social behaviour on to her daughter, or that the daughter has learned this by watching her mother. As children, both mother and daughter were strongly influenced by their respective grandmothers, which is associated with Uranus.

In Daniel's case, Moon/Saturn stand in conjunction in the 10th house, in opposition to Mars and with blue aspects to Neptune, Moon Node and Pluto. Here, the Saturn position in the family development moves from the collective upwards into the conscious area, now near the 11th house cusp. The role function of the mother has changed. Probably the mother noticed over the years that basing her thinking and behaving on the collective did not bring the desired security. Saturn at the top of the horoscope indicates fears; in the 10th house stress area it indicates experiences of powerlessness and attempts to compensate for this.

The Moon/Saturn conjunction also indicates that the mother would like to have had a particularly good and decent son – in the individual space all the others are looking at me, so that it is important to be a loving and obedient son. The conjunction indicates a very close and possibly complex maternal bond. Actually, mother Ingrid and son Daniel do feel very closely connected.

Daniel left home at age 20 only to move in with his girlfriend immediately, and soon to marry. Children came along, a house was built and the family is perfect. The right-side emphasis of the aspect pattern indicates that Daniel is very focused on the You and on his environment. It is therefore understandable that it is difficult to differentiate between Moon and Saturn, i.e. between his experiences as a child and those of his mother. Mars in opposition to Moon/Saturn is a significant disturbing factor for the close bond between mother and son. Mars is connected with Daniel's own experience of his masculinity and the close mother-child bond probably finds it a threat.

For the younger daughter Laura, Moon and Saturn are in a square aspect to each other, Moon in the 1st house and Saturn in the 10th house just after the Low Point. Mother Ingrid's Moon is also in the 1st house. We are already familiar with the Saturn position in the shadow of the 11th house from Daniel's horoscope, the mother probably found herself in a similar situation as at Daniel's birth.

The red aspect between Moon-Saturn shows a tense relationship between mother and daughter with conflicts and friction. The square is one-way; energy only runs from Moon to Saturn, from daughter to mother. Laura experiences the relationship to her mother as conflictive. What the mother requires from her conflicts with her own wishes and interests. If she follows her mother's wishes, she must suppress her own, if she follows her own impulses, she must defy her mother. The former makes her sad, and the latter makes her feel guilty towards her mother, because she wants to be a good girl yet at the same time do her own thing.

The vertical positioning in Laura's horoscope reveals that she seeks conscious confrontation with this issue. In puberty, this is still very conflictive with fighting, and is occasionally linked with feelings of guilt. Over time, Laura comes to experience the relationship with her mother more and more as an opportunity to learn new things, for self-awareness and as a spur to further development. In this sense, she benefits from the red aspect, which apparently makes a harmonious mother-relationship impossible.

Sun Position

Father Heinz has Pisces Sun in conjunction to Mercury and opposition to Neptune on the 5/11 axis. There are also semi-sextiles to Venus and Jupiter. The aspect connections with sensitive planets indicate a soft, thin-skinned self-confidence, idealistic, sensitive and subtle. This does not indicate a strong, expansive and autonomous Sun position but rather to a yearning individual searching for ideal love. This Sun is less suited to assertiveness in the world, to autonomy, the development of strength and self-confidence, especially as far as the Moon/Saturn trine is concerned. Heinz's father might have been able to put more emphasis on a strong Sun position, but he was absent for most of Heinz's childhood.

Mother Ingrid has Sun in Sagittarius at the IC, with trine to Neptune, square to Jupiter/Uranus and in opposition to Moon Node. This is a very strong position, even though the Sun would naturally develop more in line with its own nature in the individual area. The Moon Node reveals that the actual developmental task takes place there. Even so, the Sun lies on a cardinal axis, so that Ingrid eventually had to take on the "Sun role" in the family.

In the children's horoscopes, this is reflected in the position of Saturn, which for the oldest daughter is still in the collective area, but for the younger children has moved to the individual area. This also shows that the younger children do not really experience an individualised mother, but a mother who suffers from existential angst and the fear of losing the achieved position and security again. This does not correspond to natural Sun autonomy, but leads to defensive, Saturnine behaviour.

Anna's Sun in Scorpio lies on the 2nd house cusp in conjunction to Neptune/Mercury/Moon Node and square to Venus. This is a strong Sun from the point of view of the house position, which enables Anna to achieve autonomy in life, even though in a defensive way in the 2nd house. Her self-confidence is oriented towards security and delimitation (fixed house and sign). The conjunction to Neptune resonates with her father's alcohol problem.

Daniel's Sun is also in Scorpio in conjunction to Neptune and sextile Jupiter on the 8th house cusp. In a strong house position, the Sun indicates similar qualities to Anna's, only under different environmental conditions – it no longer involves self-esteem as for Anna but his own position in society and complying with norms and duties. With aspect connections to Neptune and Jupiter, he looks for his own place cautiously and rather sensitively; the blue aspect does not prompt him to great or fighting deeds.

Laura's Sun lies in the cardinal area of the 10th house, with trines to Moon and Mars and semi-sextile to Saturn. This is a blue-green aspected Sun, which is also in intercepted Pisces. Relatively close to the MC, the desire for individualisation and independence is indeed great, but the equipment to do this is rather sensitive and thin-skinned. However, the Sun also has energy outlets through the trines to Moon and Mars.

Here we can see a development of the Sun function in the family. The older daughter's Sun is in the 2nd house, in the son it has moved to the 8th house and in the younger daughter to the 'ideal' position of the 10th house. Over the years, the father apparently coped more and more successfully with his role function (house position), but without the necessary inner substance "maturing", as Laura's Sun remains in a water sign with a strong Neptune connection and green-blue aspects.

Comparison of Moon/Saturn and Sun Themes

In the charts of the three children, the Sun is not optimally placed. There is no combative self-confidence, with the desire for expansion and autonomy, but instead a sensitive ego, subtle, with Neptune also "thin-skinned", permeable and sensitive.

There is a similar father-theme in the Sun position of all three children, which corresponds to the real father's problems. In this family, there seems to be a Sun/Neptune/Pisces theme, a sensitive self-awareness which makes self-assertion and autonomy difficult. All family members have either a Sun/Neptune aspect or a Pisces Sun position, or even both. In Laura's house chart, there is an intercepted Sun/Neptune trine.

Nearly all family members also have a Moon/Saturn theme, i.e. a mother/child theme, a close and influential relationship between mother and child.

The combination of these two factors: significant Moon/Saturn bond with "weak" Sun position, can be more closely examined against the background of depth psychological findings with regard to early childhood development.

Depth Psychological Consideration

In early childhood development, after an initial Neptunian phase of oneness (in the first three months of life), the next phase is a symbiotic bond between the child (Moon) and its mother (Saturn), which is fundamental for the child's emotional development. This experience of unity should, among other things, provide basic trust, which is necessary for the later separation from the mother ("emotional birth").

A Moon/Saturn connection in the horoscope can show how the child has experienced and internalised the symbiosis and subsequent separation from the mother. Conjunctions can indicate a "prolonging" of the symbiosis beyond the normal duration; the mother and/or the child do not want to leave the bond. Blue aspects can have a similar, but not quite so binding, effect. A red aspect can deeply disturb the symbiotic bond and inhibit the development of basic trust. The child may have had the impression that they did not receive enough love and that they were not "satisfied" in their emotional relationship with their mother.

During later developmental stages in which the child separates from the mother, in a way cuts the emotional umbilical cord with her, the paternal role becomes more and more important. The father takes over a vital role, which helps the child to find their own position within the family and not to feel so united with the mother. The father can encourage independence and autonomy, self-confidence and individuality, discernable in the Sun position. The child learns that it can not only have one close relationship (i.e. with the mother), but also a second one with the father, and perhaps a third, fourth or fifth with other people...

A weak Sun position shows that the so-called "triangulation" (the father joins the mother-child relationship as the third force) has been unsuccessful or at least not optimal.

The father, or more precisely the paternal attachment figure, was not able to give the child sufficient self-confidence and desire for autonomy, because he himself did not possess these qualities or because he was emotionally or actually absent (e.g. too busy working). Consequently, the child found it difficult or impossible to separate from the mother, and also as an adult strongly identifies with the maternal theme. The person is not able to realise their potential and gain self confidence (the real significance of the Sun). This also affects later relationships in adult life.

Family Moon Node Charts

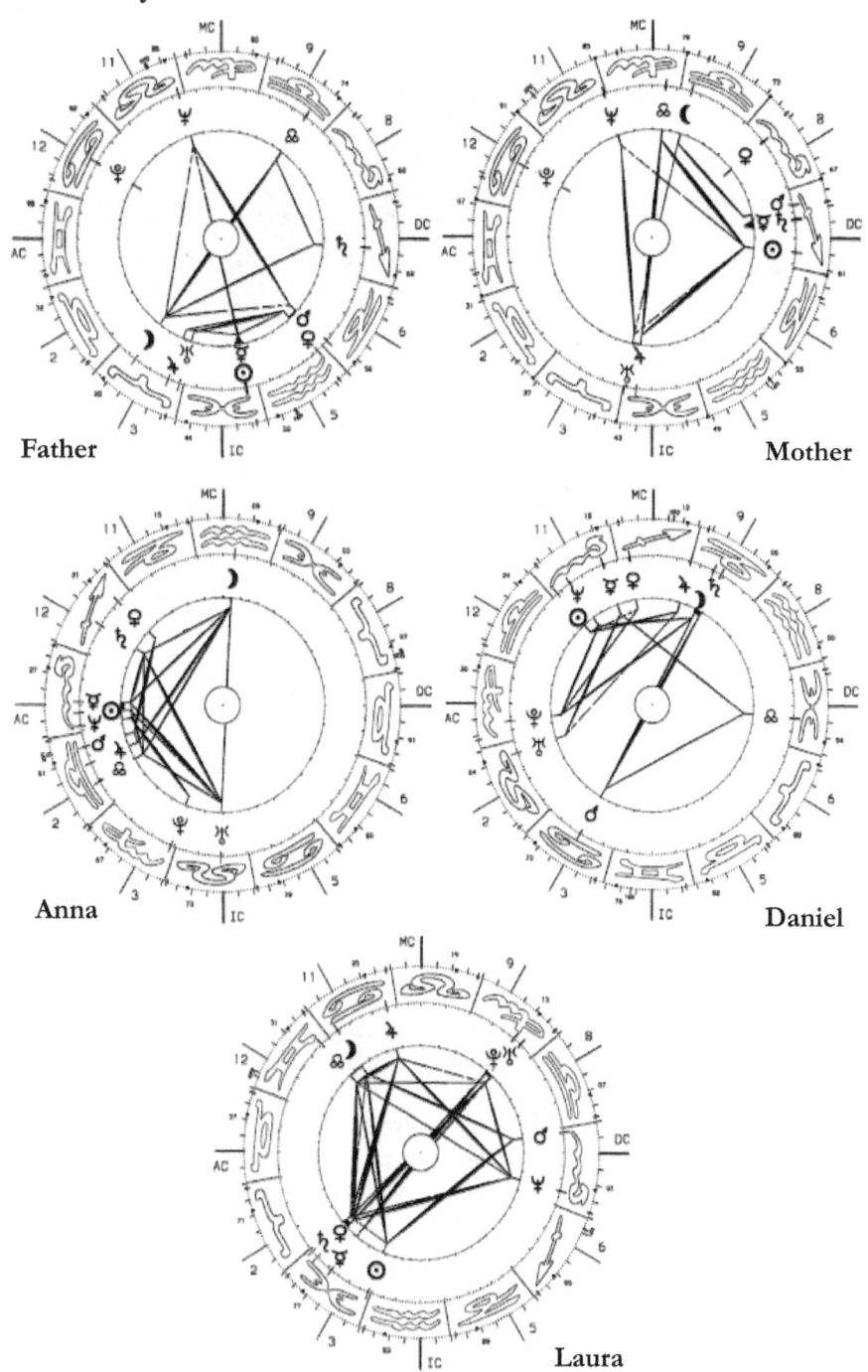

Comparison of Individual Click Horoscopes

Looking at individual click horoscopes gives further important clues.

Father Heinz and Mother Ingrid

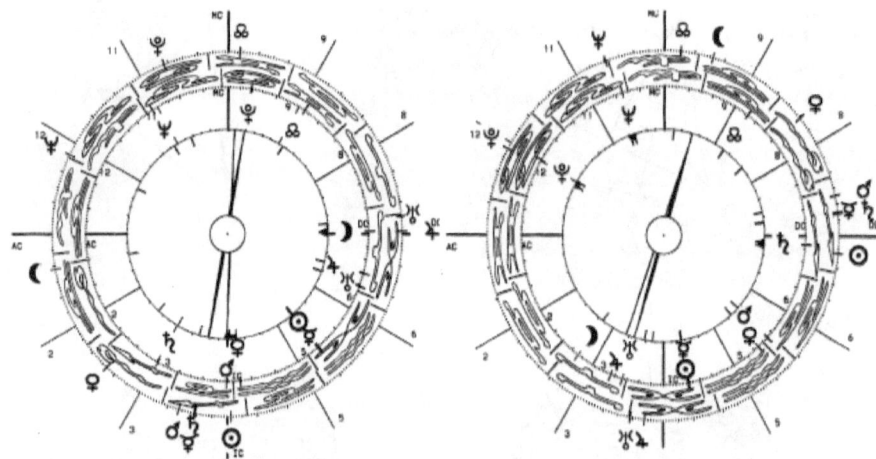

Clicks: Father-Mother house   Clicks: Father-Mother moon node

In the house click chart, we find a conjunction click between Ingrid's Sun and the Heinz's Venus/Mars conjunction, whereby Heinz's Mars lies opposite Ingrid's Moon Node. Ingrid is initially deterred by Heinz in this point from the learning task of the Moon Node; the path towards it becomes more difficult and only possible after a lot of experiences. Heinz's Moon lies in conjunction to Ingrid's Jupiter/Uranus conjunction. This is probably experienced ambivalently: on the one hand as a welcome and valued sense with Jupiter, but also with a portion of unpredictability and agitation with Uranus.

In the moon node click chart, there is a Sun/Saturn conjunction at the DC, which could indicate a "karmic" relationship. At least there seems to be some "history" to this relationship, which can now be drawn on in the moon node chart. In addition, Ingrid's Moon is in opposition to Heinz's Jupiter/Uranus conjunction, and therefore involves the same issue as in the house click with the signs reversed.

Both Ingrid and Heinz have ego planets that "click" with other planets, an indication of the significance of the relationship for their personal ego development.

Father Heinz and Daughter Anna

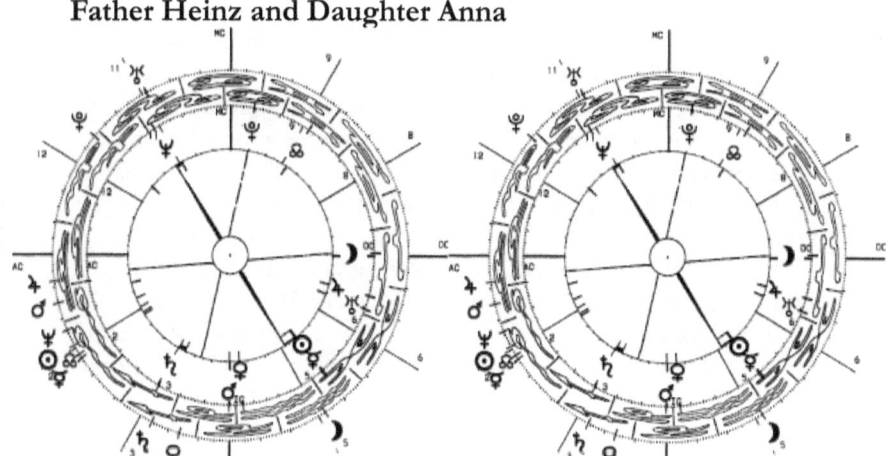

Clicks: Father-Anna house   Clicks: Father-Anna moon node

In the house click horoscope, we find a Saturn/Saturn conjunction click in the 3rd house and a conjunction between Anna's Moon and Heinz's Sun, the classical attribution Moon = child and Sun = father.

In the moon node click horoscope, there is an opposition between Anna's Sun and Heinz's Saturn. Here too, aspects between the ego planets are emphasised, i.e. this family relationship emphasises ego development.

Mother Ingrid and Son Daniel

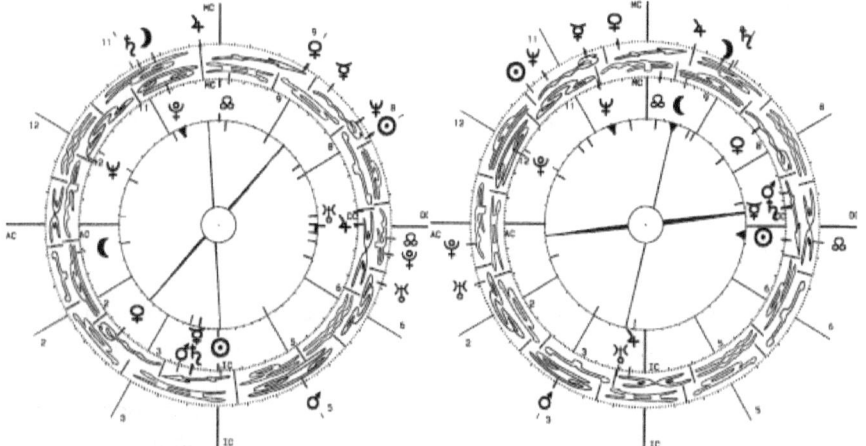

Clicks: Mother-Daniel house   Clicks: Mother-Daniel moon node

In the house click chart, Daniel's Moon is in conjunction with his mother's Pluto. This greatly intensifies the effect of Daniel's radix Moon/Saturn conjunction, and indicates a very close maternal bond.

In the sign comparison, Ingrid's Pluto lies in Cancer in conjunction to Daniel's Mars and in opposition to the Moon/Saturn conjunction in Capricorn. The Pluto-Moon/Saturn aspect is repeated both in the house and sign comparison, which underlines its significance.

In the moon node click chart, there is another opposition, but this time between Daniel's Pluto in the 1st and Ingrid's Mars and Saturn in the 7th house. "Before", the role allocation may have also lain in reversed signs.

Finally, there is a reversal of ascendants in the basic chart, i.e. Ingrid's AC at 24° Virgo lies opposite Daniel's AC at 19° Pisces. The Meridian Axis is also reversed: Ingrid's MC at approx. 22° Gemini lies in opposition to Daniel's MC at 25° Sagittarius. This is another indication of a very strong attraction and a kind of rivalry between mother and son, which could perhaps be helped by the growing awareness of Daniel's Moon/Saturn theme.

Mother Ingrid and Daughter Laura

Here in the house click chart we see a Moon/Moon conjunction click, which both enjoy and which can provide Laura's love-needing Cancer Moon with important relationship experiences with her mother, even though this bond will always be disturbed by the opposition of the maternal Uranus (the father also experiences this with his Moon in conjunction click to the mother's Jupiter/Uranus). But perhaps Laura's childhood experience of oneness with her mother ("symbiosis")

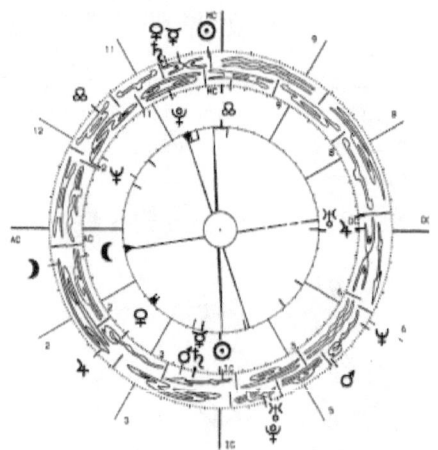

Clicks: Mother-Laura house

was so close that the only way for differentiation to take place was through conflict; sure enough, a square between Moon and Saturn is found in Laura's radix.

The strong blue emphasis of Laura's aspect pattern, particularly the exclusively blue aspected Neptune, can be seen as an indication of being spoilt, and of a connection to so-called paradise fantasies in early childhood, meaning that there was a lack of the "optimal frustration" which is necessary to enable separation from the mother. As suggested at the beginning, Neptune symbolises the early childhood phase of oneness, the feeling of being at one with everything, of unity with the whole world. In the case of harmonious experiences this can correspond to a kind of paradise fantasy, which one might be unwilling to relinquish with only blue aspects. The experience of red aspects in the chart will then be particularly painful if they are not strong or numerous.

Finally, there is a house-click conjunction between Laura's Saturn/Venus and Ingrid's Pluto. As for Daniel, this is an indication of the strong effect and influence of the mother on both children. For Laura however, with Venus, her self-image as a woman and her personal libido is affected, and there is also the opposition of Uranus/Pluto to Ingrid's Pluto to consider. This is also an intensive power theme on the 4/10 axes where Laura's Sun is situated.

Laura's Sun in the house click lies opposite Ingrid's Sun and in conjunction with her Moon Node. The daughter gives the mother important individuation impulses; we remember that she could not understand why her mother did not leave the difficult marriage and stand on her own two feet. The mother believed that she was not in a position to due to her inadequate education. However, the daughter knew that she was the one who guaranteed the survival of the family of five during difficult times.

Family and Development

In this work, not all important and notable points in the comparison of the horoscopes of the individual family members can be addressed. There is just too much material. It is, for example, also interesting that the parents both have a dynamic aspect pattern, with triangles and linear figures, while the children's aspect patterns are static. The parents' aspect patterns are tri-coloured, while the children's are almost completely red-blue with just one semi-sextile.

It is also notable that the opposition on the relationship axis 5/11 of the father continues in the charts of the three children. If we look at these four charts from the point of view of this opposition, we discover that for Anna the opposition on the axis 5/11 blocks the aspect pattern on the You side, while for Daniel the aspect pattern is blocked on the I side. For Laura the opposition is at the Low Point 4/10 and in the shadow of 5/11 and forms a symmetry axis or even a pivot, a thorn in the side of the blue kite, which allows no peace and harmony. All three children try in different ways to address and master the relationship theme, which they have already observed in their father.

This view of the family shows that, within a family, certain themes and developmental patterns can be repeated with variation from generation to generation. All the family members discussed here share an emphasis on the theme of ego development. In the comparison of the charts between parents and children, there is a notable emphasis on Sun, Moon and Saturn. In this family, Neptune is also highlighted; in other families there will probably be one or several other planetary characteristics.

In Heinz and Ingrid's family the main development themes are found in the Moon/Saturn aspects, which indicate a close maternal bond, perhaps even a fixation in the symbiotic phase, and in the comparatively weak Sun positions, which show that the father offers the children few possibilities that could have helped them to separate from the maternal bond.

The fact that this problem can apparently continue from one generation to another raises the question as to whether such fixations in the emotional development can be "inherited". Similar constellations also occur in previous generations of this family, which we will not go into now, as it is beyond the scope of this work. It may for example be possible that parents who themselves remain stuck in a certain point of their early childhood development (fixation) in the upbringing of their own children repeat the same "mistakes". They cannot give their children something that is strange and unfamiliar to them, in this case a strong sense of self-confidence.

From an esoteric perspective, we can also imagine that in this case, the three children have "sought out" this couple with a suitable ancestry in order to experience and revise their own Moon/Saturn and Sun problems from a new perspective in this family, but that their actual causes may be found in previous incarnations and are not caused by their current family situations.

The question arises whether this repetition or even passing on of "problem themes" can be stopped at some point. I imagine that this may happen when a family member starts to consciously confront the theme and tries to solve the problem individually. In this case, the overcoming of conflicts would not only be an issue of personal mental hygiene, but also a form of family hygiene that has an effect on generations to come.

▫ ▫ ▫ ▫ ▫

Part 2: Children and Upbringing

This second part of the book contains four articles on the growing child and its upbringing.

The Child's Horoscope as an Aid to Upbringing, by Louise Huber
In this article from 1995 Louise Huber sets out some key factors in the approach of astrological psychology to the interpretation of the horoscopes of children to help the process of bringing them up, with particular focus on parental roles and stages of personality integration.

The Child's Horoscope, by Holger Oehmichen
Gives an simple overview of the use of children's charts from the perspective of a practising therapist.

Children's Horoscopes, by Rainer Bauer
A comprehensive exposition of the interpretation of the horoscopes of children which marries astrological psychology with the educational understanding of Rudolph Steiner.

The Horoscope as an Aid in the Teaching of Gifted Children, by Karin Goebel
A teacher considers case histories of three gifted children ('Indigo children') and their learning needs, how these are reflected in their birth charts, and points the way to further research.

The following Huber books give details of features of astrological psychology that are of particular relevance to the context of children and education:

Aspect Pattern Astrology, by Bruno & Louise Huber
  Covers the significance of aspect patterns, their shaping, colouring, etc.

LifeClock, by Bruno & Louise Huber
  Covers the technique of Age Progression and its association with the developmental stages of life.

The Planets and their Psychological Meaning, by Bruno & Louise Huber
  Considers the pychological meaning of each of the planets and their significance in the growth process.

The Child's Horoscope as an Aid to Upbringing

Three Basic Motivations

Louise Huber

First published in AstroLog Issues 85-86, April-June 1995

Introduction

To get the most out of a child's horoscope, we must start by examining our own attitude towards the child. What kind of child is it, what role does it play in our lives, where has it come from and where does it want to go, what kind of relationship do I myself have with my child and what does it require from me? What place does it have in the sweep of human development?

In the foreword of her book *The Secret of Childhood*, Maria Montessori wrote: *"it is not the physical child that can give a powerful, even decisive push to the betterment of mankind, but the child's spirit. The spirit of the child can bring about real human progress and perhaps even the dawn of a new culture."* The investigation of the child's spirit and the recognition of its special, innate quality and its mission in the world is the most profound significance of a child's horoscope.

Over the last hundred years, the relationship of adults to children has changed greatly due to man's awakening consciousness and the gradual development of science and psychological understanding in general.

To make sure that we enter into the spirit of this special relationship with the child from the outset, I would like to quote a few fitting words from Kahlil Gibran:

> YOUR CHILDREN ARE NOT YOUR CHILDREN,
> THEY ARE THE SONS AND DAUGHTERS OF LIFE'S LONGING FOR ITSELF.
> THEY COME THROUGH YOU BUT ARE NOT FROM YOU,
> AND THOUGH THEY ARE WITH YOU YET THEY BELONG NOT TO YOU.
>
> YOU MAY GIVE THEM YOUR LOVE BUT NOT YOUR THOUGHTS,
> FOR THEY HAVE THEIR OWN THOUGHTS.
> YOU MAY HOUSE THEIR BODIES BUT NOT THEIR SOULS,
> FOR THEIR SOULS DWELL IN THE HOUSE OF TOMORROW,
> WHICH YOU CANNOT VISIT, NOT EVEN IN YOUR DREAMS.
> YOU MAY STRIVE TO BE LIKE THEM, BUT SEEK NOT TO MAKE THEM LIKE YOU.
> FOR LIFE GOES NOT BACKWARD NOR TARRIES WITH YESTERDAY.
>
> YOU ARE THE BOWS FROM WHICH YOUR CHILREN
> AS LIVING ARROWS ARE SENT FORTH.
> THE ARCHER SEES THE MARK UPON THE PATH OF THE INFINITE, AND
> HE BENDS YOU WITH HIS MIGHT THAT HIS ARROWS MAY GO SWIFT AND FAR
> LET YOUR BENDING IN THE ARCHER'S HAND BE FOR GLADNESS
>   KAHLIL GIBRAN, *The Prophet*

Appreciation

By considering the child in this way, we bring the same respect for and appreciation of its individuality and innermost being as we would to a cherished guest in our house. We know that children harbour within themselves their own life secret, which can reveal the mystery of the human soul, that it contains something unknown which enables adults to see their own problems in a new light. This point of view can form the basis of a new direction in the raising of children and the study of human life and existence. This approach can influence and improve the social life of all humanity.

The Uniqueness of the Child

Our assumption is therefore that every child already contains a uniqueness, an individual self, like a seed that develops according to its inner image. Just as in nature every plant has its seed that grows into a plant or tree, in every child the germ of his inner being is sown, which wants to develop according to its latent potential. It is our responsibility to find this individual talent, this originality. In every horoscope, this uniqueness is revealed in the individual aspect pattern. For the inner person to develop and thrive it is vital to acknowledge this.

Individual differences can already be seen even in young babies. Many mothers with several children say spontaneously: "This child is different from his siblings." Some are lively, open, and interested in people and their environment, while others are calm, more self-involved, anxious and shy. Some children can adapt to changes in the environment more easily than others. When they grow up, some children are more active, courageous and persistent, and others lack thoughtfulness, caution and restraint. The child's particular nature can be discerned in the horoscope, and this knowledge used in the upbringing, as it enables a better, conscious understanding of the child's personal qualities and allows it to be correctly guided. From this point of view, a child's horoscope is very valuable for its psychological development and reveals much of how its inner character will develop.

Psychological Findings

According to psychological findings, the inappropriate attitudes of many young people are usually the result of difficult early childhood experiences. The child naturally learns to expect that the world will correspond to his innermost ideas. If he is not let down by his parents, the key attachment figures, his ego will grow undamaged until a state of complete self-confidence is reached. This in turn will lead to the development of a healthy overall attitude towards life, and the child will be able cope with life's tasks and obstacles.

However, if the child's basic trust, faith and security are let down by the failures of the parents or the educating collective, he is thrown back onto his own resources. He builds a form of defence for his own protection, a so-called "false ego". Later on, this must be recognised as such and the difficult task of dismantling it must be undergone. Conversely, parents can also project their own ideals onto the child, who is unable to fulfil them because they do not correspond to his innate talents.

At some point, the maturing young person must also liberate himself from his parents in order to become himself.

That is why it is better to be guided by the child's true potential and talents right from the beginning. A horoscope is a neutral instrument and cannot be swayed by wishful thinking; it is objective and reveals the subject's true nature.

Of course, many problems in a child's upbringing are caused by the parents themselves; by their own inadequacies, worries, disappointments, unfulfilled expectations of life and marital problems. In these instances too, it is useful to consult a horoscope for it is incorruptible.

A Better Understanding for a New Age

The consultation of a child's horoscope can make it easier to understand the child, his needs and the conditions under which he grows up and develops. It also enables an understanding of the spirit of the age, the hitherto undiscovered inner needs and images of the new man. By studying the child's horoscope, and therefore his character, more closely, we can not only adapt well to the child and his innermost character, but also to the 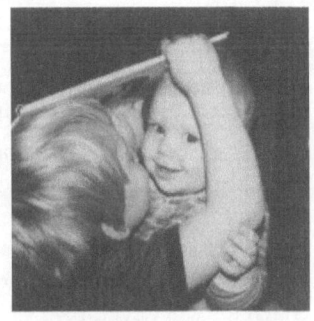 *zeitgeist*. This will enable us to recognise our own perspective through examination and correction of ourselves and our own attitudes.

It is true that all parents compare themselves with their children. Many are proud and happy if the child takes after them, others are upset if their children do not take after them. Many parents think "my child should have a better chance in life than me and should have more than me," and so on. However, we should bear in mind that such ideas may be beyond the child's actual potential, which can lead to disappointed parents and criticised children.

It is also the case that we pass on uncritically to our children the general norms and cultural values that we have absorbed in a certain period. People's quick, possibly even shocked reaction to this is that "It's understandable though, it has always been like this." However, cultural and societal structures are constantly changing. The change in the approach to what for example was good, right and desirable fifty years ago is proof of this. The ideas that "That's how I was brought up" or "It wasn't any better for us" are not realistic and only show an inability to keep up with the times.

The assumption of behavioural psychology, that the child is a blank slate upon which genetic make-up and conditioning (nature and nurture), upbringing and adaptation to the environment then shape the person, is also mistaken.

It is very important in this new age that adults accept the concept and understanding of a child's true nature. Then the child will no longer be seen as a possession with which one can do as one pleases, but as a guest, a gift, whose spirit has an innate mission to usher in a new age, a new culture. This will enable many problems to disappear by themselves or be solved much more easily.

Individuality

The most important factor in bringing up a child is therefore to understand and be sensitive to the child's uniqueness. Mothers often have this inner understanding of what is good for their child, what he really needs. If they followed their instincts or their heart much more, it would avoid so many mistakes being made in the child's upbringing.

This acknowledgement of the uniqueness of the child's developing ego also changes the way standards are set for and demands are made of the child. In the child's horoscope, intrinsic basic motivation can be immediately seen in the graphic structure of the aspect pattern. Knowing this, we will then not demand or expect something from the child that he cannot achieve because it does not correspond to his abilities. Expecting something from the child that he cannot do is a heavy burden for him to bear, an inhumane form of torture, and is essentially a human rights issue. The child has the right to develop in his own individual way, and has long been denied this.

Life Motivation

The child's horoscope also reveals basic life motivation in the graphic form and colouring of the aspect pattern, as well as its position and direction in the house system. In this process we distinguish between three possible structures and colours, analogous to the three crosses, cardinal, fixed and mutable.

Three Graphic Structures

Quadrangular Motivation – Security (Fixed)
The quadrangular aspect pattern strives for security and corresponds to the fixed cross.

Triangular Motivation – Love (Mutable)
The triangular aspect pattern corresponds to the mutable cross, which is primarily interested in interpersonal relationships, love and contact.

Linear Motivation – Will/Power (Cardinal)
The linear pattern is more will-oriented and corresponds to the cardinal cross. It strives for power and influence and its motivation is the dynamic achievement of objectives.

This distinction alone gives an important key to understand and develop the child's basic motivation. For example, we cannot expect a child with a triangular aspect pattern (oriented towards love and contact) to be motivated by financial considerations; he can only be motivated by love.

The main task of the child's upbringing is therefore to find out his unique, innate, even pre-ordained character. The child's right to self-confidence, self-actualisation, to exercise his own free will and have his own ideality must not be denied. We should accept that the urge for self-actualisation is a profound psychological drive intrinsic to each one of us. It is, however, all too often repressed by our upbringing and the cultural norms of the time or the life situation and is not allowed to develop freely.

The individual creative will is directly dependent on self-confidence. In the process of upbringing, self-will should be treated with great care, be developed and nurtured if it is to evolve. The child himself usually knows what is best for him, as long as he is in touch with his innermost being. If we realised how easily we can hinder this process with our intellect, with our petty, formalistic fears and apprehensions, then we would treat these precious young shoots of life with more care.

If we accept that every child harbours an individual will or plan, we can allow him to develop according to his own ideas. What tends to happen is that this inner, knowing will is broken during children's upbringing. We tell them: "what do you know about that? First you must become someone and achieve something before you can join in the conversation," which means that eventually the child no longer knows what he actually wants.

Career Choice

The choice of career is a key area where the young person is often told what to do. This is another situation where it is helpful if the young person is allowed to make their own choices according to their own abilities and potential. It is not even advisable to predict a child's career based on the horoscope. Premature choice of a child's future profession by the parents is unwise, as it leads to certain abilities being emphasized and encouraged by the parents at the expense of others that are neglected or repressed. The child will then not develop freely and uninhibitedly, but instead is unconsciously prematurely pushed in a certain direction, which may not correspond to his own character and is experienced as a constraint or restriction. The horoscope can definitely indicate potentials and aptitudes, but they are just general tendencies. Specialisations and choices should be left for the young person concerned to make later on. This means he will do his job better and more successfully because he chose it himself.

Lifecycles – Developmental Bursts

The inclination for development of will and self-actualisation is stronger in some life phases or situations than others. There is an interesting biological discovery that states that in development there are quite distinct periods of sensitivity or intensity of receptivity. These are temporary and enable the child to acquire certain skills, such as speech. Once this has happened, the sensitisation switches off. Every character trait and ability develops in this way, i.e. from a particular stimulus during a limited time span. This stimulus is provided both by the child's own instinctive nature and by the environment. The life clock, or the age progression, is the key to this, for we know that the progress of the age point changes the basic psychological inclination or sensitisation every six years. Birth starts the process at the ascendant, and with the progression through the first house, the child has a strong urge to manifest, to take his place in the world. He does all he can to establish himself **physically** in the world. He draws attention to himself by crying. His body needs feeding and caring for and the focus is on developing the physical aspect of the personality.

Age Progression

The second sensitisation phase affects the psyche, and begins right after the Low Point of the first house at about 3½ years. The child becomes more spatially aware and tries to claim his own living space. He becomes more and more possession-oriented, the nearer he gets to the second house cusp. He now grows into the **psychic** world and develops affection for things and people.

In this phase, the child can suffer if his things are taken away, as they belong to his psychological living space, one could even say, to his psychological body. The habits he is starting to form in these early years should not be repressed either, because these habits also form a part of his living space, providing needed security and thus affirmation of his existence. This is all connected with the theme of the second house. Also at this age, around 4 years old, the famous age of defiance sets in, when the child starts to vigorously assert his ego.

This is when most mistakes occur in upbringing, due to the assumption that the child must be tamed, as in every phase when the inner will manifests itself, such as later on during the pubertal or post-pubertal phases. (This always happens in the phase after the Low Point in the mutable houses in the will-forming area of every house axis.) If the child's horoscope shows a conglomeration of planets in the first two houses, or on the opposite side in the seventh and eighth

Part 2 – Children and Upbringing

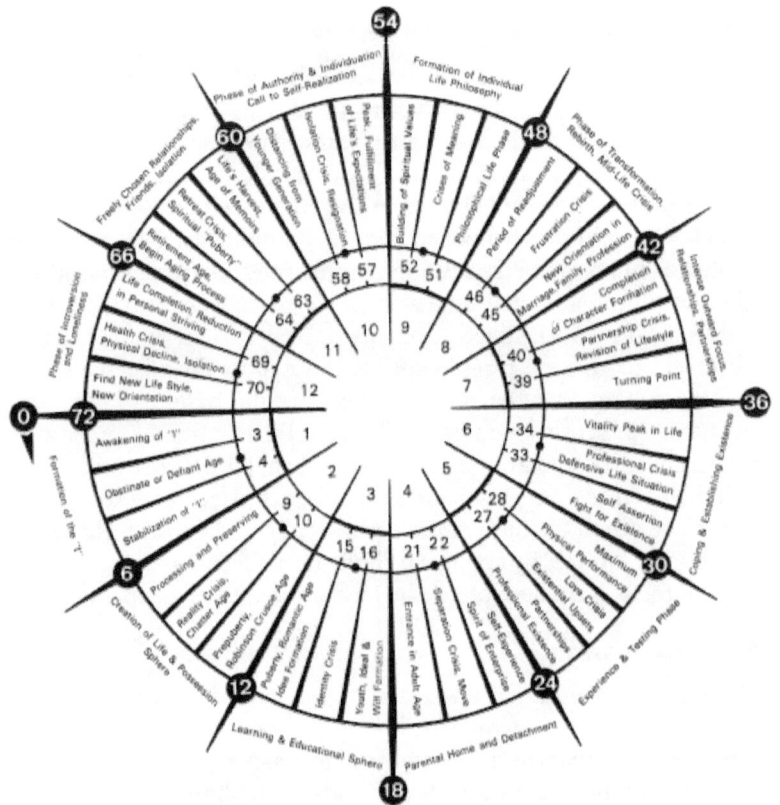

Life Phases from the book *LifeClock*

houses, it indicates more intensive learning phases in these life areas and at these ages. If we also know which planets and aspects are involved, we can adapt the child's upbringing accordingly. Although the intensification and therefore the increased developmental dynamic cannot be avoided, a better understanding is often sufficient to keep things flowing and stop any traumatic blockages building up.

Understanding the Character

It is very important for the harmonious development of self-confidence to recognise these developmental surges and laws, and adapt the upbringing accordingly. The child's horoscope shows how this self-confidence progresses and which possible dangers or inhibitions could arise, and we can make sure that the demands and expectations we make of the child correspond to their potential capabilities. We should study, encourage and support those attitudes that are likely to encourage the child in his ongoing encounters with the world and with himself, his abilities and potential. The individual can then form an early, resilient self-confidence and self-awareness that constitutes the cornerstone of any developing personality. The young person is sure of himself and this inner security enables him to know what he wants and stops him from being led astray by passing fads, drugs or criminal activity, because he has developed a strong core within himself and has a strong sense of values and decency.

He is therefore morally well-adjusted and automatically acknowledges the rights of others, for his own inner authority tells him the difference between right and wrong.

The correct understanding of the child's character and innate uniqueness is then what our pedagogical insight and approach to upbringing should focus on. Once we have done this, our attention should turn to the aims and nature of the upbringing, the educational path, or in a wider context, the value given to the child by our culture. By accepting our children, by respecting their individual liberties, we can enable and promote this process of self-discovery and the development of the personality.

The child's horoscope shows both the uniqueness of the individual and his strengths and weaknesses, the obstacles and restrictions that may inhibit the development of his innermost nature, so they can be avoided.

This is indicated primarily by the layout of the horoscope, the contrast between zodiac (genetic make-up) and houses (environment), and in the aspect pattern. How it is placed and which energy losses the inner self, the centre circle, must incur in its transition to the outside world. In addition, the intelligence planets in particular are an indication of the abilities, where they are situated in the horoscope, how they are related to each other and so on. We will go into this in more detail in the following.

The Five Levels of the Horoscope

1. The Centre Circle
   Core being

2. The Aspect Pattern
   Consciousness structure

3. The Planets
   Life or function organs

4. The Signs of the Zodiac
   Abilities (genetic make-up - nature)

5. The Houses
   Behaviour (environmental influence – nurture)

The Three Personality-Forming Factors: Sun, Moon, Saturn

Experience has shown that, where upbringing is concerned, it is helpful to have some knowledge of the development of the self, the gradual development of ego consciousness and the real implications of different developmental crises. This enables the child to be helped to find and to become himself.

I would therefore now like to explore in more detail the three personality-forming factors, whose gradual development should be the main focus of the upbringing.

We know that the personality consists of three layers of being: physical, emotional and mental, or body, soul and mind. In each of these layers or personality areas, an ego centre is developed during the course of development – a kind of focus of consciousness. Saturn represents the physical body, Moon the emotional body and Sun the mental body. The positions of these three planets in the horoscope tell us a lot about these ego functions.

In adults, the three ego functions should interact as an integrated whole, which constitutes the autonomy of the personality or the individuality. This three-layered, integrated personality can then be permeated and guided by the innermost self, by the soul or the centre circle. This is called the evolution of the self and is characteristic of the self-aware or spiritually-infused personality.

In the child's horoscope, we are interested mainly in the relationship with the parents, whereby Saturn tells us about the mother, the Sun about the father and the Moon about the child himself.

Three Phases of Ego Development

As mentioned above, these are characterised by the three ego-forming planets Sun, Moon and Saturn. The position of these three planets indicates the relationship to the parents as archetypal role models for development of the ego. The position of Saturn indicates the relationship with and influence of the mother, and the Sun that of the father. The Moon represents the child himself, his own feelings and experiences. They tell us where development of the child's personality will progress harmoniously or where it will be problematic. There are different areas in the horoscope in which these main 'ego' planets can be situated. A strong position for Saturn is at the bottom of the horoscope, for the Sun at the top and for the Moon on the contact level in the middle.

People's egos go through different stages and forms of development. Three main phases should be highlighted, as has been clearly identified in psychological research. These three phases are not clearly delimited, but overlap and take place at various times in our lives according to an individual rhythm, depending on the progression of the Age Point and its aspects to the three ego planets.

1st Stage: Saturn – Body – Mother

Astrologically, we can compare the first stage of physical self-awareness with Saturn. Here the childlike ego is still symbiotically connected to the mother. It is even said that the two first years of life are a continuation of the embryonic state. The child's ego is merged with that of the mother: it lives through and with the mother as a unit of life and cannot yet be separated from her. In the unitary field of this primal relationship (symbiosis), there is no psychological delimitation, as would be present in the adult personality. That is why there is no perceptible individualisation of the psyche. This interrelatedness only disappears slowly as the individual ego consciousness develops.

In this symbiotic phase with the mother, the child is affected by the mother's psychological and physical states. For example, the mother's anxiety at the birth is indicated by Saturn or Mars at the ascendant and is communicated to the child; conversely, the mother senses when the child is in danger without needing to be told directly or indirectly. That is why it is important that the mother knows the position of planets near the ascendant in the child's horoscope. The birth circumstances are indicated by any planets at the AC or DC and those of the first year of life in the 1st house. The mother should be very aware of the responsibility of such an intense relationship and work on herself. She should teach herself to be a controlled and loving person, who radiates peace and security and provides creature comforts with a skilled hand. Every child also educates their parents, who can learn a lot from them if open to it. The mother's treatment of the child not only affects his health, but also his attitude to life and to the material demands of life.

If there is poverty or instability in the family and making ends meet is always a worry, this fear, uncertainty and inability to master the material side of life are transferred to the child. This is again visible from the positions of Sun, Moon and Saturn in the first quadrant as well as in the rest of the horoscope. [You can read about this in more detail in *LifeClock:* early-childhood conditioning.]

In astrology, Saturn is known to represent form; the physically and materially established and delimited world. It is also the symbol of the mother, who protectively wraps the child within herself and sets the necessary boundaries for life to develop. From the point of view of the ego, Saturn is physical awareness, the ability to perceive, experience and preserve one's body.

The Physical Ego

The physical side of formation of the ego and its survival therefore depend to a great extent on the mother relationship in the first phase of life. If this relationship was negative, i.e. the mother was not able to provide adequate loving care, then the child unconsciously assumes that other people must take care of his creature comforts in later life; he becomes unable to cope with life. The position of Saturn in the child's horoscope shows the nature of the mother relationship, whether there were conflicts, problems, uncertainties, repressions or states of anxiety, neglect or separations that hindered the child's development.

If the mother relationship was positive, which is naturally indicated by a good Saturn position (often at the bottom of the horoscope), the child also has a basic trust in the life-sustaining forces of nature. Such a person knows that he is at one with everything, with nature, with his own self out of which he exists. He also knows that he will get everything he needs to survive. From this he also develops a faith in God, a healthy and positive attitude to life and the necessary self-confidence for his ego to develop. This is a strength that is critically important for self-assertion in the world and finding happiness. We all know people who do not worry too much about the material side of life, who are carried as if by a mysterious power and who also actually always have what they need.

Where there is a problematic Saturn position, e.g. at the top of the horoscope or on the You side, we can deduce that the child has lacked security and the protection of a nurturing environment in the first years of life. In later life it also transpires that the instinct of self-preservation is undeveloped and the person finds it hard to survive.

2nd Stage: Moon – Feelings – Child

This is the psychic or emotional phase of ego development, which corresponds to the Moon and is of the utmost importance for the child, as the Moon represents the childlike ego. It shows how the child feels and how he reacts to the environment. In the "anonymous phase of the primal relationship", the unity of consciousness is responsible for the child's healthy sense of existence and basic trust. If circumstances dictate that the child was removed from the primal relationship with the mother too soon, he suffers throughout life from a lack of basic trust.

In the second phase an I-You relationship with the mother, and with the environment surrounding the child, slowly begins to develop. The experiences of these first contacts have a profound effect on the child's psyche, which is still unformed and wide open. If they were loving, considerate, tender and understanding, then the child's own later contact with the You and his love relationships develop correctly. If this first contact was harsh, scolding, loud and inconsiderate, then this behaviour will be carried over into later relationships. This emotional phase is therefore also important for the child's social and human development, and for the development of correct social behaviour. As we know, we can tell a great deal about this from the Moon's position in the horoscope.

It tells us whether the childlike ego has felt protected and secure, accepted and understood, or whether there has been exclusion, rejection, separation or divorce in the family. It is important that the child feels included in the family circle, for this is his natural protection where all his needs should be met. If there are constant disputes between the parents or irreconcilable differences, then the child easily loses faith in love and the supporting and protective power of a communal life. How many children suffer when their parents split up and they are moved back and forth between them and sometimes even used as transmitters or buffers for their own unsatisfied feelings. Then very often the child's natural feeling of security and protection breaks down, which is the basis for later problems in love, partnerships and social attitudes. Every doctor and psychologist can confirm that some spiritual disturbances and abnormal behaviour in later life have their origin in this kind of childhood experience. Such problems are usually indicated by tension aspects between Saturn and the Sun or Moon in the horoscope.

So that the ego sense can develop harmoniously, the child should not be exposed to sudden separations, abrupt frightening influences or be left alone. One phase should lead smoothly onto the next.

The Feeling Self

The Moon as symbol of the feeling self is a reflective principle that is analogous to watery substance. The feeling self initially experiences itself without boundaries. Just like water, which flows wherever it is not blocked, the feeling self drives the child to blindly follow its instincts. The lack of boundaries or restraint of the child's world is also due to the fact that it is not restricted by the reality principle, which initially must be provided by the mother, the environment or carers, i.e. by Saturn. The child still knows nothing of the dangers around him. He must first learn by experience that he can fall from the tree he climbs, or that fire can burn.

However, he is driven by his feelings, his desire to move, his urge to get to know the world, which is expressed as curiosity. In the process, he repeatedly comes up against certain boundaries which hold him back and guide him along a certain path, and which are unavoidable. In this way the child learns not only how to adapt to the realities of life, but this collision with boundaries leads to his first awareness of himself. This is experienced as opposite and different to the environment, and in the process becomes conscious. The ego-experience therefore only becomes possible, even if still only on an emotional level, by colliding with Saturn, with necessary restraints and laws.

Ego Formation

Through friction, conflict and pain the ego awakens from its deep sleep and experiences itself with increasing consciousness as an ego in relation to the world, to objects, to people. In this way, the child learns the difference between itself, other people and the objects around.

The boundary-setting in the first years of life is almost exclusively determined by the mother. Her **protective function** makes the child aware of life's dangers. How often does the mother say: "Don't do that," "Stop that or you will fall or get dirty." This constant "boundary setting" has affinity with the quality of Saturn. From the position of Saturn in the horoscope we can determine which constraints, obstacles, restrictions, dangers and burdens have been imposed on the ego for it to overcome and to mature it.

But sensitivity is also required in this phase of the upbringing, a loving heart with empathy. Instead of gently giving the necessary restrictions it is all too easy to forcefully impose boundaries, which represses the life of the spirit and the emotions and causes the child to be afraid of its own experiences.

Constantly being told not to do things, with an emphasis on the moralistic conscience, can be escalated to depressive guilty feelings in the mental and intellectual world. This can easily produce a negative attitude towards life, which bitterly rejects everything living. The childlike emotional self becomes impoverished and dried out. We are then left with the true Saturnine type, who mistrustfully gives up in advance without trying in order to save himself suffering – and in the process does not notice that he is missing out on life.

The other extreme development would be if the feeling self were not restricted at all. The child could do anything and get anything he wanted, thus eliminating all hardship, all experiences that could mature him. Such a child would live without boundaries and remain stuck in an immature or infantile state. He has no inner strength and is torn between internal and external voices. It is hard for him to grow up and leave the phase of childhood behind – the person remains infantile in many respects.

It is important that the child understands and processes the limitations in the right way. If he realises that they exist to ensure his survival and also therefore his needs, then they will be quickly and willingly accepted. However, if they work against his ego development, then he must necessarily oppose them. In the confrontation with the realities of life, with boundaries, the ego is constantly changing and adapting to these realities. The correct adaptation to reality involves the ongoing establishment of the **sense of reality**, and with it the ability to deal with life. If this reality is hard, chaotic, hostile, friendless and problematic, then it is naturally difficult for the child to identify with it, to love the world, to adapt positively to life and to love willingly. He then constantly longs for an unattainable state of happiness and from an early age fantasises about an illusory, imaginary world where all his desires will be satisfied.

This creative fantasy is necessary up to a certain point. But when it becomes excessive, the child will lose touch with reality, in which case there is a split between reality and the imaginary world. Later the child lacks the **ability to implement** his ideas and plans. He suffers from the inability to use his inner strengths in the real world and to be successful, which has a negative effect on his self-esteem, with all the psychological consequences. We often see this with tension aspects between Saturn, Neptune and Moon. (An example could be the drugs scene.)

The child should always be given joy, attention, variety and praise where it is due, so that he is happy and retains his love of life. This is the only way his ability to love can thrive and mature and also remain intact should he ever get into difficult situations in life. Only the naturalness and security of the understanding and protection provided by loving parents and the family give the child the strength to cope with the tensions, problems and adaptation to the environment.

The foundation for the development of the self is not punishment or the withdrawal of love, not feelings of guilt and fear, but security and positive relationship through the emotional devotion, love and understanding of the parents. Only the experience of emotional fulfilment, i.e. through the calming of the drives, through the constant supply of confidence, love, security and protection, will the child acquire the ability to develop his own ego – such that he can later transcend his own limitations and be able to bear greater responsibilities and take on tasks for the community. An upbringing with punishment, fear and the withdrawal of love is the worst foundation for truly human and social behaviour. This produces only aggression, hostility and hypocrisy. The main effect of feelings of guilt is to bind the child to the authority figure. Feelings of guilt therefore prevent the child from becoming independent. They create a vicious circle of rebellion, repentance, submission and renewed rebellion.

The feelings of guilt of most people in our society are not so much due to their own conscience as to the feeling of disobedience to an authority and the associated fear of punishment.

In this development of the emotions in which the emphasis is on the Moon self, the ego mainly experiences itself as a reflection of the interior and exterior worlds. This reflecting principle is also the cause of the imitative instinct, the pride of identity that is strongly characteristic of the early years, along with curiosity. They are all crucial as future willingness and ability to learn depend on them.

In this phase the child adapts simultaneously to the activity of his body and the assimilation of his environment. It is completely immersed in imitation. Naturally adults and playmates are the most important people it wants to copy, but the child still does not yet have the capacity for mental contemplation or moral discrimination, which is why the only effective educational aid is a consistent role model or good example of the educators and the environment, for here the child is mainly conditioned by the environment, by nurture.

3rd Stage: Sun – Self-confidence – Father

This brings us to the phase of ego development that can be likened to that of self-confidence and therefore the Sun. In this phase, we are dealing with the child's thinking ego, which comes to dominate the world of the feelings and the body, so that ideas can be converted directly into physical action. As the autonomous principle in the horoscope, the Sun always represents vital self-experience.

The life habits are formed, the fundamental basic attitude, the temperament, in short the character or the mentality in the real sense, which can be determined from the Sun's position in the horoscope. Its position by sign/house and its aspects tell us how the person thinks and what kind of mentality they have.

Through learning, experience and memory, the intelligence functions continue to develop. Intellectual performance begins with the ability to understand, which is constantly developing from simple perception to concentrated observation. Memory, or the ability to remember, enables the child to retain what it has absorbed, and to compare it with new experiences. Through practical experience, it brings order to the tasks of daily life and can then deal with life in a coherent, logical fashion.

This leads to development of the **ability to judge and evaluate**. The child can draw consequences from his experiences, make relationships and make certain judgements that guide his actions.

The Thinking Self

With the progressive development of the self, the personal thinking function starts to develop and to mature into an independent and autonomous individuality. This is the prerogative of each one of us and should be the goal of development. This development requires the initial role model of the father or a person who the child can look up to or admire, and whom the child can trust unconditionally. This role model usually has masculine characteristics in both genders. It contrasts with the hitherto dominant primal relationship with the mother, against which the struggle for liberation by the emancipating ego is directed in this phase.

Usually between ages 6 and 16, the child begins to identify more and more with the father image. This is quite natural and should not be opposed by the mother, whether out of jealousy or because she no longer plays the leading role. It is always important to respect this natural phase and to adapt to it.

When the Sun is at the top of the horoscope, there is usually a father full of inner dynamism and a positive will to live, able to ensure the family's survival. The child can depend on him. From the Sun's position in the horoscope, we can see what kind of role the father played as a role model. If the Sun is in a strong position, then it is good if the child is guided and taught by the father. On this strong foundation, the desired ethical and intellectual faculties can develop, be practiced and become habits in the child. At the end of this learning phase the autonomous mind has developed, allowing the individual to come into his own.

Straight after early childhood, the child is ready to recognise an authority, i.e. to place particular trust in an individual or a few people, to be guided by them and agree to obey them and do what they ask. The best person for this is the father. If the father has that natural personal charisma

The three stages of life: one living, one dead and one petrified tree (horizontal). The petrified tree has turned to pure agate in 200 million years. ("Agate Bridge" in "Petrified Forest National Park" in Arizona USA; photo B. Huber)

then the growing person will recognize this and willingly follow him and his own self-confidence can develop without inhibition. If the father cannot think for himself, jumps on bandwagons to whatever is popular at the moment, lacks integrity, is sycophantic and fails to cope with life, then the child will reject and fundamentally disrespect him. His own inner self-esteem also suffers in the process and his ego cannot develop without inhibition. The secret of the true evolution of the self lies in the role model of the father, who as a real personality has the courage to be completely "himself", who is in a position to be responsible for himself – and neither in his work nor in his dealings with others does he rely solely on commandments, regulations, prestige and expediency nor make his actions dependent on the opinions of others. Such a father is perceived by the child as a true authority and he can build his own self-confidence in such an image. How often do hear one young person say to another: "My father said it so it must be true!"

While the child in the Moon phase looks at a person's visible actions, a child in the ego formation phase of self-confidence looks at and reacts particular strongly to that which is true to a person's own nature and what they really feel.

From this representation we see how important it is to study the influence of the key figures, the parents. It clearly illustrates the fact that education must start with the parents, so that both of the child's archetypical role models provide what is beneficial for his personal development.

Personality Formation:
The Urge to Experience – Separation – Becoming Independent

Eventually the great hunger to experience presents itself, which makes the maturing young person want to experience things for himself. This tumultuous phase usually starts with the transit of AP through the 4th house and has its high point in the 5th house, between ages 18 and 25. It also involves separation from the parental home.

If the child is to develop into a healthy adult, one day he must renounce the primal relationship with his parents and become completely independent. He must learn to cope with the world as an individual and make decisions not guided by other people, but as a result of his own opinions. All his powers must be directed towards adapting to the world, not seeking security by dominating or being subservient, but by being self-sufficient.

The desire for personal experience and self-actualisation aids this process of liberation or self-evolution that turns young people's lives upside down, and usually causes internal and external crisis. This power comes directly from the innermost self and must on no account be repressed or restricted by the those responsible for bringing up the adolescent; instead they should be guided along the right path with sympathetic involvement, constructive interest, broadminded openness and with clear, calm objectivity.

The young person is so grateful when he feels that adults take him seriously and try to understand him – even if he does not show it at all and hides his inner insecurity behind a mask of boorishness, suspicion or brusque rejection.

This process is a kind of "creative self-actualisation", a primal human urge, which comes directly out of the person's core being, which is initially rather chaotic, but which contains so much potential, the like of which he will never find again. It is a massive concentration of living creative power. Anything can come out of it, the best or the worst, depending on how this power is channelled.

All human creativity, from the simplest manual action via the most complicated intellectual performance to the greatest work of art come from this inner source. Particular attention should be given to this **"urge to become" of the inner self** in the upbringing. It should be treated with intelligent responsibility so that the young person can develop to their full individuality. This is the principal task of the upbringing, in which the psychological interpretation of the child's horoscope can be helpful. By using astrology in this way, we can make a contribution to a new age of the history of humanity.

Real progress always starts with the upbringing. Our children are the adults of tomorrow and determine the culture of the future. If we are aware of this responsibility and can encourage them towards true self-actualisation today with great understanding and love, we can contribute towards making the world a better place to live in.

¤ ¤ ¤ ¤ ¤

Beauty, Growth, Joie de Vivre
Photo by Andreas Lott

The Child's Horoscope

How Astrological Psychology can help Improve our Understanding of Children

Holger Oehmichen

First published in AstroLog Issue 91, April 1996

In the past, as now, parents worried about whether they could teach their children the things they would need to be able to cope in society as adults. Obedience and adaptability used to be the main requirements. It was the role of educational institutions to reinforce the authority of adults.

Today, individual initiative and responsibility are valued in the workplace, so that increasingly, parents would like their children's individual qualities to be nurtured. This development means that educational institutions now have the task of reinforcing the authority of the child.

Personal and spiritual awareness have changed enormously in the last 50 years. The structures within the family are dramatically different from those in previous generations. The role of women in society has also changed and is still changing. Holistic perspectives are spreading e.g. into the fields of economics, ecology and medicine. We increasingly feel the need to find a balance within ourselves and have a greater understanding of the importance of letting a child be itself and having its needs met. Parents want to know where their child's abilities lie and how they can be applied in everyday life.

This is where astrology comes in. A horoscope reading can reveal individual energy patterns that are unique to the person concerned.

Is there anything special that must be borne in mind during an astrological consultation when looking at a child's horoscope?

When each person is born, a unique horoscope is formed that indicates the person's developmental potential, but not their developmental path. If a person in their 50s comes to see me, I can establish to what extent their developmental potential has been exploited and used. This will become clear during the course of the consultation. In the case of a child, this question is still completely open.

As with every horoscope, we can discover basic motivation in the horoscope of a child by looking at the shaping and colour of the aspect pattern, by its position and direction. In astrological psychology we distinguish between three possible graphic structures and colours. This tripartion is echoed in the cross qualities of cardinal, fixed and mutable. As far as the shaping is concerned, we distinguish between quadrangular or polygonal figures, triangular figures and linear figures that do not form a geometric shape.

Quadrangular or polygonal aspect figures can be compared with the qualities of the fixed cross. These children strive for a final, calm, harmonious and perfect state and are constantly wondering what they need to do in order to accomplish this. For them, life is about security; they find it difficult to cope with loss. Parents should prepare these children very carefully for changes. Such children may find it hard to cope with changes of scene, even rearranging their room.

With predominantly **triangular** aspect pattern, the child concerned must be able to understand the meaning of something when dealing with it. They constantly wonder why they should do this or that, why is it so. There is an affinity with the mutable cross. This motivation arises from the desire for contact, learning, communication and love. These children are usually interested in many things, particularly inner connections and laws. It is difficult to get them to do things just because they have to. Parents and teachers must appeal to the child's curiosity or draw attention to the significance of a thing in life.

Linear aspect patterns indicate basic attitudes that are comparable with the cardinal impulse principle. These children want to achieve their objectives. They are motivated to accomplish something special and want to win and to be the best. They have a strong will and take risks, but also have a tendency to overdo things and perhaps also to overestimate themselves. They can act impulsively and energetically, but not necessarily lastingly. When dealing with these children, parents need a good sense of what kind of challenges they can set for their children and which they cannot.

Colour

If we find combinations of these graphic figures in a horoscope, it can indicate that the child's motivation is confused. Just as we interpret the three graphic structures differently corresponding to the motivations of the cardinal, fixed and mutable crosses, we also distinguish between red, blue and green aspects.

This resolution of the duality that we still find in classical astrology, the overcoming of polarised thinking, is perhaps the most valuable contribution of the Huber School to the development of astrological thinking. Classical astrology only recognises difficult and favourable aspects, those which would appear in red and blue, if shown in colour. When he introduced green, Bruno Huber not only added another colour, he also recognised that the red aspects (oppositions and squares) not only bring conflict and tension, but can also be a source of strength. The energy potential that we find in the red aspects is ultimately necessary for the processes of development and growth.

The same thing happens with the blue aspects, sextiles and trines. The German Astrological Association calls them "harmonious aspects", and at the very least creates the misunderstanding that a person who has many blue aspects and no red aspects in their horoscope is believed to be happy. Rubbish! Admittedly, these blue aspects do provide opportunities for relaxation, pleasure and joy, but there is also the danger of inertia and stagnation.

There are two sides to every coin, as the saying goes. Polarised, black-and-white thinking does not reflect the real complexity of life. Reality is made up of shades of grey, while pure black and pure white only exist in our minds, i.e. in theory.

In our lives, when we are caught between two alternatives, there is often a third way. And so in our astrology there is also a third colour, green, that is used for the semi-sextile and the quincunx. Green aspects correspond to the mutable cross. Here we find in the child the ability to learn perceptively and consciously from experience and to constantly update their understanding of life. If there is a lot of green in the horoscope, it can lead to indecisiveness and agonising doubts and questioning.

Position

The shape, direction and colour of the aspect pattern already provide us with a vivid impression of the child's basic motivation. Discovering the position and direction of this pattern deepens our understanding of his or her motivation.

If the horoscope has a horizontal orientation, the motivation will clearly be towards human contact. If the orientation is vertical, there is a desire to be freed from the chains of traditional or family expectations in order to be able to live as a free individual.

If the planets are grouped in the bottom half of the horoscope, there is a strong need for trusted people and situations.

If nearly all the planets are situated in the top half of the horoscope, the child will have a minimal sense of the desires and requirements of family or the collective. And if the emphasis of the aspect pattern is on the left I side, the child will place importance on independence and "being itself", while an emphasis on the right You side indicates a need to live through and for others.

Sign/House

Every horoscope tells us something about the talents the child may have, which are found in the emphases on certain signs in the horoscope, whereas expectations of the social background are reflected in the qualities of emphasised houses. Such a contradiction contains both the possibility of overloading or the non-acceptance of the child's abilities, and the opportunity to develop the child's behavioural repertoire thanks to the conscious encouragement of the environment.

This process has already provided us with interesting information about the child's basic motivation, so that we now already know a great deal, and fundamental things at that, about the child's needs and the structure of its consciousness. The beauty of this is that the child is still treated holistically. We have not analysed it in its individual parts, but have looked at the holistic, overall picture. In a deeper study of the birth chart, we usually look at details such as the position of a certain planet in a sign and house, but by this stage, the danger of allowing details to obscure the bigger picture is significantly reduced.

We will now take a look at how the child experiences their mother and father, as reflected in the horoscope by the positions of the Moon, the Sun and Saturn.

Family Model

Here there is another significant departure from the symbolism of classical astrology. Although attempts were made to identify the mother and father figures in the horoscope, no such attempts were made with regard to the child itself. At the beginning of the 1960s, Bruno Huber carried out extensive research that yielded the following results:

> In the horoscope, the way the horoscope owner experiences their father and mother can be seen from the positions of the Sun and Saturn (particularly their house positions).

> The position of the Moon does not relate to the mother figure but to the receptive, inquisitive, open and dependent child. The child's experience of its relationship to its parents and the relationship between the parents can be deduced from the aspecting of the Moon, Sun and Saturn.

> Finally, the location of these planets in the house system indicates the family hierarchy, i.e. who is in charge.

The Moon versus Saturn as Mother

Far be it from me to impress you with the results of scientific research, if they do not appear significant with regard to our experiences and observations of life, but here are a couple of thoughts on this:

a) For more than 2000 years, we have been living in a patriarchal, male-dominated world shaped by men. Is it not then typical that lunar qualities were attributed to the wife and mother? Qualities that do not take into account their organisational and supporting role in the family and at best reflect their dependency (the only reason we are able to see the Moon is that the Sun shines on it.)

b) The maternal role primarily consists of feeding, protecting, teaching us how to protect ourselves, giving us security and teaching us discipline. These are indeed the positive Saturnian qualities, which can only be acknowledged when we abandon the one-sided view of Saturn as the frightening evildoer in favour of a more sophisticated attitude.

I personally found the research results immediately appealing and spontaneously convincing. With my Sagittarius Moon and my exact Sun-Venus conjunction, I am apparently particularly open to the female perspective. Despite the Arian emphasis of my horoscope, this has enabled me to learn a great many things from women, in particular from my female life partner.

To conclude, I would like to present some issues that could be particularly relevant to the horoscopes of children.

Parental Guidance

When parents come to me wanting an astrological consultation for their child, I understand my task to be to tell the parents what kind of environment is necessary for the child so that it can develop according to its individual abilities and needs. To this end, I first consider the basic motivation as described above, I then look at the child's ascendant (AC), Moon Node and Moon qualities. These could be particularly important for the way in which the child explores its world. Why is this?

The sign characteristics of the ascendant are, according to my observations, more influential in the first years of life than the characteristics of the Sun sign. To what extent the Sun characteristics determine a person's behaviour and consciousness obviously varies from person to person. The person's karmic maturity could also be revealed here. If ascendant and Sun are in the same sign, then the same characteristics are expressed in both cases, but there must be an examination of how the child can live out its very egocentric self-expression so that its development is also encouraged by its environment. The sign characteristics of the ascendant determine the way the child reacts and also reveals something of its inner needs. This is the location of the Age Point at the moment of birth, so that the ascendant not only appears as a developmental goal, but also as a starting point. In the first years of a child's life, it is constantly facing new and unfamiliar situations, to which it reacts according to the characteristics of its ascendant.

Leo AC

A child with a Leo AC may make early efforts to gain attention from those around it with beaming smiles and oodles of charm. Such a child prefers to risk trouble or punishment than to be ignored. Parents can therefore avoid trouble by constantly trying to devote their undivided attention to their Leo AC offspring. In kindergarten and nursery school, it is a good idea to allocate a small job or responsibility to these children.

Virgo AC

Children with a Virgo AC are quite different, as too much attention confuses them. These children need a lot of time to find their feet in new situations. A duty or a little job can also be beneficial though, for they want to be useful and to be needed, but due to their great need for perfection they may be afraid of making mistakes. Parents must watch out for this.

Libra AC

With a Libra AC, children find it particularly hard to cope with tensions and arguments within the family. They try to act as mediators and are perhaps all too willing to put aside their own wishes and needs. Parents should make sure that they do not abuse this willingness. They should constantly ask their child what it would like and also allow it enough time to come to a decision.

Scorpio AC

Children with a Scorpio AC also want a lot of attention, but at first glance appear shy. They do not show it as much as the "Leos". These children are shrewd observers and perceive things (and perhaps also draw attention to them), that others would prefer to keep quiet. They show interest in taboo subjects (like death and sexuality). They give little away about themselves though. They like to delve into a subject, and parents should give their children the opportunity to report on the outcomes of their research.

Sagittarius AC
With a Sagittarius AC, the child is concerned with independence and freedom. They have their own ideas as to what should be done and how. They always need to find the deeper meaning in things. Parents hear questions like: "Why should I do that?" or "Why is that so?" all too often from these children. They would achieve more with their children if they always explain the significance and meaning of a task.

Capricorn AC
Children with Capricorn AC want to feel that they are special. They like to be assigned a special task within the family or at school, if they feel it can make them stand out. It helps them if at the same time they also have the feeling that only they could do it. If parents and educators bear this in mind, they will save themselves and the child a lot of stress and frustration.

Aquarius AC
If the AC is in Aquarius, the child will attach great importance to having a few selected friends with whom they together indulge in often very particular hobbies. Having to be with a lot of children in a group they have not chosen themselves (e.g. in kindergarten and school) easily overwhelms these children. Here it is helpful to offer them smaller interest groups in which they can collaborate safely with more motivation.

Unfortunately there is not the space here to give tips and advice for the other AC positions and consider the temperament and cross quality of the sign concerned.

The Rising Moon Node
Another special feature in the consideration of a child's horoscope can be the special way in which the Moon Node theme is assimilated. The rising Moon Node is particularly worthy of our attention where children are concerned. This indicates properties and abilities that the child inherits at the moment of birth. We can imagine this like a kind of shaping that takes place on the spiritual level as the child is born. In order to understand the inherited shaping, it is always helpful to take a look at the moon node horoscope. The child seems to have inherited certain aptitudes, abilities and preferred ways of behaving from former lives, and then by developing the themes of its rising Moon Node it can find its life task. During childhood, the behaviour patterns caused by this Moon Node are usually still decisive. Parents and educators can better understand their child's behaviour when they know the consequences of the house and sign position of the rising

Moon Node. The house in which it is situated indicates the areas in which a child feels particularly at home.

In stressful situations, the child often reacts with needs and behaviour that are indicated by the position of the rising Moon Node.

The rising Moon Node in the 12th house indicates a child that likes to withdraw into a world of fantasy and dreams. This child would certainly prefer being read to or making up its own stories than rough and tumble play.

If this sensitive point is situated in the 1st house, the child is very selfish, perhaps egocentric, thinks the world revolves around him, likes to look for trouble and finds it hard to compromise.

With a rising Moon Node in the 2nd house, he clings to what he knows and possesses and tends to err on the side of caution.

In the 3rd house, he will be sociable and inquisitive and may take school very seriously.

With rising Moon Node in the 4th house, we find children who are very affectionate and unwilling to leave the family environment because they need to feel that they belong. Basic tendencies can also be found for the other positions of the rising Moon Node.

The sign characteristics of the Moon Node also indicate how the child implements these tendencies. Combined with the qualities of Sagittarius, perhaps spontaneously and self-opinionatedly, in Capricorn responsibly and independently, in Aquarius originally and idealistically, in Pisces sensitively, empathetically and helpfully, to give just a few examples.

Moon Position

As a child is still very identified with its Moon in the first years of life, special attention should always be paid to the Moon position in the horoscope, and to the position within the above-mentioned Family Model (Moon-Saturn-Sun).

The characteristics of the sign in which the Moon is situated shows what the child reacts most strongly to, what it needs in order to feel protected, and how it will express its feelings and needs.

Fire

With a fire Moon, he will be alert and attentive, and be happy when there is a lot going on around him. These children usually need less sleep than others and are very vocal in expressing their great need for activity.

Earth
Children with an earth Moon react strongly to physical contact. They want lots of cuddles and need the presence of someone they trust. When they are a little older, these children like to have one or more fluffy toys or their own room or a special corner of the house. They like to have their own permanent place at the table.

Air
Air Moons are usually lively, interested and inquisitive children who like to have a lot of interaction with their environment, in which listening, talking and seeing are very important. They enthusiastically imitate the speech and sounds of adults and are therefore often early talkers. These children can adapt well to a changing daily routine. In contrast to earth Moons, they even find it boring if the daily routine is always the same.

Water
A child with Moon in a water sign needs less physical play in order to be happy. They need a harmonious atmosphere. These children react to the emotions surrounding them. If their parents feel unwell, sad or angry, the child will assimilate and express these feelings. These parents should confide in their children when they are angry or hurt. In this way they help their child to take his perceptions seriously and help him to deal with unpleasant feelings. A water Moon child needs to be encouraged to express their feelings, otherwise they may adapt excessively to conform to other people's expectations.

A Concept of Children

I would like to complete these observations of my experiences with children's horoscopes with a few fundamental thoughts. If we can manage to abandon the traditional idea of children as incomplete adults, and instead see the child as an individual personality, we can learn much from them on a daily basis. C.G. Jung recognised that archetypal deep access to the essence of the human soul already exists in children's dreams. The American pedagogue Thomas Armstrong reported children's intuitive insights and subtle perceptions and proposed the theory that alongside the development "from the body outwards", there is a simultaneous development "from the essence downwards". That means that we come into the world physically immature, but develop throughout the years, only to decay again physically at the end of our lives. While we seem to be born spiritually fully developed, this spirituality is quickly lost during the course of our lives (because it is not used), only to be cultivated once more in old age. The legendary Chief "Black Elk" put it like this:

"Adults can learn from very small children, for the hearts of small children are pure and the Great Spirit can therefore show them many things that older people cannot see."

Take a look at a newborn baby as it calmly watches you and its environment and you will see what he means.

Accompanying children on their developmental journey is for many of us a profound experience. The same is also true for me, and I am constantly learning new things when I meet them as a therapist, friend or father on their journey.

◻ ◻ ◻ ◻ ◻

Children's Horoscopes

A Systematic Approach taking Temperament into Account

Rainer Bauer

First published in Astrolog Issues 141-144, August 2004 - March 2005

Why are children's horoscopes important?

Children are our future, and represent our hopes for a better world, and for this reason alone they deserve all our love, attention and understanding. However, children can also be very challenging, relentlessly demanding everything we are willing and able to give. They want to be seen and heard. How can parents do the best they can for their children?

What kind of image of humanity and worldview do the parents have? Are they conversant with ideas of reincarnation, incarnation and the laws of karma? Do they have answers to the questions: "Who am I?" "Where do I come from?" "Where am I going?" "What is the meaning of life?" Do they know that they are incarnations of an immortal soul? Parents need to be aware of the existential implications of these questions and how to answer them. Parents, and all of us, need a connection to the spiritual world and access to our souls, to our higher selves. This is the only way we can truly understand ourselves and the world around us. Man is capable of authentic thought once he has the inner freedom to become creative, and has learned how to free himself of all dogmatic and atavistic belief systems, whose only purpose is to subjugate and enslave mankind.

The School of Life

Both sides – parents and children – have already reached an agreement in the spiritual sphere that is often rooted in a fateful intertwining of previous incarnations. Seen in this way, the parent-child encounter is an ancient karmic game with new or exchanged roles. The purpose of the whole thing is to acquaint both parties with their special learning task. We parents can be absolutely sure that our children have deliberately sought us out with our approval. However life, in its wisdom, has so arranged things that children and parents have no memory of this, for this knowledge would only get in the way for both parties. We should therefore have complete confidence as parents that everything happens for our own good and should therefore also be willing to do our best for our children.

Learning to Understand our own Child and our Inner Child

The challenge presented by this encounter consists of unconditionally accepting the other side, i.e. the child must accept the parents and the parents the child. This is where the Family Model comes into its own: it shows us how the child (Moon) would like (radix) its relationship to the father (Sun) and mother (Saturn) to be, and how it subjectively experiences the relationship between father and mother (houses). In addition, the family model can also be drawn upon for the "inner child" of the parents. For it is often the case that parents unconsciously project the experiences of their own inner child onto their actual child, which leads to tensions and conflicts. This can be prevented by also taking the parents' horoscopes into account when considering the child's. If we have learnt as a parent to see and understand our own inner child, to become reconciled with it and redeem it, we have created the best conditions for a free and unrestricted encounter with our own actual child.

How important the redemption of the inner child is can be gauged by how deeply injuries and traumatic experiences can be embedded in the human soul, and how they can unconsciously affect our behaviour. Critical for this are the initial contacts of the Age Point in the first half of the life. A sensitive child cannot avoid picking up on the unhappy child within the father and mother. If a corresponding aspect is present, it starts to burden itself with feelings of guilt, and believes that it is responsible for the mother's unhappiness or the father's frustration. To the extent that we have freed ourselves, we can encounter our children freely and with an open mind.

The Temperaments

The temperaments are vitally important, yet receive little attention in the upbringing of children. How many parents have actually seriously thought about which of the four temperaments predominate in their child's character and how they should specifically deal with it? They are not only important in the development of the child but also later on in adult personality development. Identifying and understanding the temperament and dealing with it appropriately are essential for enlightened parenting in the truest sense of the word. Enlightened here means a humanistic perspective, as expounded by Rudolf Steiner. This means no more and no less than understanding our evolutionary purpose and task and internalising it, which enables the process of self-actualisation and the increasing awareness developing from this understanding. The aim of this process is freedom, and the improvement of man so that he approaches the divine, in accordance with the words of Jesus: *"Be perfect as your Father in heaven is perfect."* If we choose not to make this our highest priority, we should not be surprised by, never mind complain about, the frustration and suffering we encounter. Only by acknowledging our true selves, or by acknowledging that we are love, can we cope with the task of implementing Christ-awareness in and around us, in the process also redeeming Mother Earth and her children.

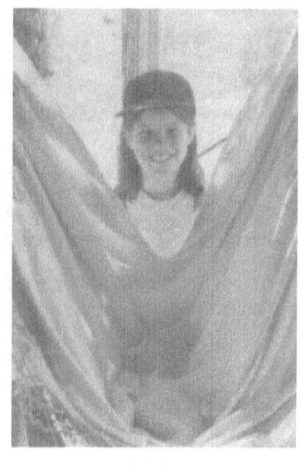

Indigo Children – the Time of Awakening

A phenomenon that Nancy Ann Tappe from the USA first drew attention to in the 1970s was that of what she calls Indigo children, due to the presence of the colour indigo in their aura. In her book *Understanding your Life through Color* (1982), she describes for the first time the typical behaviour patterns of this new generation of children, which seem to be completely different to those of previous generations. Their behaviour and intelligence are exceptional. They often possess special abilities and talents that cannot be explained biogenetically. They themselves feel that they are special and suffer greatly from being misunderstood by others. They reject any authority that tries to stop them from doing something that they have more knowledge of. They tend to get frustrated if their creativity and abilities are not taken seriously, and become antisocial and turn inwards if they are not understood. It is not easy for them to be accepted, as they do not correspond at all to established ideas of what children should be. It is therefore hard for these above-averagely gifted children to find their purpose and role in life, as their environment cannot figure them out. Most children born since then are these kind of highly gifted, exceptionally talented souls. They have come here to help out in these difficult times so that we can all enter a New Age, in which a New Man will be born. It is a time of global awakening, of a growing awareness of unity. It is a time of a great process of inner and outer transformation – a time for the rejection of falsehood, injustice and power in which all structures impeding the good of humanity will dissolve. We find ourselves at the start of this new understanding of human nature in which creative impulses in the form of awakened mental capacity, willpower and love are perceived in us and flow through us.

As parents, we should welcome these special children, but are we really in a position to do this? The less we ourselves know about the significance of these children, the less chance they have of developing their true potential. For what also characterises them is their great sensitivity and empathy for the need and attempts of others to bring light into the darkness of life. Ultimately, all awakened souls will be bringers of light to our inhumane Earth, which eagerly awaits the enlightenment of its children. For man is not only a child of God (Son of God), but also a child of Mother Earth (Son of Man), which is both a great heritage and responsibility. Now is the time for him to fulfil this spiritual legacy in the form of his awakened responsibility to himself and to the world.

[This article included the quote from Kahlil Gibran's *The Prophet*, given on page 68.]

The Aspect Pattern

The aspect pattern reveals the structure of the individual consciousness, the person's core life motivation. Before starting to analyse this, we first give it the opportunity to inspire our imagination. These structures often create imaginative associations that reveal something of the character or subjective affectivity of the person concerned. Interestingly, this first, subjective impression is often confirmed and better understood after analysis of the horoscope. It is an intuitive assessment of the person, and a connection on the soul level. The aspect pattern also reveals the person's growth potential and destiny. It is the quite personal oscillation of love, which is what we are all made of, and which sounds like a chord played on a stringed instrument. Every chord sounds different and is a harmonic consonance of all the aspects which life has in store for him. We should listen to it with our hearts.

Positioning and Alignment of the Aspect Pattern

The positioning of the aspect pattern (top or bottom, right or left, which quadrant it is in) tells us a great deal about the person's orientation. The same is true with regard to the alignment of the aspects, whether it is predominantly horizontal, vertical or diagonal. The size of the aspect pattern and the important issue of coherence should also be considered.

Shape of the Aspect Pattern

We first look in the radix, where the aspect pattern reveals the child's basic motivation. Comparing the different shapes of the pattern helps us to easily identify the child's basic needs. Linear figures convey a cardinal, triangular a mutable and quadrangular a fixed motivation. The way the ego planets (Moon, Sun, Saturn) are aspected in a figure attributed to the cardinal, fixed or mutable cross should also be taken into account, e.g. it makes a big difference whether the Moon features in a cardinal, fixed or mutable figure. The same is true for the other ego planets. It is also important to bear in mind the attributions of the ego planets: i.e. the Moon corresponds to the mutable principle and the triangular figure; the Sun to the cardinal principle and the linear figure and Saturn to the fixed principle and the quadrangular figure.

A child whose ego planets are predominantly linked to one or even several cardinal linear figures will present itself as naturally active. He is busy, imaginative and strong-willed and needs relatively little sleep.

However, if the ego planets are in one or several triangular figures, the child is inquisitive and sociable. He enjoys experimenting and likes to learn. He has a lively imagination, loves fairy tales and stories and is a great animal lover.

A child with the ego planets in quadrilaterals has a strong need for protection and security. He requires a regular rhythm, is happiest being at home and knows how to amuse himself. Such a child is usually easier to manage than one with a cardinal motivation.

Aspect Pattern Colour

The next step is to consider colour in the same way as shaping. While shaping tell us about the causes and motivation of behaviour, colour tell us about the way in which this motivation is displayed. We differentiate three colours: red, blue and green, and the ideal numerical ratio of the colours is 1:2:3 for green:red:blue, which should indicate a balanced and harmonious nature, and enables us to identify when one colour is over- or under-emphasised.

Green Aspects (semi sextile and quincunx) awaken curiosity and longing (tendency to dreaminess). The child appears to be thoroughly interested in his environment. He frequently likes to ask questions. Connected to sensitive planets, this indicates a lively imagination and love of knowledge. Green aspects correspond to the mutable principle and indicate sensitivity and awareness.

Red Aspects (opposition and square) enliven and energise. Through the inner pressure of red aspects the child seeks confrontation, conflict or competition. He wants friction, rivalry and likes to measure his achievements against other people's. He learns to assert himself and hold his ground on a lasting basis. Red aspects correspond to the cardinal principle and indicate achievement and energy.

Blue Aspects show substance in the sense of talent that has already been acquired (trine) or that is still to be actualised (sextile). Unlike red, blue aspects are not stimulating. They confer tranquillity and calmness, but also a tendency towards laziness. "Why should I make an effort?" Blue aspects correspond to the fixed principle and indicate pleasure and substance.

Colour combinations of blue and red indicate ambivalence, blue and green sensitivity and red and green excitability.

Understanding the Relationship between Radix and House Horoscope (HH)

While the radix indicates inherited talents, the house horoscope describes the way the child is influenced by the family environment. This social critical phase began in the prenatal stage and usually ends after the first, or at latest the third, year of life. During this period, the subconscious of the embryo and later of the child are shaped by certain inner images. The behavioural patterns they give rise to are reactions to the environment. The child adapts to it and learns to come to terms with it in order to survive. However, in the long term, the person may not be happy to have to make these adaptations, i.e. to the structures imposed by the environment. He must now – often painstakingly – learn how to find his way back to himself, in order to reestablish his own, original structures (aspect pattern in radix). For only in the radix can the person experience his own authenticity, self-love and finally his destiny. Only then will the patterns learned in the HH be available to him on a higher developmental level as alternative and more enriching opportunities for his being.

The way back to the self is initially full of pain and suffering, combined with fear and guilt. But if this way is followed with awareness and using all the senses, it also provides much insight and therefore healing, which aids our understanding of our relationship to the world and to ourselves. This way to our own self is the way of self-knowledge and therefore also the way towards reconciliation with ourselves and with the world. It leads us from dependency to independence, from adaptation to freedom, from guilt to redemption and from anger and hate into love. Everyone must go down this path sooner or later. Depending on their living circumstances, modern children are usually able to find their way back to the radix much more quickly than those of previous generations. This way from the HH back to the radix is revealed in a graphic fashion in every horoscope and the Age Point often indicates the timing of certain processes (development of awareness and transformation) initiated or triggered by this return.

Just as everyone's aspect patterns in the HH and radix are different, their way back to the self is different. It is ultimately the restoring of the person's different partial personalities to their original authenticity that first enables them to attain individuation and self-actualisation. For only as a mature, independent and responsible personality can the person experience reconnection with his soul or his Higher Self. Psychosynthesis considers this integration process to have five stages: identifying, accepting, learning to manage, integrating and transforming.

Comparison of Aspect Patterns in Radix and House Horoscope
The comparison shows to what extent the child has adapted to its environment and which survival strategies it has developed in order to meet the expectations and demands of the parents and the world. The differences between the aspect pattern in the HH and that in the radix often brings surprising discoveries to light, which are particularly important when it comes to the parents' understanding of the child. This comparison is particularly important for the Family Model.

Questions of holistic, i.e. 'Jupiterian' perception
* Does the HH have significantly more or less aspects than the radix?
* Do certain aspects change their colour?
* Do whole aspect figures or individual aspects shift, change, appear or disappear?
* Is coherence maintained, or is incoherence resolved?
* Are there unaspected planets?
* How do both aspect patterns influence me?

Questions of the detailed i.e. 'Mercurial' analysis
* the position of the ego planets in the chart, and in house and sign
* the position of the Moon (to determine the temperament)
* ascertaining the strongest ego planet
* the position of the 'instinctual' planets Mercury and Jupiter (to determine learning and communication style)
* the position of the libido planets Mars and Venus
* the position of Saturn in house and sign
* the position of the spiritual planets
* dynamic calculations
* the dynamic quadrants.

The Family Model (FM)
In the radix, the FM shows us the relationship of child (Moon) to mother (Saturn) and father (Sun). The aspect pattern shows what the child hopes for and expects from the relationship with its parents so that it can develop in line with its karmic task. In the HH though, we are usually confronted with another, sometimes very different aspect pattern, which, unlike the radix, reveals what this new arrival really has to come to terms with. The more different the two aspect patterns are, the more the child's external behaviour deviates from its inner needs. The comparison of these two reflects the discrepancy between inner will and outer duty, between external adaptation and personal needs. If this discrepancy can be correctly identified in good time by the parents, and is taken into consideration during the child's upbringing, early on the child can be given the possibility to find his own strengths and weaknesses and thus his own, free and meaningful life. For the latter is only found when the child or the adult discovers their radix, i.e. when identification with the radix is achieved.

The comparison of the two aspect patterns of the HH and radix therefore reveals the extent to which reality deviates from what the child expects, and we must pay great attention to how the child copes with this deviation. The FM can show us the child's inner wants and what it needs for healthy development. However, it only shows the subjective feelings on the part of the child and not the objective truth of the relationships concerned.

Position of the Ego Planets (EP) in the Charts
The position of the EP is important for accurate analysis and evaluation of the FM. Its location in the chart should first be established (top, bottom, left or right). While the preferred location of the Sun (father) is at the top in the conscious and individual space, i.e. is seen as free and independent, Saturn (mother) is out of place at the top, i.e. it is

experienced as controlling and domineering. It is more at home at the bottom of the chart, where it dutifully fulfils its caring role within the family. This is completely opposite for the Sun, which feels dependent and trapped down in the unconscious, collective area. If it is situated at the right, near the DC, then it is dependent on the approval of the You; but if situated near the AC it demands attention. Saturn behaves the same way. If it is near the DC, the child may find that its mother wants to choose its friends and control its relationships, and is experienced as being restricting and suspicious. However, if it is near the AC her influence will be responsible, serious and prudent.

A Moon at the top of the chart will be admired and needs acknowledgement for its exceptional achievements, but in reality for a lack of closeness. In the bottom, collective area, the Moon looks for protection and security and would like to lean on others. On the left side, it often feels alone or seeks out solitude. However, on the right at the DC, on the You side, it livens up and is sociable and friendly.

The Ego Planets in the House
The area in which the EP is situated in a particular house tells us something about its effectiveness. In the cardinal or cusp area, a Sun appears strong and self-confident. In the fixed area, it has trouble asserting and standing up for itself. It has a restricting and inhibiting effect; at the LP it is even frustrated or resigned, with no real chance of asserting itself because it is misunderstood. In the stress area, the Sun is stressed or tense because it has to prove itself.

In the cardinal area Saturn as mother appears dutiful and busy (house theme). In the fixed area insecurity and doubt prevail as to the mother's quality. At the LP the mother is usually too self-involved to offer the child the necessary attention; she feels powerless and at the mercy of external circumstances. In the stress area she is under strong pressure, wanting to show herself able to cope with the demands placed on her. The child could experience a mother who is constantly stressed, always trying to please everybody but consequently never providing the right closeness to herself and the child.

A Moon in the area of a cusp simply does not want to show any weakness to the outside world; it acts as though it is strong and self-confident and does what is expected of it; a nice, obedient child. Nobody knows what is going on inside. In the fixed area the Moon is bothered by the pressure to adapt: it often feels that it is not good enough and is constantly giving something of itself away just in order to be loved. At the LP it feels passed by or rejected and resigned, because it cannot receive the love that it wants. In the stress area the Moon does everything just in order to be loved, totally overextending itself in the process.

The Ego Planets in the Sign
The sign in which the Sun is situated tells us about the basic character of the father; that of Saturn about the mother and that of the Moon about the child.

Interpretation of Aspects to Ego Planets in Family Model
Moon-Sun aspects describe the relationship of child to father. **Red aspects** indicate a tense relationship, which does not mean that it is not a loving one. Love can be expressed fundamentally in either a harmonious or a tense constellation. In the process, we should always bear in mind that the relationship behaviour is chosen consciously here, and we have entered into it voluntarily and with good reason. Therefore the conflict shown in the square (weight of expectation), from the father was consciously chosen, to allow the child – for whatever reason – to learn something, to step out of his father's shadow, to find his own point of view and learn how to stand up for it. For women, this potential conflict can often only be dealt with in a relationship. In the opposition, the child learns to confront the father, in order to represent itself as an equal partner or rival. Through such a challenge, the child can quickly develop and strengthen its personality. Unlike the square, there is more possibility for mutual consideration and respect. The child encounters the father more freely than with the square, in which case the child must fight for freedom.

Blue aspects indicate a harmonious relationship with the father. A sextile signals inner connectedness and mutual goodwill; with a trine, the child is burdened by the desire to please, which may discourage it from spontaneously following its own developmental impulses. Unlike with the opposition, the child is here emotionally strongly connected to the father because it is firmly attached to this love. Such a father must be careful about what he confides to his child, so that he does not run the risk of hurting it too much. However, it is often precisely this hurt and disappointment that cause the child to disengage from emotional dependence and find its own freedom. With a sextile, the child might find any support it can think of insofar as it is desired. However, a certain "no strings" love prevails between the two, indicating a friendly relationship.

Green aspects tell us something about the father's accessibility. Unlike the semi-sextile, the quincunx indicates independence.

This consists of a longing for more closeness, because the father apparently pulls away from the child or cannot be present for it (work, separation, etc.) In a certain sense, the child is not free either, because it constantly suffers from this longing. In the semi-sextile, this means of communication with the father does exist, but it is up to both sides to decide how to use it.

A **conjunction** of Moon and Sun is indeed the New Moon, which means that the Moon is hidden, not visible. The child can therefore hide behind his father, idealise him without actually making an appearance himself. This child finds it hard to discover its own independence, particularly where emotions are concerned, as he is too easily guided by his father and literally internalises him.

Moon-Saturn aspects describe the relationship of child to mother. Here too **red aspects** are tense, but are represented and felt in a qualitatively different way. With a square there is potential conflict between mother and child, which usually means that they want to fight – fight in the sense of using provocation in order to feel strong. The same applies for men as well as women: this conflict is usually unconsciously continued in romantic relationships in later life, especially if the relationship with the mother cannot be lived out for some reason, either because the child has dutifully adapted (in the HH this red aspect becomes blue) or because the mother – for whatever reason – has rejected the desired confrontation (the red aspect disappears).

With an opposition, the child is painfully aware of the mother's distance, which is perceived as hardness or coldness. A pronounced antagonism prevails, which can be expressed in the form of violent reactions in the phase of defiance.

Blue aspects have a close relationship with the mother, usually indicating a 'low maintenance' child who adapts well. With a sextile this relationship is particularly loving and the child is considerate towards the mother. With a trine the relationship may be even closer, where the child is very adaptable but in the process also makes itself very dependent on the mother – almost a symbiotic relationship.

Green aspects search for closeness and communication with the mother. Here too, for the semi-sextile there is no dependency. The child is always able to communicate with its mother. With a quincunx the child finds the mother inaccessible and suffers in silence from its longing for closeness and understanding. If it does not receive the desired protection and warmth from her, it tends to withdraw into the dream world of its own imagination.

In the **conjunction** of Moon and Saturn, the child's experience of symbiosis with the mother is usually painful – or even exhilarating. It would be exhilarating if the mother had already attained a high state of development and could align herself completely freely and lovingly with her child. Otherwise it is the highest degree of dependency of child on mother, and consequently the path to independence should be particularly painful for the child. Even more than with a trine, this child feels responsible for its mother's wellbeing, suffers if mother suffers and is happy when mother is happy. This also means that it is burdened with guilt and anxiety, but can also be richly blessed by the mother. The precise circumstances can never be ascertained exactly, as we know little or nothing about the karmic background. In a general article such as this we cannot go into specifics, as concrete cases are always required for this.

Sun-Saturn aspects describe the relationship of the parents to each other. With **red aspects** the child picks up on a tense relationship between the parents and an often-oppressive atmosphere. With a square there is usually conflict between the parents, or the child senses subliminal resentment or resistance between them. With an opposition the child feels torn between the two and tries to act as a go-between, but should make sure it does not get caught in the crossfire in the process. If the child is connected to one of these red aspects, it will suffer more than if it were not.

Blue aspects indicate a harmonious and loving relationship between the parents, particularly a sextile. With a trine this harmonious relationship may well be just a sham, because one party shies away from conflict. The child may be able to sense this very well. The parents try hard to pretend to be a harmonious and idealised couple. If the latter is the case, it is very probably that in the HH this aspect changes colour (conflict instead of the expected harmony) or disappears (separation of the parents).

Green aspects tell us about the parents' willingness and ability to communicate with each other. With a semi-sextile this ability to communicate definitely exists. Whether it is used or not is another story (see HH). With a quincunx the child senses coldness and distance in the parental relationship. Warmth and familiarity are lacking and it senses that they are not really interested in each other.

With a **conjunction** the child senses that the parents are united. This may make it more difficult for the child to distinguish between the paternal or maternal roles, which can happen where the parents share childcare duties equally from the start. But this is not necessarily so; this constellation can also be positively understood as evidence of real solidarity between the parents.

One-way aspects indicate a one-way street. That means that only one of the two planets involved makes the effort to reach out to the other, and that nothing is forthcoming from the other in return, which can be very frustrating (LP position).

If there are **no aspects** between the Moon and Sun/Saturn, this means that there is no system of dependency between child and parents. The child moves freely and independently in this relationship framework. It is literally unattached and only communicates or states its needs if it can do so voluntarily. It is under no pressure and goes its own way independently of its parents. The parents only offer it the framework and external conditions for its development. The child does not need more than this, which would be perceived as an unwelcome invasion of its privacy. There is particular respect for the child's dignity, as in the case of a good friend that one would want to avoid hurting or even losing under any circumstances.

Additional Comments on the Family Model (FM)

The Special Situation of the Family with two or more Children

All direct aspects between ego planets indicate a particularly close relationship. The child is born into this world with these constellations and the parents cannot be blamed for them. Every child in a family has a different relationship to their parents. What applies to one child can be quite different to how the other child behaves with respect to the same mother and father. It should therefore always be borne in mind that when considering the FM, it only concerns the subjective perception of the child concerned.

The FM shows early childhood influences up to the end of the first year of life, which have a significant effect on interaction patterns in later life. These early childhood experiences directly affect the unconscious and are then expressed as specific behaviour patterns of which the person themselves is only rarely aware. This explains common statements like: "I married my father or mother." We tend to seek out a partner who corresponds to the relationship pattern of our own family model. At the same time, the all-important EP has a thoroughly archetypical significance, insofar as the mother image (Saturn) or father image (Sun) can also be represented by someone else. The person undergoes the associated experiences again and again until he has learnt to examine them consciously, accept them and transform them.

The FM is not only fundamentally important for understanding later relationships, but also for dealing with a child. The great danger for parents is to suddenly and uncontrollably fall into behavioural patterns that they once experienced themselves, and of which, being just a child, they were very afraid. When discussing a child's horoscope, it is therefore advisable to also take a look at the horoscopes of both parents. A profound self-knowledge is a pre-requisite for parents to be able to understand how their child would like to relate to them as indicated in their horoscope, and to treat them accordingly.

Other important planets in the consideration of the FM can be: Pluto for a grandfather, Uranus for a grandmother, Mars for a brother and Venus for a sister. In addition, for women Venus symbolises the girl and for men Mars symbolises the boy.

Ascertaining the Strongest EP

Our ego identifies with the mental body (ideas) via the Sun, which stands for self-confidence and the integration of the personality. The Moon symbolises the astral body (feelings) and our unconscious. Saturn represents the physical body. In the early phase of development, it indicates inhibition, which is why it also has an important role to play in the interpretation of the child's horoscope. Until the age of puberty though, the child primarily experiences itself via its Moon. Feelings and actions are still one here. Only later, after puberty, do the integrating personality force of the Sun and also the other planets become increasingly important.

From the position of the EPs it is possible to ascertain which is the most strongly placed, and therefore plays a key role in integration of the personality. A long process of maturing and development of awareness is required to gradually integrate all elements of personality. In order to do this, the person must have a good understanding of his ego  structure, i.e. knowledge of the relative strengths of the EPs. The aim is to harmoniously reconcile the different ego elements and place them under the guidance of divine will, with which the personal will merges. The person should deliberately focus on their strengths so as to continue to develop them, and not on weaknesses to try to eliminate them. Focusing on the latter would only bog the person down further.

That is why we should continue to work calmly and joyfully on our good qualities, as indicated by the strongest EP, which prevails over the others and could be called their leader. A healing process is thus initiated, which gradually soothes our hurt and pain, and produces an integrated, self-aware personality.

If Saturn is the strongest EP the person is sensitive to need. Saturn is always looking for suitable structures, to be able to put something into practice or to compensate for a deficiency. That means starting by developing physical awareness of the body. "Listen to your body. Develop a healthy physical awareness." should be our watchwords here. The body is a useful tool for self-actualisation for these people. Saturn works primarily with the senses, not the intellect. Such people are well advised to confront fears and limitations to liberate themselves from them, learn to separate what is important from what is not, put external conditions into perspective and open up to that which is greater and more powerful than oneself. They will want to acquire virtues such as: individual initiative with regard to personal needs or what is required in the way of material or intellectual abilities; the willingness to spontaneously approach others and let them take what they need; helping people to help themselves. Saturn rules the need for protection and security and associated utilitarian thinking. These can be fully lived out once the remaining ego elements are acknowledged as equal aspects of the personality. If the person manages to do this, he will be able to recognise the needs of others and react appropriately to them.

If the Moon is the strongest EP the emotions dominate. Such people should be particularly aware of their feelings and learn to deal with them lovingly. "Listen to your feelings and learn to take them seriously." is the watchword. That means making the time to find tranquillity and calmness. The person learns to let go of fears and listen more to their own needs. The abilities to communicate feelings, wishes and needs to others and to approach others spontaneously and openly are essential. Communication is spontaneous; stale old contacts are sidelined to broaden their horizons. The task set by the Moon is to be authentic, to lead a free and independent life in harmony with one's feelings and to develop an open heart and understanding for the needs of others and the world (empathy).

If the Sun is the strongest EP the special task entails the development of a healthy self-confidence which knows how to be autonomous and independent. This involves developing mental abilities in order to be able to see things as they actually are. "Learn to use your mind, not just your lower intellect, but also and above all your common sense. Learn how to think freely and creatively, allowing you to see the truth for yourself and not rely on other people's opinions and dogmas."

This requires a disciplined will and great awareness of self and others, which means questioning oneself and forming one's own opinion. The Sun, more than any other planet, represents individuation. It should enable us to distinguish between what is true and what is false (artificial) so that we can judge clearly. It communicates and reflects the relationship between subject and object and is responsible for weighing things up. Finally, it is the coordinator and integrator of the ego, even if at first it is less dominant than another, stronger EP. The Sun provides information about the heart, the inner motivation and one's unique individuality. The thought and willpower associated with the Sun enable people to discover themselves and the world. With a fully awakened Sun, the person is connected to all living things. Light, love and divine power flow from his heart, enabling him to come nearer and nearer to the quality of his Creator.

The Sun wants something to happen. The Moon asks how and Saturn asks why it should happen.

Of course there are cases where two EPs are equally strong, in which case these two planets must be developed to strengthen the weaker one. Very briefly, a weak Saturn requires an increased awareness of reality; a weak Moon improved social skills and loving awareness, and a weak Sun increased self-confidence through self-knowledge.

The Child's Temperament

Another essential factor to be considered in the horoscope is the child's temperament. According to Rudolf Steiner, there are four types of temperament associated with the four elements: choleric (fire), sanguine (air), phlegmatic (water) and melancholic (earth).

Below I describe the origin and function of the temperaments in general, the nature of individual temperaments in particular, and how a parent or educator should deal with a child according to their prevailing temperament. The associated comments are courtesy of Rudolf Steiner (*The Secrets of the Human Temperaments*), who, unlike the Huber School, associates water with the phlegmatic temperament and earth with the melancholic temperament. From a humanistic perspective, the attribution of the temperaments must be based on an understanding of the essence of the temperaments and its connection with the four essential human elements. These four essential human elements are the physical body, which corresponds to the Earth; the etheric body (contains the form-creating forces), which corresponds to water; the astral body, which corresponds to air and the ego, which corresponds to fire.

To discover the essence of the temperament, one must first have a fundamental knowledge of human nature. In this regard, Steiner talks of **two life currents**, which the person must combine within himself when he takes on a physical form or becomes incarnated. One is the **line of inheritance** and the other comes **from the person's innermost spiritual essential core.**

It is important to note that Steiner describes this inner essential core as "the fruit of former lives", thus emphasising the significance of the Law of Karma and the associated Theory of Reincarnation. If we want to accurately understand the essence of the temperament, there is no way of avoiding dealing with the fact of rebirth, of the repetitive nature of life on earth.

The temperament therefore interfaces between the two fundamental currents, that of the inner qualities the person brings with them from previous incarnations and that which he inherits. Elsewhere Steiner also calls the temperament the "physiognomy of man's innermost individuality".

We should therefore conceive the temperament as a kind of buffer, which is placed between our actual essential core (the central core of the chart, the Higher Self) and our inherited abilities. This should in a way cushion our incarnation and bring about a reconciliation with what the person expects from their appearance on Earth. The temperament enables our individual essential core to adapt to the specific conditions of the line of inheritance that it meets on its arrival. According to Steiner, the person's spirituality radiates through their temperament, thus displaying their uniqueness and individuality.

There will be a description of how the temperament reconciles the eternal with the past. This reconciliation occurs when the person's four essential elements, i.e. the physical, etheric and astral bodies and the ego, relate to and interact with each other in a quite specific way, featuring a special relationship between the astral body and the ego. As the person enters the physical world, one of the four essential elements then prevails over the others, colouring and thereby determining the corresponding temperament, so that a dominance of the physical body (earth) gives rise to a melancholic individual, that of the etheric body (water) a phlegmatic individual, that of the astral body (air) a sanguine individual and that of the ego (fire) a choleric individual.

Although no temperament exists in its purest form, one will always prevail over the others. Dealing with this in an appropriate way is the great task and pedagogical challenge of the educator, and therefore of prime importance to parents. Once they understand the spiritual background to human development and the nature of the temperaments, and if they are also able to correctly identify their child's temperament and deal with it appropriately, they have all they need to give their child a healthy and effective upbringing.

As for the question of the correct way to deal with children according to their temperament, bear in mind that: **One must always work with what is there, not with what is not there.**

The Sanguine Temperament

"THE SANGUINE SKIPS EASILY OVER THE STONE, BOLDLY AND GRACEFULLY. BUT IF HE TRIPS OVER IT, HE DOES NOT DWELL ON IT."

The sanguine temperament is ruled by a preponderance of the astral body. Such a child is prone to a certain flightiness. He is very natural and flexible, is usually slim and skips or even dances as he walks. His face is mobile and expressive with an alert look. His interest is easily sparked, but not for long. He soon moves onto new things, like a butterfly fluttering from flower to flower. Although quick to pick things up, he forgets them again just as quickly. He is not very persevering and finds it hard to concentrate on something for long.

Counteracting this does not mean teaching the child to be something he is not, but shaping and reinforcing the qualities he already has. For parent or educator, this means paying attention to the child and trying to find something he is particularly interested in that is likely to hold his interest. The thing concerned must be something special, to which the child can dedicate himself and which allows his temperament to blossom. This may be a pet that the child looks after, or later on a specific hobby he is particularly interested in, or a specific sport, etc. The important thing is that the child must be able to form a close, trusting and loving relationship with the person who is trying to help him; otherwise any efforts to guide him in a certain direction will be in vain. The child must develop an attachment to a particular key figure, via whom the attachment can also pass onto other things.

However, for the child to be able to live out his sanguine disposition completely freely, he should have a range of toys that are rotated. This means that he can turn from one to the other and that his interest is constantly being reawakened, when after a while he rediscovers an "old" toy and starts to play with it again.

In the pedagogical handling of the sanguine character, we are reminded of the signs Gemini and Sagittarius: the superficial and dispersed interests of Gemini with its mercurial talent but erratic character is transformed by the targeted and positive ambition of Sagittarius, which can totally dedicate itself to one thing, one person or one goal. There is also an affinity with air (Gemini) and fire (Sagittarius) signs. The airy sanguine temperament is transformed by the influence of the fiery choleric temperament. Conversely, the same is true for the choleric temperament. That exactly corresponds to Steiner's representation of the interaction of astral body (sanguine and air) and ego (choleric and fire) for the purposes of mutual regulation. This temperament is supported by the corresponding motivation of the cross, which in this case is mutable.

The Choleric Temperament

"THE CHOLERIC POWERFULLY KICKS IT ASIDE AND HIS EYES TWINKLE AS HE ENJOYS HIS MOMENT OF TRIUMPH."

The ego predominates in the choleric temperament. A child with this prevailing temperament is burning for action, strong-willed and persevering, so does not give in easily. Above all he wants to excel by virtue of his achievements. He is less changeable and can focus completely on one thing. In external appearance the choleric is often small and stocky of stature, has sharp features and a sparkling and often penetrating gaze. His step is hard, firm and heavy.

The concern here is whether or not the child can develop strong inner ego powers. The child must be acquainted with the kind of difficulties that he may have to face in the outside world, so that he can learn how to implement his strength. Difficult tasks, obstacles, and resistance must be placed in this child's path so that he can thoroughly test and live out his temperament and discover his limitations. By making life easy for this child, one is certainly not doing him any favours. On no account should one try – and this applies to all temperaments – to suppress the characteristic behaviour of the temperament by threatening punishment or deprivation and the like. This would only weaken his temperament and thus his strength and life motivation.

The choleric child needs a credible authority figure to guide him during his upbringing. The parent or attachment figure must be absolutely respectable and reputable in the highest sense of the words. The child must be able to take them seriously and look up to them. The educator should not, as in the case of the sanguine child, try to be the child's friend. One should always behave with dignity in front of this child, show that one knows what one is talking about and never drop one's guard. This requires a significant amount of self-confidence on the part of the educator, and above all discipline and the apparent ability to cope with anything. One should never lose control. This child should be taught self-esteem, self-respect, patience and discipline but also respect and understanding for the requirements and needs of others.

The choleric child should pursue activities that suit his temperament. This includes competitive or combat sports, any committed action against violence and social injustice or artistic activities where his creative energies can be deployed. The child needs the opportunity to feel like a soldier or an artist and a field of activity where these feelings can be lived out in a concrete and meaningful way. Even small opportunities to express his strength, determination and enthusiasm are welcomed.

There is also an astrological affinity with the fire signs here, particularly the Aries – Libra axis. The untamed, wild and impetuous nature of Aries (fire) meets the civilising and therefore inhibiting power of Libra (air), whose authority enables a framework to be created in which the Aries temperament can blossom. The challenge for the choleric temperament and therefore the Aries nature is to learn to identify, understand and integrate (respect) the justified claims and needs of the You in order to be able to place his impulsive creative and will powers at the service of his fellow men and the world. This process is supported by the cardinal cross quality of Aries and Libra.

The Phlegmatic Temperament

"THE PHLEGMATIC FEELS LAZY, HE CASUALLY STOPS WALKING – HE DOESN'T AVOID ME, I JUST GO AROUND HIM."

Like the melancholic, the phlegmatic child is introverted. This child seems indifferent, apathetic and dreamy and likes comfort; quite unlike the extraverted sanguine and choleric temperaments. He avoids anything that takes him out of his comfort zone. He does not go outwards but dives deep down into his own interior. It is hard for him to connect with the world. In physiognomy, he is usually stout with a healthy appetite. He has indistinct features and a dull, apathetic gaze. The gait is more shaky and slow and the step is unsteady, because he does not want to appear steady in a rigid sense.

Here too it is completely counterproductive to persuade the child to take up certain interests. He must discover them for himself. The best approach is for the parents to give the child the opportunity to socialise a lot with other children. For no other type of child are playmates so important, as from them he learns a wide variety of interests and his curiosity can be awakened if their interests rub off onto him. The right way to bring up this child is therefore to let him be inspired by the interests of others.

If such a child suddenly – encouraged by others – starts to become enthusiastic about something, however strange, then the parent should on no account step in and try to talk him out of what they see as an absurd pursuit, for this would only extinguish his vital flame. Such a child must always allow himself to be inspired only by others, to emerge from the protection of his comfort zone. As the sanguine child needs attachment and love to his attachment figure, the phlegmatic child needs friends. The effort of coming out of his shell and turning towards the world must be worth making, and indeed it is to receive the gift of joy and friendship. For this child, the benefit of being interested in others is being able to share their joy and interests. This nicely illustrates the quite special quality of the phlegmatic character: the joy of sharing, mutual cooperation in thought, action and being.

Like other children, this child also needs things around him that allow his temperament to blossom. Objects that also satisfy his indifference should be chosen, for example the items used for everyday activities and all things used for practical survival. It may be hard for the phlegmatic child to learn how to use these, for they offer him no spontaneous reason for giving up the comfort of his own well-being in order to expose himself unnecessarily to the demands and inconveniences of the outside world.

The phlegm causes etheric body to dominate, which is why such a person instinctively strives to enjoy life. Children and adults with this disposition tend to be overweight, because eating makes them feel good; or they are picky about what they eat. Or they spend the whole day alone at home, dreaming, diving down in the realm of imagination until they become fed up with themselves and start to complain about being bored. Feeling bored is a sign of inner change and transformation. The child then starts to renounce precisely the things that have hindered his interest in other things that are now important for him. He learns to reason and to utilise his practical intellect more and more.

The person who feels at home in his etheric body initially uses all his energy to hold on to his inertia and sense of comfort, which seems to suit him. There is initially no reason to give up this state and take an interest in other things, much less to become something that he is not already or to give something up for something else that he does not already have. Going out into the world and exposing himself to the inconvenience this entails is the great challenge for the phlegmatic temperament. Only when his sense of the everyday needs for practical survival is sharpened and he has been almost imbued with an interest in the world does he manage to break out, and may actually go on to achieve great things. For it is only after his own feelings and an interest in other people are awakened that he can discover his own individuality and ultimately his freedom. By letting himself be impressed by others and utilising the intrinsic emotionality of the water signs, he can implement his vision of a better world.

The phlegmatic temperament therefore has an affinity with the astrological water signs. It is supported by a cardinal, fixed or mutable impulse, depending on the motivation of the axis on which the sign is situated. The phlegmatic insists on looking inwards, always in search of a newer and better vision of himself – he just needs to act, and for this he needs time. From an astrological point of view, the direction of development of the phlegmatic temperament clearly goes from the quality of the water signs to the earth signs. Unlike the previously mentioned temperaments, whose typical external manifestation is usually associated with a particular cross motivation, the phlegmatic identifies equally with all the crosses. As still, calm and deep water, it is the lake (Scorpio), as flowing water whose form is constantly changing it is the stream and then the river (Cancer) and as the accumulating, simultaneously all-uniting and all-dissolving water it is the sea (Pisces).

Such a person needs to be grounded and to turn outwards and not in on himself, so that his heart and feelings can flow practically and usefully into action. A healthy physical awareness is essential here. Physical equilibrium is vital for the phlegmatic temperament, particularly if a strong Saturn prevails. This can be done by engaging in sports, skilled manual work or other practical activities, any kind of physical therapy such as yoga, which helps the person to establish an energetic balance with their physical body.

The Melancholic Temperament

> "THE MELANCHOLIC STANDS STILL BY THE STONE. HE PONDERS AND SPECULATES, UNHAPPY OVER HIS ETERNAL MISFORTUNE."

The melancholic temperament suffers from the barriers produced by the physical body. In other words: the physical body stands in the way of the ego; the ego feels that it cannot handle the suffering experienced by the physical body and the pain this causes. The person is disappointed, feels powerless and becomes contemplative and suspicious. The outside world causes him pain and he feels rejected. In physiognomy, this is indicated by a lowered head, a sluggish, often hesitant walk and a lowered, usually dull gaze. The melancholic tries to avoid looking others in the eye, so that they do not notice his insecurity and pain. Such a person has an innate fear – more than the others – of penetrating the depths of their own soul.

We should not make the mistake of thinking that we can as it were graft something onto the melancholic child that he does not possess. Such children have a particular tendency to obstacles and barriers. They are very introverted, and the parent/educator would be well advised to guide their attention and interest outwards, to develop their willpower, to motivate them, keep them busy creatively and above all provide them with opportunities to socialise with other people, so that they do not fall victim to brooding or even melancholy. This child's latent pain and sorrow cannot in any case be talked or educated away. If one should try to do this, the child will only sink deeper into himself. This inner pain, also called world-weariness, characterised by taciturnity, is based on insecurity caused by the dominance of the physical body. The melancholic gives the impression that he is not really comfortable in his own skin; that he has not really learnt to inhabit his own body and is standing beside it. That is demonstrated in mediocre sporting performance, particularly in gymnastics.

So how should a parent/educator treat such a child? They will focus on showing the child that there is suffering in the world and teach him about social issues.

The melancholic child has a high capacity for pain and distaste, or what could be called the capacity for suffering. It is therefore only logical that he has an unerring feel for the sufferings of the world. The parent or attachment figure will therefore try to channel his interest into affairs of the outside world that cause people to suffer, where he can see that pain and suffering are really justified, which helps him to see his own pain in perspective. The educational approach to this temperament should now be obvious; it consists of introducing the child to things with which he can most easily identify. This is what particularly characterises his temperament.

We are not overwhelming such a child by showing him the illness, poverty and misery that exists in this world. Far from it, as in this way his attention is awakened and his interest in it justified; it is the only way to distract his attention from his own melancholy. On no account should one make the mistake of artificially cheering the child up or wanting him to show obvious *joie de vivre*. That would be shortsighted, for it would just make the child close up even more. He would say to himself: "What do they know of how I feel."

The only magic formula that helps here – for the sanguine it is love, for the choleric it is credible authority – is a personality that has been so tested by life, who has gone through the purifying fire of suffering and can speak and act based on these experiences. The child must sense that his attachment figure has had experience of what he himself unconsciously perceives, and what worries him. This person should tell the child about all the things that determine his destiny, and by doing so help the child to look out into the outside world, to understand it, accept it and transform it. The child should sense that he is dealing with a kindred spirit.

As with the above-described temperaments, the parent's fundamental task is to transfer. They guide and transfer the experiences it produces in the child into the outside world in order to counteract the child's unhealthy introversion. A child with this temperament should be encouraged by confronting him with appropriate everyday instances of suffering and pain. They can be little community tasks, such as running errands for sick elderly people, taking care of the weaker and disadvantaged members of a group, a job in an animal sanctuary, etc., or being given some other kind of responsibility for others, to be there for others in their time of need. Because of their own suffering, these children are able to empathise with the suffering of the world, and in turn make a contribution towards helping to save the world. For the melancholy temperament, saving oneself by gaining self-awareness and self-knowledge also always means helping to relieve the suffering of the world. This happens if such a person can let the love he finds in himself and the resulting empathy for all living things flow freely. For what is very characteristic of the melancholy temperament is the love borne of genuine empathy, which should not be confused with pity. A child who is so sensitive to the suffering of the world will be in a position to listen to others, suffer with them and empathise with them and will preserve these valuable qualities into later life, where he can put them to meaningful use.

The astrological correspondence for the melancholic temperament can be found in the earth signs, particularly in fixed Taurus with its opposite counterbalance, Scorpio. Taurus (earth) clings firmly to the material, because it identifies too strongly with possessions and therefore with the suffering and pain associated with "not being able to let go". The melancholic

person is disturbed by the obstacles and difficulties forced upon him by his physical body, just as the phlegmatic temperament is disturbed by the dominance of the etheric body. Just as the Taurus person has a tendency to build a wall around his possessions to provide security and defence against external attack and interference, the melancholic takes refuge deep within himself. Here he can indulge in pain and suffering – if he is not encouraged by the opposing sign Scorpio (Water) to raise his head and take a look at life in the outside world, examine it and take responsibility for it. In Scorpio, as in other water signs, the person experiences the deep mental-spiritual transformation process. The hard, experienced and fossilised structures of the earth in Taurus are softened, dissolved and made fertile by Scorpio's water. The hidebound, fossilised Taurus self has no defence against the deep, clear insight of Scorpio, who is well acquainted with human transformation. This whole process is supported by the fixed cross.

Identifying the Temperament in the Horoscope

We now come to the exciting question of how temperament can be identified in the horoscope. The initial answer to this question must be hypothetical. After weighing up all the factors that can be considered, the principal indicator of temperament is the position of the Moon in sign and house.

However, there may be cases where this is not completely satisfactory, in which case the positions of the other ego planets should be examined, particularly if they are very strongly placed and form oppositions with other planets. Apart from this, it may happen that a second temperament also dominates alongside the prevailing temperament. In addition, other perspectives, factors and criteria should be verified. The end result is that the parent/educator not only knows the child's temperament but also knows how to treat the child in a pedagogically meaningful way.

On the basis of this interpretation model, the Moon's position indicates one pole of the so-called temperament axis. On the other side we have the complementary pole, providing a balance. This balance indicates the developmental task that this temperament must take on, especially if there are oppositions to the Moon or other ego planets. This means that every axis links two mutually balancing temperaments: fire (choleric) – air (sanguine) or water (phlegmatic) – earth (melancholic). The attribution of the temperaments is clearly based on the interaction described by Steiner of the four essential elements of the ego (fire) and astral body (air) and the etheric body (water) and physical body (earth) for the purpose of mutual regulation and balance. There are therefore two possible temperament axes, which multiplied by the three cross qualities cardinal/fixed/mutable gives a total of six temperament axes.

The idealised representative of the choleric with Moon in Aries is on the fire-air temperament axis occupied by cardinal Aries/Libra. This axis can also run in the mutable fire or air signs, which represents a weakened and changed form of the temperament. We can thus identify each of cardinal, fixed and mutable choleric temperaments. The same applies to other temperaments. Finally, the axis quality should be considered – in which of the cardinal, fixed or mutable crosses is the corresponding temperament axis situated? This is particularly helpful when it comes to answering the question of degeneration of temperaments. For the cardinal cross, this means manic-depressive (1/7 – 4/10), for the fixed cross paranoid-catatonic (2/8 – 5/11) and for the mutable cross epileptic and hysterical (3/9 – 6/12).

There is therefore a total of three levels which determine the temperament: the sign level, the house level and the level of the cross qualities.

Depending on motivation cardinal (c), fixed (f) or mutable (m), there are 12 possible temperament types. This initially applies to the sign level. If the house levels are also taken into account, we have a total of 12 x 12 = 144 possible temperaments. Every temperament can theoretically feature 36 shades or nuances.

The Moon as the Indicator of Temperament		
Water-Moon c/f/m	Phlegmatic Dominance of etheric body	The phlegmatic should be shown the benefits of being interested in other people and things. He should not withdraw, but must come out of his shell and approach others and be interested and enthusiastic about new things.
Earth-Moon c/f/m	Melancholic Dominance of physical body	The melancholic should detach from its own pain and develop empathy for the fate of others. He should act with joy, empathy and love.
Fire-Moon c/f/m	Choleric Dominance of ego	The choleric should be able to develop esteem and respect for the achievements of the personality. He should have self-control, self-discipline and respect others.
Air-Moon c/f/m	Sanguine Dominance of astral body	The sanguine should be able to develop love and attachment to one person. He should concentrate, trust and love.

More Questions on the Subject of Temperament

How is it represented outwardly (developmental tension on the house level)? How does it develop and what support does it receive (Moon aspects)? How can it be balanced (temperament axis)? Is there a second, co-dominant temperament? These questions should be answered from a holistic perspective, also taking into consideration other horoscopes such as the HH, moon node horoscope (MNH) and soul horoscope. Other interpretation methods that help in the interpretation of the temperament are dynamic calculations and the dynamic quadrants. The latter in particular tells us a lot about the person's behavioural process.

Developmental Tension of the Temperament

Hereditary Disposition (Sign) – Environment (House)

The Moon, with its temperament, is subject to a specific developmental tension that results from the discrepancy between its position by house and sign. The child must first learn to accept and understand his temperament before he can start to compensate for it. For the Moon this acceptance, or growing into the temperament, is often combined with enormous inner distress and problems, not only for the child, but also for the parents who have to support him. This applies to the first year of life in particular, as long as the structure of the HH is visible.

Luna 1528

Of the four temperaments, fire and water are I-signs; earth and air are You-signs. In the zodiac, fire–air and earth–water always lie opposite each other. These pairs complement each other. Less complementary, but not totally incompatible, are the pairings: fire–water, fire–earth, air–water, air–earth.

Developmental Tension – Fire Signs

In the Fire Houses
Harmonious. The temperament finds approval and acknowledgment in the environment and can enjoy life to the full and be happy.

Everything you do, you do with joy. Others encourage and stimulate you. Into battle.

In the Earth Houses
The fire in the oven or in the forge, which is beneficial for the implementation of inner goals. The fiery energy is shaped into the

correct form by the constant requirement for implementation. The ability to empathise and judge is necessary in order to be able to act appropriately. Create discipline and endurance.

Do not give in and stick bravely to personal tasks and ideals. Hang on in there. Understand and accept reality for what it is.

In the Air Houses
Complementary function. The hot air balloon. The ideas workshop. Ideas rise up. The intuitive dynamism of fire reacts quickly with the mental demands of the environment. The willpower of fire merges into the intellect and imagination of air.

Transfer the willpower and flights of fancy into workable ideas; inspire with one's ideas.

In the Water Houses
A difficult match, as both elements are extremely suspicious of each other. However both sides benefit from the transformation of personal passion, whereby water is warmed by fire and then turned into steam. The individual wishes and goals (volition) conflict with the emotional demands of the environment. Not being able to or not wanting to adapt or react to the emotional needs of others means that the other will get hurt. Can stir up and inflame emotions.

Learn to be considerate and understanding of others. Be patient. Achieve emotional awareness and interact with caution.

Developmental Tension – Earth Signs

In the Earth Houses
Harmony. One trusts one's senses implicitly and does what appears to be sensible and useful; very autonomous; one knows what should be done and what should not. One appears to be stable and reliable. However, there is a tendency to be self-involved.

Learn to be of value and use to others – you will be useful.

In the Air Houses
Earth and air can coexist harmoniously. The air wafts over the earth. The nose inhales the smells in the air. The dissemination of concrete ideas. The sowing of seeds. However, the earth suffers if the air becomes stormy. The practical intelligence of the earth temperament will usually cope with the challenges of the air houses.

Learn to bring others back down to earth or allow them to inspire you. Be open and receptive to the ideas of others.

In the Water Houses
The earth is made fertile by water and starts to bloom. However, there is a risk of flooding. Do not overindulge in emotions, to avoid

being washed away. On the other hand, water can dissolve and wash away old soil and old, inherited structures, as in the cleaning of the Augean Stables in the Labours of Hercules.

Be true to your feelings and let people help you, then you will experience something fantastic and create a thriving garden of life.

In the Fire Houses
Earth gives substance to fire. However, the two do not entirely trust each other. If fire burns too strongly, it can dry up or destroy the earth. A constructive and creative interaction would be the baking of clay. This process always represents a great challenge for both sides, as it requires optimal synchronisation.

You must know what you want and what you are getting involved in and what is required to be successful.

Developmental Tension – Air Signs

In the Air Houses
The qualities of both temperaments are enhanced. Verbal and intellectual exchange is vital for these people. They tend to take off, lose touch with reality and build verbal castles in the air.

Never use your intellect just for its own sake.

In the Water Houses
The air moves the surface of the water, but cannot stop it moving. It is hard to put feelings into words. What one says and thinks may evoke powerful feelings and strong emotions in others, resulting in stormy waters. The ability to address others on the emotional level. But it is also difficult to make something last more than a moment or to create something of lasting value.

Learn to develop tact. Be cautious with your words and thoughts, for they make waves, also including waves of self-awareness.

In the Fire Houses
Complementary, however it is worth bearing in mind that the wind may fan the fire or blow it out. Inspiring ideas find the creativity and willpower they need in the fire houses. However, if the wind blows too hard, the flame disappears. The right amount of air is needed to let the fire burn calmly and constantly, thereby providing warmth and light and allowing the intellect to expand and become creative.

Learn to commit to your ideas.

In the Earth Houses
The artist. Airy ideas come down to Earth where they are turned into concrete facts. Putting theory into practice. May initially be perceived as constraining or restricting before the anticipated satisfaction is

acquired. One must do something with one's ideas or get involved with others' concrete concepts or needs in order to turn them into something substantial.

Carve yourself out a pipe and start to play a tune with it. Think of a way of putting your ideas into practice.

Developmental Tension – Water Signs

In the Water Houses
Feelings flow constantly and strongly. This person has a rich emotional life, frequently prone to emotional fluctuations. They usually have a subjective view of reality. There is a tendency to relate everything back to themselves; overreaction and self-absorption are common.

Transform your lack of interest in the world into genuine interest and understanding. Educate your inner observer so that it can describe your feelings, gain objectivity and implement your visions.

In the Fire Houses
Water and fire are afraid of each other. Fire is afraid of being extinguished by water and water is afraid of being evaporated by fire. It is an extremely tough yet effective transformation process. Great benefits can be derived from getting involved in and yielding unconditionally to it.

Be brave and trust in something that is greater than you.

In the Earth Houses
Water and Earth get along well. The earth useful for water because it acts as a vessel. Irrigation techniques. Earth understands what is really important in life and keeps the overflowing emotions under control. Clear structures are needed in order to be able to guide the powerful emotional currents along the right channels. The earth protects its people from the annual floods by erecting dykes along the rivers to protect from overflowing.

Very adaptable. Do not worry, but have confidence in outside help – you are safe.

In the Air Houses
Water finds it hard to cope with the intellectual demands of the air houses. Emotions and intellect, closeness and distance conflict with each other and cannot find common ground. The visceral and the intellectual have not yet discovered that they can be linked via the heart. Subjectivity and objectivity find themselves in painful opposition here.

Discover and uplift yourself with the power of your thoughts. Only by thinking with your heart can you reconcile your feelings with your mind.

The Tool Planets
Mercury, Jupiter, Venus and Mars

During the young person's development, the tool planets activate other functional parts of the personality which need to be integrated. To start with, the child identifies almost exclusively with its Moon nature, i.e. it is primarily guided by its emotions. It approaches the world emotionally, and it is only later that the conceptual intellect gradually emerges.

Intelligence, Learning and Communication Behaviour

With Mercury, the child wants to learn to understand the world and itself, utter words and express itself linguistically and form concepts in order to communicate with the world. Mercury provides the ability to make contact with the world, to form a relationship with it and learn from it. Mercury, Jupiter and Saturn involve the child in a process that enables the development of individual, free and creative thought. This process is led by the Sun, Jupiter and the spiritual planets.

It is above all the ability to learn, which the child must demonstrate from the time it starts school. By this time, a process of disengagement from the Moon temperament must have started in order for conceptual thought to become part of the child's practical survival skills (at school and at home). Thanks to the teaching and integration of Mercury,

Merkur und seine Kinder 1503

the young person comes closer and closer to his Sun, or the core of his personality. However, this entails separation from his Moon nature. During puberty, this conflict between Moon nature and the incipient Sun nature becomes particularly evident. Young adolescents increasingly identify with the light and awareness of the Sun, and their search for their own identity is supported by Mercury, Venus, Mars and Jupiter. The Moon temperament is then relegated to a shadow role, but should be integrated nevertheless. In this phase of increasing intellectualisation and individualisation, it is very important that the needs of the inner child are not neglected.

Mercury in the Temperaments
In Fire Signs

The child appears particularly alert, interested and sociable. He wants to investigate everything and try out new things; he is quick on the uptake; enthusiasm and indifference are closely related; he has spontaneous ideas and develops artistic forms of expression; he thinks intuitively.

In Earth Signs
The child seems nondescript, even awkward and shy; slow on the uptake; initially finds it hard to make contact with the world; new impressions often seem to overwhelm him; therefore needs time to process things; wants to learn by doing; does not want to be shown anything and wants to do everything by himself; desires independence from an early age; healthy understanding of human nature; thinks practically.

In Air Signs
Here, Mercury is in its element; the child is sociable and enjoys being stimulated by his environment; he learns easily and likes to talk; has a gift for languages, has a thirst for knowledge and is inquisitive; likes reading and books; has an easy time in school; wants to do everything right; can communicate; his understanding is often only superficial, otherwise his thinking is differentiated.

In Water Signs
In order to relate to his environment, the child needs emotional harmony and a warm atmosphere; if something is wrong on the emotional level, then learning is also blocked; he has a lively imagination and can create images; deep understanding, does not remain on the surface; tendency to wishful thinking.

The Two Libido Planets
Venus and Mars
While Sun and Moon guide the search for personal identity as far as the intellect is concerned, Venus and Mars take over when it comes to understanding one's own and the opposite gender. After puberty, both planets indicate the desired image of the opposite sex. This means that a girl or woman's ideal type of partner is indicated by the position of Mars in their horoscope, and the same applies for the man's position of Venus. In addition, both planets symbolise the two essential elements of the masculine (or animus) and feminine (or anima) which should be brought into a harmonious balance.

Irrespective of gender, **Venus's** main requirement is self-esteem. The position of Venus shows the observer the preferences, the way in which the child expresses his creativity and aesthetic sense. In Venus, the child expresses e.g. his preferences for certain foods, for certain clothes, certain works of art, certain people he likes or dislikes, certain ways of behaving when interacting with the opposite sex, etc. It is the power of selection, but also that of synthesis, as the Venus principle is primarily interested in the creation and preservation of substance for the purpose of physical and psychological enjoyment. A strong Venus wants to enjoy itself and be happy.

Venus in the Temperaments

In Fire Signs
Is passionate about what it likes, has a predilection for the theatrical; likes to exaggerate; values extravagance and loves the out of the ordinary; likes to be at the centre of things; tendency to arrogance and pride; finds it hard to put own sensation and hedonism into perspective; likes colours and artistic structures.

In Earth Signs
The appearance is nondescript, but he knows very well what he wants and is very determined; he has a pragmatic disposition, not as selective as the fire Venus. In Taurus, this child develops a high degree of aestheticism and sensuality; needs time to express himself; prizes physical closeness and tenderness; is loyal and reliable; artistic activity with tangible materials.

In Air Signs
Contact with others is important for these children; they are very selective; communication is essential for survival. He is very demanding of his selected friend or partner, who must be able to tolerate disagreements; he is charming, likes to flirt, loves good manners; does not like commitment; enjoys cultural activities, particularly aesthetic literature.

In Water Signs
Requires a lot of sensitivity in order to become aware of his own worth; very selective, but emotionally intense, devoted and very passionate; everything must be in harmony with his own feelings; great longing for a partner; creates the image of a knight in shining armour or a dream wife; likes to believe in his own illusions; likes to makes himself dependent on others; sense of romance and fantasy.

Mars is the will impulse and the engine that drives us to satisfy our needs. It symbolises the power and decisiveness that turn ideas into action, which is why Mars energy is part of the child's development from an early age. Crying to get attention is how the baby first expresses itself, and the early defiance phase is where the child's will is asserted for the first time. It is therefore possible to cope with a consolidation of Mars in its early stages by correctly picking up on what is driving the child and

Mars 1553

understanding how to react appropriately. Here, the question for the parent/educator must be: should I offer the child a framework in which it can offload its aggression and energy potential in order to transfer it constructively and playfully? Mars is able to develop its energy if it is set worthwhile goals and challenges. The simultaneous integration, i.e. conscious awareness of Venus interests is essential, so that the Mars energy does not get out of control or have to hide if for some reason it cannot be lived out. The unredeemed Venus or Mars is therefore often projected onto the future partner and the failure of these relationships due to these expectations not being fulfilled comes as no surprise. Hence the importance of the development of the child's Mars and Venus energy on the part of the parent.

Mars in the Temperaments
In Fire Signs
Here Mars is in its element. He can easily develop his energy; a very active child; likes to demonstrate his strength and will; spontaneous outbursts of anger that vanish as quickly as they come; not vindictive; very egotistical during puberty; assertive and considers himself to be irresistible; must learn to develop endurance and to use his mind; likes to be independent; high energy potential.

In Earth Signs
Compulsive, desiring nature; otherwise rather placid, hesitant, cautious and concerned with his own well-being; gives himself time and can be very tenacious; rather shy during puberty; does not like flamboyance; knows how to treasure the sober and practical Earth qualities; should not sell himself short or show false modesty but must learn to appear self-confident.

In Air Signs
Prefers to set himself goals requiring mental rather than physical strength; is slow to crawl and run; enjoys talking; prefers to avoid conflict; in puberty is diplomatic and charming; shows little tendency to be tied down at an early age; wants to impress with mental brilliance; must learn to get more deeply involved in relationships or tasks.

In Water Signs
Great emotional intensity; at a very early age learns that everything in this world is connected to pain and suffering; no really deep experience is in vain; it is hard for him to avoid that which is expected of him by others; a dark horse who is easily underestimated as his strength is neither physical nor mental, but spiritual.

Profession and Vocation

A whole range of factors influences the choice of profession and training, and it could be said that they are all revealed in the horoscope. However, the complicated and corrupt nature of our economy and society make choosing a profession difficult. It is often impossible for young people to find a training course that corresponds to their interests and talents. They make the best of the choice available and, if they are lucky, something may come of it. If they are unlucky, they come away empty-handed. Nevertheless, there is sufficient margin for error to ensure that far-reaching mistakes are avoided. The important thing is that the decision that is taken suits the child, otherwise frustration and suffering are guaranteed. It is better to wait than to decide in haste. It is essential to trust in life and not to let oneself be uniquely guided by the head, but also by the truth of the heart.

The Position of Saturn in the Houses

Along with the above-mentioned planets, the position of Saturn in the houses also plays an important role. Saturn provides structure, stability and security. Together with Mercury it influences the balancing and refining of temperament. Long before it appears on the scene as *Dweller on the Threshold*, it sets the child certain tasks that help it to disengage from the still-unconscious attachment with temperament and grow increasingly closer to its Sun nature.

The house where Saturn is found usually represents the life area in which the person's particular strength and ability lie, especially with regard to refining its temperament. It is a special kind of learning programme, beneficial for the personality as a whole. But at first it is hard to cope with. The child experiences constraints, comes up against obstacles or just feels inhibited. Secret recriminations are directed against this area until he realises that they are his own imperfections and inconsistencies. The child is initially critical and suspicious of this life area and prefers to avoid these issues, although he suffers from them and secretly longs for them. For he will gain maturity by completing these great challenges or learning tasks.

If the parents are aware of this beforehand, they can teach the child from an early age how important it is to accept his weaknesses and work on them, although this process requires greater integration of the personality, i.e. not before puberty and possibly even later. If the adolescent or adult eventually masters Saturn's hard learning programme and the problems this may raise, then this produces a certain quality of security and composure, which they should be proud of. So, what to the child first appear to be restrictions and problems should have been transformed into special abilities and strengths as the he matures.

Coming out of Weakness, Insecurity and Doubt into Strength, Security and Certainty.

The position of Saturn in quadrant/house is of great importance here. It is noticeable that people with Saturn in the 1st and 3rd quadrants have consciously experienced the house theme during childhood. With Saturn in the 2nd and 4th quadrants the associated house theme only becomes a serious issue later in adulthood. This is linked to the first contact with the Age Point.

There follows a brief description of the inhibitions that correspond to the house theme and the associated learning task, also taking the sign and temperament into account.

Saturn in the 1st House

It is hard for the child to act with confidence and assurance. There may have been aggravating circumstances during the first six years of life that made the child feel that he was not wanted or which inhibited his development. He shows mistrust, fear of being hurt and a deep sensitivity that he tries to hide behind a mask of toughness and seriousness. He has difficulties expressing spontaneous impulses. He is scared, insecure, depressed, joyless, listless and unenthusiastic, burdened with cares and woes. He also lacks assertiveness. Such a child suffers from himself. He may well ask itself: "Do I have to be as I am and am I welcome here?" This child should be told: "Look the world in the eyes and don't be afraid." If this child manages to control his Saturn, then in later life he will also have gained the ability to express himself, to be himself, to articulate his needs and to set boundaries. He will have become a person who knows what he wants and who is no longer so easily intimidated.

Saturn in the 2nd House

The child probably finds it difficult to enjoy and accept himself. His sense of self-esteem is inhibited; he may have the feeling that he gets a raw deal in life. This sense of lack or neediness may be on a material, emotional or spiritual level; it is important that the corresponding values are explained to the child so that he can relate to them. The other side of the coin is that he has to struggle with the fear of loss and learn how to let go. If this child has learnt his lesson, then as an adult he will always ensure that his basic material and emotional needs are satisfied. The talents and abilities acquired serve to raise his self-esteem. In later life, he will mature into a person who has gained inner freedom, who is efficient, conscientious and thoughtful.

Saturn in the 3rd House

This child does not find it easy to relate to others, and probably also takes longer than other children to grasp connections and learn new things. He is slow-witted and rigid-minded. Such a child must be handled very patiently. He is slow on the uptake and often appears to be a late bloomer. He wonders: "Why is everything so hard for me? Why can't I do things more easily?" However, as he matures, such a child will learn to express himself clearly and precisely and understand how to get to the crux of the matter instead of beating around the bush. His thoughts and speech become clear and structured, focused and profound, and he turns out to be a very studious adult.

Saturn in the 4th House
It is hard for such a child to find the protection and security he needs within the family. This position often indicates a difficult childhood. Spiritual hurt, rejection and repression have beaten this child down. To get attention, he thinks he has to offer something in return. He will therefore be afraid of intimacy and closeness, and also have difficulties accepting and expressing feelings. He will wonder: "Why did I have to come here? I wish I had never been born." However, once this child matures and develops his Saturn, he will find the security and protection that he so sorely lacked as a child.

Saturn in the 5th House
This child feels inhibited as soon as he is the centre of attention. While it is true that he secretly wants attention, when he receives it he finds it overwhelming. He lacks self-confidence and usually takes life too seriously. He will wonder: "Why is life so hard on me? What have I done to deserve it?" There is a lack of lightness, humour and sense of fun. He is reserved and often seems self-conscious, strict and fussy and must go through a few disappointments in love before he learns to come to terms with himself. As an adult, once he has transformed his Saturn, he is able to come out of his shell and unselfconsciously express his uniqueness with awareness and even spontaneity, thus becoming a friendly, warm and open person.

Saturn in the 6th House
This child wants to make himself useful from an early age. He likes everything to be tidy and clean. Later, this child can always be given the most difficult tasks. He has to do the work that nobody else wants to do. Because he believes that he has to deserve the recognition and love of others by doing favours and practical chores, he makes himself dependent on others, but also tends to control others and can be pedantic about it. At first he will not really enjoy everyday duties and homework, finding it hard to deal with them. He will therefore try to avoid any responsibility and obligation. As he gets older and manages to transform his Saturn, he will get a clear sense of what he is prepared to take on and what he is not. He will also have learnt how to say what he wants and to conscientiously fulfil his everyday obligations and professional responsibilities.

Saturn in the 7th House

This child probably finds it hard to mix with others easily and unselfconsciously and to socialise, although this is important for him. He needs close and not just superficial friendships, but may initially appear to be suspicious of others. His fear of intimacy or getting hurt makes him seem reserved and cautious in social situations. He prefers to avoid relationships rather than get involved, and makes a quick retreat in face of the slightest disappointment or for fear that he might get drawn in. Such a child finds it hard to believe that he can be loved for himself. He is therefore always, even after puberty, looking for reassurance or constantly requires new proofs of love. He places great value on external show, even if everything is already dead inside, which leads to the danger of dominating and controlling the partner in adult relationships. Such a person will first have to learn to see through their own avoidance strategies, to open up their heart to others, to be able to convert their mistrust into real trust. Then he will become a loyal, reliable, caring and responsible partner.

Saturn in the 8th House

This child (and the adult) finds it hard to get in touch with his own, deep feelings and to delve into himself. Related to this is the fear of losing control, of failing, and being totally at the mercy of others (power-powerlessness problem). Such a person is inwardly inhibited, stiff and never really relaxed. However, if he starts to get involved with the deep, existential issues of life and has accepted life's uncertainties, he then acquires a deep inner peace that allows him to get in touch with his feelings and relax. Then he can also understand life's deepest secrets, thus enabling him to give spiritual support to others.

Saturn in the 9th House

This child quickly learns right from wrong and what is fair from what is unjust. At first he is quick to judge and condemn because he believes he knows what he is talking about. High ideals and dreams are checked for their practicality. In youth this person may tend to form a rigid worldview with strict values, featuring a 'black and white thinking' style. He refuses to accept life's absurdities and may struggle with the question of meaning. Strangers are initially treated with scepticism, even hostility, until at some point a clear and above all tolerant worldview starts to emerge. He then has a firm and unshakeable inner belief in freedom, love and justice.

Saturn in the 10th House

Saturn is in its own house. Such a child will probably appear serious and ambitious to the point of obsession. He refuses to accept help and wants to do everything himself. This child (also the adult) has a tendency to focus on his own failures, mistakes and weaknesses and those of other people. At work he is very demanding both with regard to himself and other people. If these demands are not met he is harsh and becomes unfair and lacking in humanity. Such incidents are painful for both sides. Discipline and structure, concentration and endurance are the values this person most prizes, which make him a credible authority. However, sensitivity should not be neglected to avoid becoming ruthless and dictatorial.

Saturn in the 11th House

At first, this child may have a fear of groups. With time, he will probably make a big effort to make suitable friends and in any case to cope with the demands and expectations of the group to which he feels he belongs. He has the urge to be something special and will expend a great deal of attention and energy in living up to this role. Otherwise, he shows little need to comply with externally imposed norms and standards. In the bottom of its heart, this child is looking for good friends, but initially finds this difficult. He is suspicious, reserved and prefers to take refuge in solitude until loneliness again makes him emerge from his hiding place. However, once this person has mastered the tasks set by Saturn, he knows his own worth and uniqueness without being arrogant or overbearing. Then he can move safely and self-confidently within the group, where he is a natural authority other people can listen to and rely on.

Saturn in the 12th House

This child usually finds it difficult to relax and let himself go. He is afraid of losing control, giving in or losing himself. He always needs firm and reliable structures that give orientation and security. If they are lacking, he can easily panic. He is afraid of the great unknown, the infinite, the unfathomable (irrational fears) and of the all-one-ness. However, this person secretly longs to allow himself to fall into this infinite sea of existence, where he will be able to find love, protection and salvation. Saturn's task is to develop his trust in the higher and guiding forces of his existence so that the child can become increasingly open to them. If the child rises bravely to this challenge, then the Dweller on the Threshold will become his trusty guide through the spiritual worlds.

The Task and Position of the Spiritual Planets (SP)

The goal of personality development is to gain the freedom to be able to get in touch with the soul. If the ego has grown to the right size and strength, then thanks to developed mental capacity and willpower this ego strength can be utilised not only to satisfy personal needs, but increasingly in service of the world (influenced by the soul). The spiritual planets (SP) are responsible for this. They connect the lower self to the higher self/soul. Their selflessness enables them to lead the person to altruism, where his/her soul's task can be clearly seen and aligned with the divine plan. Then the person becomes a voluntary and loving servant of the world.

The planetary model shows Pluto as the higher development of the Sun. It strongly influences the formation of the ego and the strengthening of willpower and finds its principal expression in the power-powerlessness theme. Neptune is the higher development of the Moon and works via the imagination producing images, visions and ideals in the soul that purify the astral body. Uranus, the higher development of Saturn, works in the ethereal sphere. It has a direct influence on the form-creating forces, the subtle energy system of our bodies. All three communicate the higher ideals of the spiritual world: Pluto the ideal of the perfect person, Neptune ideal love and Uranus the ideal of the perfect society. Collectively, they represent the Christ ideal. The Christ is the perfect role model; the goal of evolution for humanity, the human psychological/emotional/physical matrix, and this ideal has universal validity. The three SPs are therefore the impetus for man's spiritual awakening. However, their house position may initially cause them to be significant stress factors in the developmental process; as guiding principles and ideals they overstimulate the ego and never leave it in peace. The person then experiences the SPs as a powerful superego, an inner compulsion to fulfil these ideals.

A child at the start of its development is totally absorbed in its Moon nature. The ego is only just starting to form and the above-described transforming energies of the SPs are not expressed so strongly. Here, Saturn's role as the *Dweller on the Threshold* is to keep watch over the child. Nevertheless, they can decisively influence the structure of the child's consciousness, depending on the way they are aspected and their position in the houses. If the SPs are incorporated into the aspect pattern, are coherent, and form aspects with ego planets, they can be better processed and integrated than if they develop a dynamic that is completely detached from and uncontrolled by the ego planets.

The **position of a SP in the house** indicates the source of its stimulation. It is like an antenna that can be directed either inwards or outwards. If in the fixed area or at the LP, then the child tends to be cautious. The planet then has a strong inward effect and tries to access the soul. Basically it can be said that the best place for SPs is near the LP or in the fixed area of the house, for there they mobilise spiritual forces in the form of an inner ability or aptitude. However, if they are at a house cusp, and especially in the mutable stress area, the child is subject to greater inner anxiety and pressure. The planet(s) behave(s) like a superego, constantly bombarding the child with new impulses in the form of demands and expectations. This pressure to perform comes from within, not from outside, and makes the child feel that he has to behave in a certain way that is expected by the environment, without realising that the cause can be found in the exposed position of the SP(s).

This feeling is reinforced if a **SP is in conjunction with an ego planet**. The ego planet then constantly feels it must transform and barely has the chance to develop a healthy ego awareness. His own needs are not taken seriously or are constantly questioned and overlooked. Instead he overexerts himself for the environment, leading to what we call an exploitation of the ego, which is usually the result of low self-esteem.

The other extreme would be an **unaspected SP**. At the LP this should not cause any trouble, and may only be noticed when the AP crosses over it, and as it were wakes it from its slumber. However, the situation is very different if the SP is at a house cusp. There it can lead to activities that are completely beyond control of the ego, which the person will find hard to cope with. These outbreaks suck him in like a vortex and the associated experiences must be endured. Every time it is as though his former life is being put to the test and nothing is sacred. At these times the person needs to be treated with understanding and sensitivity, and should on no account be criticised, for his suffering is much greater than that of those around him who may be affected by his behaviour.

With **Uranus at the house cusp**, instead of a spiritually oriented intuition, he has a constant stream of new whims and crazy ideas. He wants to be original and shock others, is unpredictable and has a predilection for unusual, eccentric activities. This person often shows a penchant and aptitude for technical matters. The special qualities of **Uranus at the LP** may find expression in artistic activity, especially music or esoteric science. Uranus is active wherever old traditional structures must be broken down (Saturn) in order to make room for new ones.

With **Neptune at the cusp,** he always feels called upon to help and get involved irrespective of personal feelings. There is great empathy which is hard to switch off, developing a superego that tells the person what to do and how to behave – good, kind, caring, fair, etc. He is too quick to put himself out for others, without adequately considering his limitations, so that he does too much and ends up hurting himself. The stress area is most dangerous, as here he has the feeling that he is indispensable to the environment. He feels needed and hopes to gain approval, but should be careful not to get completely overloaded and burnt out. **At the LP** Neptune is able to clearly distinguish what is true from what is not and what is appropriate from what is not. Here it stimulates the longing for transcendence and unity in others.

With **Pluto at the cusp,** the person is inextricably entangled in the power-powerlessness theme, but to a lesser extent than at the LP. At the cusp, he has problems with authority. He either plays the role of offender or victim. As offender, he acts with authority; as victim, he has to endure it. It is important here to realise that he tends to delegate, to give away the power that he has from Pluto in this area because he feels too weak to exercise it himself. Only when he has learnt to reclaim this power instead of giving it away, and learnt how to master it, can he leave his state of powerlessness and become powerful. Pluto's transformation task is fulfilled when the person has learnt to deal responsibly with power.

As well as house position, we should take into account the position in the chart as a whole. As far as age progression is concerned, it is significant whether the SPs are all in the first quadrant or in the bottom hemisphere or the top. If AP in the period up to adolescence only runs through spiritual planets, the child will find this very challenging, particularly if they are also situated in critical areas. In this case, special attention and a great deal of empathy are required on the part of the parent/educator.

Moon Node Axis and the AC

In my opinion, consideration of the axis of the rising and descending Moon Node is of less importance in children's horoscopes, as the child only becomes aware of the Moon Nodes and the developmental task set by the AC later on, but it should absolutely be included for future reference.

◻ ◻ ◻ ◻ ◻

The Horoscope as an Aid in the Teaching of Gifted Children

Karin Goebel

First published in AstroLog Issue 136, October 2003

As a teacher, I recently had the opportunity to teach three obviously gifted children in my class. They presented a special challenge. They were desperate to learn, but in their own way. They only accepted something from me as their teacher if they were convinced that it would help them to continue learning and would not overly restrict their creativity. Over time I increasingly came to see myself as their partner; I tried to understand their motivations and to progress with them. Anything else would only have ended up in an exhausting power struggle.

Despite their giftedness, these children still needed a sense of belonging and support. Their ideas on philosophical and religious matters indicated a deep spirituality, which I found touching. It made me search for activities that would nurture this spirituality. To this end, I found C. Hehenkamp's book: *The Indigo Phenomenon* very helpful.

During my training, it occurred to me that the horoscope could allow us to see the mental and spiritual world of these children, and their particular needs, the way they saw the world. In this article, I try to relate my school experiences with these children to their horoscopes. I believe that further research could be helpful for parents and children in understanding and teaching the life task of gifted children.

The Generation of the 1990s

Children with a Uranus/Neptune Conjunction

The children I had to teach belonged to this generation. Uranus is associated with technology, particularly computer technology. Another affinity is with social structures, the perfect society, but also originality and the tendency to disregard convention. Uranus is therefore the egg piercer that leads into the top of the Huber amphora into a completely new dimension of awareness. [See e.g. *Astrological Psychosynthesis*, page

131 on.] Neptune is the planet of perfect love, a love that is all-encompassing and embraces everyone, and the longing for peace in a violent world. It also symbolises profound and prophetic wisdom.

This conjunction combines a theoretical, evolutionary perspective with a mythical longing. When this generation reaches adulthood, it could contribute towards the creation of structures that make a just peace possible. Their bond with all living things could enable this generation to have completely new ideas as to how man can live and work in harmony with nature. I also see in this conjunction a spiritual task. The conflicts between religions that have already caused so much suffering could be transformed by this generation into a deep mutual understanding. Perhaps it can also overcome the division between science and religion, advancing into completely new ground.

In my teaching I have found the children of this generation to be both fascinated by computers and interested in religion and art. Their comments are often wide-ranging, sometimes characterised by a surprising wisdom.

If this spiritual approach is not seen and encouraged in the child's education, I see the danger of drug addiction, internet abuse, deception and self-destructive disenchantment.

There was also a conjunction between Neptune and Uranus in the horoscope of Karl Marx. In his work we can see the fascination and explosive power that the combination of ideas and myth can develop. We should be excited!

The Children

Felix, Julian and Britta belong to this generation. They are obviously gifted children. I would like to introduce them briefly.

Felix was in my class for two years, then he jumped the third class and went to secondary school after three years in primary school. At first he enjoyed school, but became very disappointed in the third week that, as he put it, he was not learning anything. From then on, we continually searched together for ways in which he could learn and retain his enjoyment for learning. It always came down to social skills.

After the first year, **Julian** immediately went up to class 3. According to his class teacher he had behaved arrogantly and sometimes unsociably during his first year at school. After the change, which required a lot of commitment from Julian, he only showed this kind of behaviour to begin with. He got better and better at accepting clear feedback on his behaviour and precisely defined rules. He now works well with others and makes less of a drama out of conflicts. He has also learnt to accept criticism as help. After the fourth year he will attend a secondary school with special facilities for gifted children.

Britta has been my pupil since the first school year and is now in the fourth year. In the first two years of school, she was often lost in daydreams and barely followed what was happening in the classroom. She also had little contact with her classmates. Since the third year, round about the entry of AP into Scorpio, she began to be more sociable. Since then her giftedness and high intelligence have become more and more noticeable in the classroom. Like Julian, Britta is going to attend the secondary school with special facilities for gifted children.

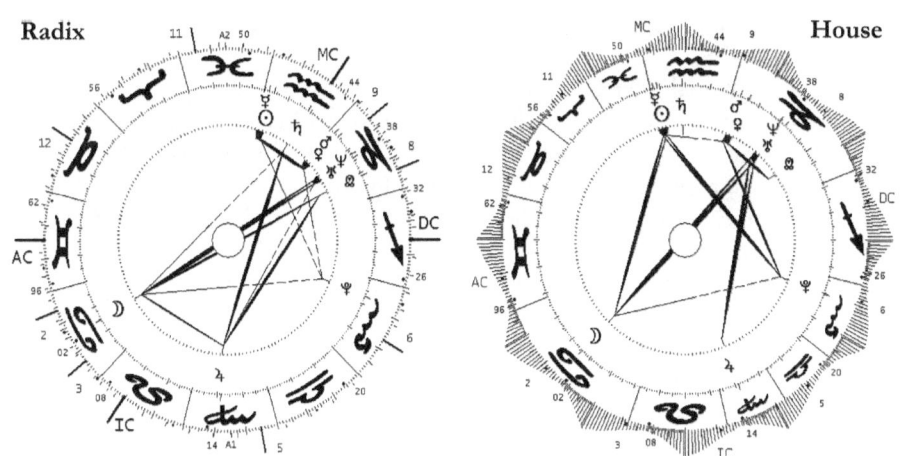

Felix, 15.02.1992, 11:34, Lichtenfels b Kassel, Germany

Creativity, Goals, Thinking

Felix was happy to get involved in making improvements for the whole class, for example he produced worksheets or puzzles for the others. The green aspecting of the Sun conjunction Mercury is reflected in a versatile mind, the 0° position of Mercury allows him to pick up nuances easily. Felix prefers to work alone (planets in houses 8-10 in Capricorn and Aquarius). The predominantly green and red aspecting of the planets could have contributed to the fact that he sometimes forgot that others could not follow his train of thought so easily.

142 Part 2 – Children and Upbringing

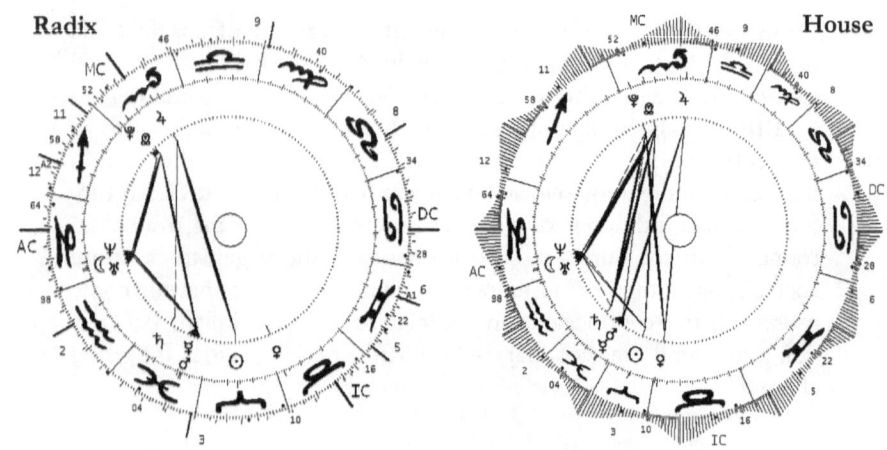

Julian, 04.04.1994, 03.39, Werne an der Lippe, Germany

Julian had a creative approach to the holistic perception and linking of subject matter. However, it took a while for him to also show this in class. In Pisces in the 2nd house we find Saturn, which may have an initial inhibiting influence. Jupiter in the shadow of the 10th could achieve lofty goals. However, Julian also had a tendency to overestimate himself, which the class immediately corrected (Saturn in 2). In his house horoscope, Julian's Mercury has a blue-green aspect, which makes him very open and receptive to learning. Jupiter in the radix is aspected blue-green, while in the house chart it is red-green, which indicates constant irritation. Julian may have experienced this Jupiter in the first class, making hasty judgements that led to conflicts.

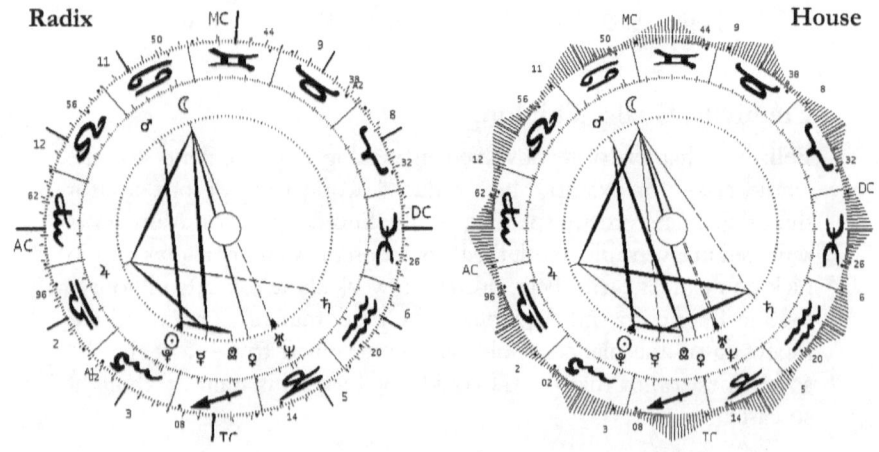

Britta, 14.11.1992, 01.55, Aachen, Germany

Britta had good ideas for the group and wanted to be recognised for this (planets in individual signs in the collective space, Moon in 10th house). Particularly in the organisational area she had many good ideas that she followed up with rigour and tenacity, even when the implementation ran up against technical problems (Jupiter in Libra with trine to Saturn). Mercury, green aspected with a quincunx, makes her thinking active and profound. It is possible that this contributed to her day dreaming, she was already way ahead. It is also conceivable that the ambivalent blue/red aspected Jupiter has a dreamy influence. Sometimes she is very astute, sometimes not. In the blue phase she then appears absent.

Interest in Justice, Philosophy, Religion, Environment and Sexuality

Felix had an early interest in newspapers, and was well-informed about political events. He loved having philosophical discussions. He was particularly interested in Egyptian mythology, which seemed to have a magical, powerful impact on him (emphasis on 8th and 9th houses).

Julian showed a particular gift for analogous, symbolic thought, which was particularly evident in religious education classes. This fits well with his small blue Talent triangle.

Britta was very interested in environmental issues. As she was always looking for something special (Moon in 10th), she became intensively involved with spiders and scorpions, a clear affinity with her Sun conjunction Pluto in Scorpio.

Perfectionism, Independent Working, Tendency to Control Situations

Felix's emphasis on the 10th house with two ego planets already prohibited him from joining in the normal learning progress of the class. He was only happy working at his own pace. He did not even mind being the only one to go into the next class up for lessons and after one year moving completely to that class.

Julian entered my third-year class after his first school year. To begin with he had problems, because he had not yet mastered certain working techniques. However, he always only needed a short introduction to them, after which he applied them logically – so that after a term this gap no longer existed. In group work, he preferred working in pairs with a weaker pupil, when he liked to determine the direction and tone (Pluto in 10th).

Britta was hard to influence when it came to the implementation of her organisational ideas, where she developed an incredible desire for perfection and enormous perseverance (Sun conjunction Pluto with trine to Mars in 11th). If things did not go as she wanted, she started to cry (Moon red/green aspects).

All three children have aspect patterns that show a striving for individuality.

Possible Indications of Intellectual Giftedness in the Horoscope

At first I wondered about the classical intelligence planets Mercury (gathering of knowledge), Jupiter (perception) and Saturn (memory). This question is most easily answered in Britta's case. In the radix, Mercury, Jupiter and Saturn are directly connected to each other. The environment seems to encourage her talents even more. In the house chart, we see the three planets joined together in a small Talent triangle. Perception, the gathering of knowledge and memory work optimally together in Britta's case.

It is not so clear for Felix and Julian. In **Felix's** radix Saturn and Jupiter are connected by a quincunx; in the house chart the intelligence planets are located in different figures, with Saturn even unaspected. This could mean that Felix uses his intelligence differently at different times, or that he prioritises the gathering of knowledge when he lives only in the house chart. He could then develop a life philosophy that knowledge is power (Mercury connected to Pluto and Moon in a large Talent triangle).

Like Felix, **Julian** has an aspect between Saturn and Jupiter in his radix, in his case a trine. In the house chart, this becomes a quincunx between Jupiter and Mercury. Depending on where Julian is living, he can switch on his intelligence planets. All three are in the element of water, so that they all have the same colouring. Julian's parents say that at home he is very difficult, verbal and aggressive (Jupiter quincunx Mars and Moon square Pluto in house chart). At home, Julian seems to live more in the house chart. At school he usually behaves calmly, and seems to live more in the radix.

Intelligence Planets in Connection with Ego Planets and the different Types of Indigo Children.

This is how Carolina Hehenkamp describes the Indigo Children:

> *"Indigo children have a hard task ahead of them, for it is they whose infiniteness can bring us worldwide peace...They sense who they are, what is right for them and what is not. They usually know exactly what they have to do and how to do it. They are filled with unconditional love, are tolerant and prejudice is alien to them."*

I can see much of this reflected in my pupils, some of it in their horoscopes too.

The section of Bruno Huber's book *Astrological Psychosynthesis* on "Intelligence in the Horoscope" and Carolina Hehenkamp's book *The Indigo Phenomenon* have encouraged me to think in the following way. These ideas are still a little speculative and the future life journeys of these children will show whether they are true or not.

The three classical intelligence planets are, as already mentioned, Mercury, Jupiter and Saturn. However, also important is how they interact with the ego planets Sun, Moon and Saturn and which conclusions can be drawn from this.

Felix's strongest ego planet is Saturn in Aquarius. Combined with a quincunx to Jupiter, he could utilise his intelligence well in structures and become what Hehenkamp calls a conceptualist. The following characteristics shown by Felix agree with her descriptions. Felix likes ideas and concepts, however he must learn to deal with details. He likes to control his parents and prefers to work on the computer. He also seems not to be very emotional. In his chart, his Moon is near the LP and in opposition to Neptune/Uranus, which could have an inhibiting effect.

Julian's ego planets Saturn and Moon seem to be equally strong, but are both in the vicinity of the LP, i.e. he must first develop them by themselves in an inner process.

He also has a trine between Saturn and Jupiter. The bond between Moon/Neptune/Uranus in the Talent triangle with Mercury could indicate relationship intelligence. The spiritual planets should at first be hard to cope with. According to Hehenkamp's description, I would consider him to be an interdimensionalist: Julian is not prepared to adapt to outdated ideas or expectations, which sometimes leads to problems in his family. He follows his thing through in class, whether people like him for it or not, and he needs clear discipline in order to be able to fully utilise his creativity. It is said that these children will bring new ideas, philosophies and religions into the world. This fits well with the small Talent triangle in his chart, which features Moon, Mars/Mercury, all the spiritual planets and the Moon Node.

In **Britta's** horoscope, the Sun is in strong conjunction with Pluto with a trine to Mars. Its house position between cusp and Balance Point is strong. Britta therefore uses a lot of willpower in order to accomplish her objectives. This and other things link her with what Hehenkamp says about the artist. I see an artistic aspect in the second house, Jupiter in Libra, and perhaps also the 0° position of Venus. Britta learns best if she can also be creative. She can paint and draw for hours. She is very dependent on me, and often comes to see me after class to chat. She sees through situations very quickly and acts accordingly. According to Hehenkamp, these children are born healers. Britta's AC is in Virgo and her DC in Pisces.

All three children have a blue or green Saturn-Jupiter connection. They consistently demonstrate the comprehensiveness of their perception and the depth of their thought.

What do Children Need?

Position and Colouring of the Moon

I asked myself this question because a gifted child is always first and foremost a child, and is dependent on having its Moon needs recognised and satisfied. Given that they belong to the group of Indigo children, they come into a world that does not understand their special life task and may even oppose it. That necessarily leads to disappointments and a feeling of being misunderstood.

All three children have tricky Moon positions in their charts.

Felix and **Britta** have an opposition between Moon and Neptune/Uranus.

Julian has a conjunction Moon/Neptune/Uranus and in his house chart the Moon has a strong square aspect.

In each of these children, the Moon must be destabilised, perhaps by much of what they sense but cannot integrate in their everyday lives.

What do these children need as children? For **Felix** it was important that his giftedness was seen and acknowledged by the collective (Moon in Cancer in 2nd house). After two weeks in the first year of school, he shouted out loudly, "But I'm not learning anything!" Despite his concentration of planets in the 8th, 9th and 10th houses, it was important for him to remain connected. He still visited me even after he had moved to the next class.

Julian's Moon is in the 1st house in Capricorn. It was important for him to be seen as an autonomous personality. Although all the football players in the class idolised Borussia Dortmund, he declared himself to be a fan of Bayern Munich. His violent emotional outbursts (Neptune square Moon in house chart), vanished if one stayed with him but did not attach too much importance to his dramas. His unpredictable emotional expression had to be lived with but not taken too seriously. Julian also liked to take responsibility for particular tasks. He wants to be respected as a person and does not let himself be manipulated.

Britta's Moon is in Cancer in the 10th house. It was indeed important for her to feel part of the class community, while at the same time needing her own performances, which she visibly enjoyed. She liked to be the little teacher who had good ideas for the coexistence of the group. Britta is only friends with a few children; she prefers the company of other gifted children.

Gifted Children, their Bodies and Basic Senses

Carolina Hehenkamp describes in her book that the Indigo children are not at home in their bodies. All three children showed evidence of partial sensorimotor disturbances.

Felix often behaved clumsily when he had to do crafts and paint. It was difficult for him to keep his work materials tidy. In his chart, Saturn is aspected in green and in the house chart even unaspected.

In **Julian's** case, a sensory disturbance had already been diagnosed before he started school. His Saturn is only weakly aspected in blue, and in addition the aspect originates from Jupiter. The sensory system is stimulated early on because children put everything in their mouths and make important sensory experiences there. In Julian's radix Venus is unaspected. Further research could clarify whether Saturn and Venus may be involved in sensory disturbances.

Britta's Saturn is only radiated on one side by Jupiter. It sometimes appears as though she is disembodied. In athletic activities she looks clumsy and stiff. She is very good at swimming though (emphasis on water element).

It was very helpful for me as Felix, Julian and Britta's teacher to see their horoscopes. I think that this helped me to avoid unnecessary conflict and thereby encourage their learning. I have learnt a lot from these children, for which I thank them. I hope that they will be able to fulfil their life task joyfully.

❑ ❑ ❑ ❑ ❑

Part 3: Relationships

The articles in this part of the book are concerned with the use of astrological psychology in understanding relationships.

The first two articles address relationships from first a psychological theoretical perspective and then an astrological practical perspective:

Some Thoughts on Relationships, by Harald Zittlau
A psychological perspective on relationships and the application of astrological psychology in relationship counselling.

Relationship as a Developmental Process, by Louise Huber
An astrological perspective on relationships, presenting the application of three levels of 'click' horoscopes: between house charts, between moon node charts and bridging across the two.

The final three articles all have a theme of 'mother-daughter' relationships. First is a real life example of a mother with a severely handicapped daughter. The final two articles both deal with parallels between the story of Snow White and the growth process of the daughter into a mature woman.

A Life Not Worth Living, by Verena Bieri
Considers the lives and relationship of a mother and her severely handicapped daughter, relating these to their radix/house and moon node charts and 'click' points.

The Transformation of the Heroine, by Dr. Reinhard Müller
Considers the often difficult psychological process of conflict and disengagement between daughter and mother using analogies in the Fairy Tale of Snow White, and relates it to Moon-Pluto themes.

Snow White, by Ruth Schmidhauser
Follows up the theme of Snow White from a woman's perspective, highlighting the significance of Moon-Saturn connections.

The following publications give detail of features of astrological psychology that are of particular relevance to the context of relationships:

Astrological Psychosynthesis, by Bruno Huber
> The third part of this psychological introduction is entitled "Love and Relationships in the Horoscope".

Partnerships and Relationship Dynamics through 'Click' Horoscopes, by Sylvia Wenk
> An explanation of 'Click' horoscopes. This publication is produced by and available from Astrological Psychology Institute (UK). [See 'Resources at the back of this book for contact details.]

Some Thoughts on Relationships

Harald Zittlau

First published in AstroLog Issues 116-117, 120
June-August 2000, February 2001

The dawn of a new century has focused our minds on the issues that will face mankind in the future. It will become more and more important for individuals, states, nations and religious groups to be able to relate successfully to ensure political justice, equality of economic opportunities, ideological and religious tolerance, the perception of cultural identity, the overcoming of xenophobia, etc.

We know that how we behave individually has an influence on living conditions on our planet and the quality of the "whole life climate". In many areas we know what kind of behaviour hinders the progress of evolution.

We have begun to think and network globally; there are no longer geographical limits to our relationships. We react to all conceivable environmental influences, often repressing the effects of how we behave in relationships in the process.

By developing our ability to relate, we will be able to live in harmony with the inner and outer laws of nature.

The Word "Relationship"

We are inextricably linked to the network of relationships into which we are born. A major part of our life energy is dedicated to getting to know these networks, changing them and adding to them.

In astrological psychology, great importance is attached to the fact that we are part of a complex network of relationship interactions on all levels. For the purposes of this article, it is therefore necessary to separate the term "relationship" from its limited use purely in the context of the couple.

The word "relationship" can be used to describe the way we relate to everything that surrounds us. (We define this "everything" as the sphere of the "You" or as a synonym for everything beyond the self.) Romantic relationships are a special kind of relationship within this general description.

Relationships on Material, Emotional and Spiritual Levels

In astrological-psychology counselling, a lot of time is spent talking about relationships, not least because the counselling process itself is an intense relationship. It should, among other things, help the consultee to gain a different perspective on the aspects of their behaviour that seem to cause conflict in relationships.

The challenge facing the consultant is to sensitively probe the themes that lead to blocks or painful experiences in our relationships with people or with the environment.

It is usually stubborn convictions, a lack of maturity or certain forms of fear (e.g. of intimacy) which make it difficult to deal satisfactorily with the "You". It is helpful to start by knowing which level is affected by conflict in the relationship.

On the **material** level, we are controlled by our one-sided ideas of how the world works or how other people relate to each other. We refuse to acknowledge certain external realities, and feel that apparently legitimate demands are unfair, or try to take advantage of others. We approach relationships as though they were business deals, i.e. only in terms of victory and defeat.

In order to overcome conflicts on this level, it is necessary to change this approach to "relationships" and to learn to behave more fairly.

The "initiation" on this level happens when we accept that we cannot understand or influence much in life, when we sacrifice our aspirations or overcome our fear in order to enable relationships, without damaging our self-esteem.

On the **emotional** level, relationships are a source of suffering until we learn how to really understand and put into practice the principle of love. Most conflicts in romantic relationship take place on this level: we cannot cope with external influences and start to hate them, or we feel at the mercy of the You due to our own neediness and burden them with our lack of confidence as a form of insubordination. We are grasping, jealous and demanding. We demand – consciously or unconsciously – affection from our partner that we ourselves are not able to give freely and unconditionally in return.

The conditions only change when we accept different forms of existence as equally valid and find the strength to structure our relationships on a basis of free will and unconditionality.

The "initiation" on this level takes place when we are prepared to give understanding and affection without asking for them in return.

On the **spiritual** level, the conflicts in our relationships with the world are characterised by a lack of guidance, identity and authority.

We want to attain genuine self-actualisation. We want to do things our own way, but so much of our time and energy is wasted on irrelevant things, and it often takes us a long time to realise this.

We see other people's achievements and allow ourselves to be guided by forms of achievement legitimised and rewarded by society. We measure ourselves by other people's standards and are inevitably dissatisfied, envious or demotivated. We allow great areas of our lives to be determined for us by external forces.

We can live our lives more authentically by using our willpower to fulfil our potential and using our resources equally for both personal and public benefit, for example if a nine-to-five job turns out to be a vocation.

"Initiation" on the spiritual level means running the risk of leaving familiar and apparently safe terrain in order to follow the path of our inner voice.

It is therefore primarily our internal conditions that provide us with experiences and challenges on all three levels of our existence and determine how we relate to the world.

Relating through Relationships

Relationship competence is not a subject that is taught in schools or universities. The archaic power of the ancient polarities (such as love and hate, friend and enemy, like and dislike) still influences the way we are socialised to this day.

If we want to transcend the pull of one or other of these poles, we must use great creative energy to take our relationships to new levels and protect them from our own emotional chaos and the resistance of the defences of those involved.

Even if it may seem almost impossible to know how to improve our relationship skills, anyone who has managed to do so will attest to the unimaginable feeling of lightness and liberation that it brings.

On the way to this experience, we encounter the most important pillars of our existence:

- The meeting of our basic needs
  (light, air, food, protection from the elements, affection and belonging, learning, meeting, exploring)

- Discovering and accepting our spiritual life goal
- The creation of a new life or new visions
- The acceptance of our physical mortality.

By working intensively with these themes, we can both put our sensitivities into perspective and distinguish what is important from what is not and what is intrinsic to our nature from what is not. By strengthening our willpower and accepting our dark side, we are able to bring love into our lives. This love, that makes a creative contribution to our relationships, allows us to experience identification and connectedness. Suddenly we see and appreciate our most sacred inner longings in the gestures of others, and find harmony, beauty and fulfilment in the process.

However, we may also come up against the greatest obstacles to the development of our relationship skills: *insecurity and ignorance.*

If we have not been able to gain any personal insight in our relationship with something, we allow ourselves to be guided by other people's explanations or adopt relationship strategies that are alien to us. We look for explanations in all kinds of belief systems, particularly with issues that we cannot explain by ourselves.

Nevertheless, it is possible to have an open mind as far as one's relationship to the eternal unknown is concerned. For example, we can answer the question: "is there a life after death?" by internalising an outside belief. However, real inner security is only attained through spiritual creativity, which addresses the issue without using an explanatory model as a crutch.

It could be that there is nothing there after death. Our emotions and spiritual and mental activities could turn out to be just the standard side effects of biologically highly sophisticated organisms. However, this would not change what we already know about the order of our world: according to modern thinking, we are made up of body, mind and spirit, although future research may produce deeper insights and other concepts regarding the interaction of these three levels.

Confidence and security are achieved via the initiative of our consciousness, rather than by going through the external motions of "assuring oneself". All we need are ever newer ways of accepting that we are part of a process of life and death, without focusing too much on definitive explanations of exactly what awaits us. There appears to be no other solution. It may be some consolation that all forms of life tread the same uncertain path. Only the affirmation of all areas of our lives that are under our control can lead us into the light and enable us to live a fulfilled life.

Why not therefore use our intelligence in such a way as to maximise the development of our potential, so that we become part of the great stream of life during the short period in which we can influence our microcosm?

What most motivates us to work on our relationship skills is the 'classical' area of the romantic relationship. Happiness, satisfaction and fulfilment are not divine gifts, but in the long run can only be achieved by active relationship work.

A New Understanding of Romantic Relationships

It is most probably an illusion that our life purpose exists somewhere outside ourselves waiting to be fulfilled or that someone will reveal it to us. It is up to us to take the decisive and vital steps towards personal development that face us all by ourselves. Nobody can learn something for someone else. Even our last great step must be taken alone.

A romantic relationship entails both partners freely deciding to share a certain stretch of their own personal life journey with another person.

The deeper purpose of such a relationship is the chance to develop through mutual inspiration aspects of the personality that would otherwise remain hidden.

The cause of most problems on this shared path is when the partners involved have differing ideas about the significance of the relationship.

In very many relationships, one partner is consciously or unconsciously 'misused' as a projection figure for the other's psychological shortcomings, and is delegated elements of their own learning task. That is why so many relationships degenerate as the partners (ab)use each other and start to panic about losing their freedom.

Conditions for Viable Relationships

All relationships, particularly romantic ones, go through different phases of varying intensities and durations:
- First meeting and awareness of each other
- Adoption of compatible forms of communication
- Experience of emotional affinity (loving each other, affection or sympathy)
- Safeguarding the quality of the relationship
- Coordination of daily routines
- Joint life organisation and definition of common objectives

- Consolidation of the daily relationship routine *creatively structuring each new challenge together, accepting the positive aspects and repressing or excluding the negative ones.*
- **Tolerating arguments (big or small), dealing with the partner's shadow side.** Growing into the relationship and redefining togetherness, or making genuine or false compromises. Getting to know each other better or growing further apart. Acknowledging or repressing problematic aspects of the relationship.
- **Transforming the relationship.** Making the relationship a source of inspiration, happiness and satisfaction, or consciously or unconsciously working towards a separation or giving the relationship some degree of ambivalence.
- **Continuity and separation**

The developed or advanced stages of relationships face the following challenges:

1. **The relationship continues to evolve to mutually desirable levels.**

   Such relationships are considered to be fulfilled. Outsiders say that this is due to the couple's "inexplicable" luck, and do not realise the work that the couple has put into the relationship to get this far on their journey together.

2. **The relationship gets "stuck" at an attained status quo.**

   The relationship usually degenerates into habitual rituals and serves to unconsciously maintain mutual demands, leading to a bond based on security and fear. (The state of our society would lead one to assume that the vast majority of romantic relationships ultimately stagnate at this level.)

3. **To break up.**

   As a conscious act, no longer being able to make the shared journey. The partners transform their relationship as a mutually positive source of life enrichment and become spiritual friends or allies for the rest of their now separate life journeys. Other forms of mutual support therefore become possible. The shared experiences often influence and enrich new relationships.

   As an unconscious act, the frustration of personal objectives. There is lasting injury and damage to self-esteem. Love can turn into hate and individuals can try to brush the experiences they have had under the carpet, thereby running the risk of "importing" the unresolved conflicts into new relationships.

Conclusion

Relationships are bonds with time limits. Their purpose is to provide mutual enrichment by spontaneous giving that inspires spiritual growth and provides emotional and physical fulfilment.

At the start of a relationship, both parties are aware that the decision to take a shared journey will be repeatedly tested.

The duration and intensity of relationships depend on the potential for mutual enrichment and can lead to a bond that lasts for a day or a lifetime.

Even in the first stage of the relationship, the partners are aware that hurt, drifting apart, separation, etc. are shared experiences and they are accepted as transformation processes.

On a mental level, the possible decision for the couple to go their separate ways is supported from the outset, even if it contradicts other personal interests and needs!

If a break-up occurs a long way into a relationship, it takes place with love and gratitude for the time and energy shared on the journey. The relationship transforms itself into a spiritual bond.

The horoscope helps us to develop our personal "methodology" so that we may enhance our relationship skills.

Types of Relationships

Many people with an interest in astrology still believe that each zodiac sign is only compatible with certain others, usually belonging to the trio of the same temperament according to "popular" astrology. The belief that underlies this assumption is that a romantic relationship follows secret laws guaranteeing automatic, maximum fulfilment once the "right" partner has been chosen, without much effort needing to be put into the relationship.

Mainstream modern attitudes are primarily oriented towards materialistic, consumerist values, and people tend to be influenced in their choice of partner by the kind of idealised personality attributes favoured by our performance-oriented society.

Most relationships that start so promisingly fail relatively quickly when they reach the inevitable stage where organic crisis management is required.

If we look at this subject in more depth, we realise the complexity of factors that affect relationships. Someone who regularly changes partner after the first disappointment will at some point start to wonder where they are going wrong, in order to be able to grow and develop their relationship potential.

As the topic of relationships is very complex, here I intend to limit myself to "classical" male-female romantic relationship, as this is an area where good and bad relationship experiences have a particularly lasting effect.

There are seven different kinds of relationship in which we are able to gain fundamental specific relationship experience and acquire the relevant relationship skills:

Seven Kinds of Relationship

Child-Parent
- daughter-mother   son-mother
- daughter-father   son-father

Siblings
- sister-sister   sister-brother   brother-brother

Parent-Child
- mother-daughter   mother-son
- father-daughter   father-son

Romantic and intimate
- man-woman   woman-woman   man-man
- and several taboo forms

Family relations
- and several taboo/incest forms

Neutral and purposeful
Neighbour, colleague, business partner, friend, contact, business meeting

Alternative relationships
To metaphysical beings, to plants, animals and objects

Five archetypal relationships strongly influence our social attitudes and behaviour, i.e. the primal relationships: mother, sister, daughter, lover, rival, or similarly father, brother, son, lover, rival (grandparents, step siblings, adoptive children, boyfriend/girlfriend, fellow citizens, etc. are variations of the above).

We are all a product of these different primary (unavoidable) and secondary (environmentally conditioned) relationships. When we come to look for a partner, we encounter different spiritual landscapes and try, consciously or unconsciously, to find familiar patterns and avoid traumatic ones.

These patterns exercise a powerful influence on how we approach life, how we behave, the kind of relationships we have and how we interpret different aspects of our experiences.

When we study our horoscope, we also find these same structures: e.g. in the form of early childhood experiences, expectations in the Family Model or guiding motivations by the spiritual planets.

For the purposes of interpersonal relationship counselling from an astrological psychological perspective, we should be aware of our own experiences and basic attitudes to these subjects. We also give our personal perspective to proven knowledge systems, which is one important reason why we study astrological psychology in the first place.

Relationship Counselling in Practice

The challenge lies not so much in the question of who or what is compatible with whom, but much more in understanding which topics and energy fields are involved in a relationship and how they creatively influence the way the relationship evolves.

Astrological rules reflect energetic potential, describe blockages, psychological complexes and strengths, which motivate or inhibit. They only provide basic principles of structures, personality profiles and life themes. Direct conversation is required to discover the levels of consciousness at which the two halves of the couple function and their real existential orientation.

The counsellor needs to have a personal impression of both individuals and needs to experience for himself how they communicate, argue, etc. Only then can he successfully establish how they deal with new insights and how their hitherto jointly travelled path can be seen in a wider context.

A relationship can therefore not be adequately analysed just by putting the two horoscopes side by side and applying relationship interpretation rules.

Below is a list of challenges to be overcome during relationship counselling:

Understand the stage each partner has reached in the development of his or her personality.

Understand each person's personality structure using his or her horoscope.

Clarify each person's expectations of the relationship.

Increase mutual awareness of each person's personality structure.

Describe what may encourage and prevent the personality structures of both parties from having a fulfilling relationship.

Developing Strategies for Conflict Resolution and Growth

Astrological psychology can provide both partners with fundamentally new insights into the most profound structures of their personality and the influence on their relationship behaviour. The counsellor can provide this by interpreting the following essential horoscope features.

The overall shape of the aspect pattern indicates whether the person's basic motivation is security-oriented, defensive, systematic and conservative (quadrangular = fixed) or risk-loving, proactive, dynamically spontaneous and action-oriented (linear = cardinal) or thoughtful, open, interested and changeable (triangular = mutable). Even these easily visible categories can significantly increase the partners' understanding of each other's basic attitude towards life.

Each partner's strongest ego planets determine whether his or her predominant self-image is mental, emotional or security-oriented (Sun, Moon or Saturn type).

This allows conflicts that may arise from fundamentally different ways of approaching daily challenges to be seen in a new light.

Aspect Pattern Position

This explains to the partners why their reactions to life situations tend to be individualistic (top of chart), sociable (right), selfish (left) or oriented towards their environment (bottom). This knowledge gives the couple new impetus for mutual support, cooperation or the division of labour.

Age Point Themes

These reveal each partner's current age development phase. This will allow them to gradually understand each other's connection lines and potential in order to eliminate any prejudices they may have.

For the purposes of relationship work, both partners need to agree on a "model" and a vision they will work towards.

The counsellor shows how the couple's horoscopes relate to each other to determine their social attitudes and their expectations of the relationship. At this point, it is very helpful to decide on a mutually acceptable "theory" regarding the desired form and content of the relationship.

The counsellor then uses both horoscopes to work out to what extent these ideas are compatible with their respective personality structures and how any discrepancies may be overcome. It may be necessary for one partner's expectations of the other's undivided attention to be qualified, if for example he has a lunar personality that is open in many directions.

Occasionally the expectations of security and loyalty one partner has of the other may need to be modified. Also both partners should agree on their concept of freedom in the relationship in order to increase mutual tolerance.

An astrological psychological partner comparison reveals the potential for growth and sustainability of a relationship.

At this stage in the consultation, astrological psychological partner horoscope comparison techniques really come into their own. The couple has understood the astrological overview of their individual personality structures and can now go on to delve more deeply into the structure of their relationship.

This process may involve consideration of the following points.

Direct Comparison of Radix Horoscopes

This reveals mental and temperamental affinities or potential complementarities. Differences in energy can be better understood and accepted using the partners' experiences of the relationship.

Direct Comparison of House Horoscopes

The partners' attitudes towards growth and their areas of interest are described as part of their life motivation. Conflicts that arise due to attempts to occupy space or to dominate (e.g. when planets occupy the same houses or areas in the house chart) can be explained and channelled. Qualities that one partner may find threatening or hard to understand in the other can now be seen as an enriching source of learning potential (e.g. complementing of empty areas in each other's charts).

Click points in the house charts can explain the mutual attraction by the planetary qualities involved, and form a lasting foundation from which the relationship can grow.

The parallelism of the Age Point path shows the partners how, by considering their own developmental themes, they can participate actively in the relationship. For this it is helpful to know at which point in the energy cycle each partner's AP is located.

If the APs are situated in the same areas of the respective houses (cardinal, fixed, mutable), the partners' current life experiences are similar as far as planning, implementation and retreat phases are concerned. If the AP of both partners is situated in the same house (i.e. the partners are the same age), it indicates that individual and joint projects can be coordinated particularly effectively. If the cycles are different, the partners can learn when the other needs motivation, support or consideration.

Click Horoscopes

These provide a deeper insight into the essential connection lines between the partners. In counselling, they really come into their own where long-term relationships or e.g. "fateful" encounters are involved, which had great repercussions on the existing relationship network of one or both of the partners. Click horoscopes enable the understanding of core, long-term theme complexes that drive the joint motivation.

Whether these connection lines are a source of strength that helps the partners grow together or a source of increasing friction that leads to the break-up of the relationship depends on the conscious creative will of both partners.

If there are deeper problems in the way the partners relate to each other, a bridge click horoscope (moon node/house) may shed some light on the karmic background of the relationship. However, this method should only be used if some progress has already been made in the astrological psychology consultation process.

Classical partnership comparison methods such as composite and combined produce abstract models of the pattern of interaction that are not very useful from a psychological point of view. The data are produced by mathematical calculation alone and produce a theoretical version of the pattern of interaction that exists in a hypothetical independent dimension and ignores the actual life reality of the couple.

Summary

Working hard to create a fulfilling relationship is more important than having a "well-positioned" Sun-Moon or Venus-Mars connection.

Open Questions on the Subject of Relationships

What makes the subject of relationships so fascinating is that everything that exists is directly or indirectly related to everything else, from the smallest building blocks of matter to the infinite number of galaxies in the universe. However, our actions would often suggest that we do not actually believe that many things are related at all.

During the course of evolution, man has discovered some of these relationship laws and allowed them to guide his conscious actions. It is probably fair to assume though that he is a long way from understanding the full range of his physical, emotional and spiritual potential.

Many aspects of human life and spiritual growth involve the discovery, experience and acknowledgement of previously unsuspected or unperceived connections.

Social relationships are part of this universal interconnectedness. Due to the subjectivity of emotional development, any problems in this area are particularly painful. This is one reason why we should be equally clear and fair in our dealings with everyone we meet. This is particularly true when children are involved, as they represent the future of personal interaction.

Modern socialisation theories and educational institutions, particularly schools, pay insufficient attention to the acquisition of relationship skills. The discussion of conflict-solving strategies in all important educational institutions could greatly increase mutual understanding and acceptance.

What I mean by relationship skills is the ability to actively structure all aspects of the interaction in all forms of interpersonal relationships. In particular this includes having awareness, understanding and consideration for other people's interests and needs.

We often have to deal with relationship complexes in our astrological work. People from all levels of society and all ages suffer from the consequences of relationships that have gone wrong. These consequences may range from a significant reduction in quality of life to psychosomatic processes.

How much creative energy is wasted to maintain a "difficult" relationship?

People usually find it draining to have to constantly overcome a cycle of misunderstandings, reciprocal pain and communication blockages. Such a situation can only be improved by changing one's personal relationship skills. A suitable approach to interpersonal relationships in all their guises, functions and ways of influencing must be developed. If the person is also willing to clear up specific sources of conflict, they will increase their chance of creating genuine and fulfilling relationships.

When counselling on relationship issues, it is worthwhile formulating open questions and helping the consultee to answer them.

In this process, the horoscope can be used as a guide in times of crisis and in the examination of the personality structure. Planets in signs, houses and aspect structures represent symbolical starting points, ways of behaving and objectives on our life's journey.

A consultation on the subject of relationships may raise the following questions:

- What kind of relationship do I have with my parents and family?
- Are my relationships active and equal?
- Can I act unconditionally in relationships?
- Am I aware of any forms of dependency in my relationships?
- How important is it for me to make compromises?
- Do I contribute productively to crisis management in my relationships?
- Do I try to experience things through other people that I could do myself?
- Can I live by myself?
- Do I make hard and fast decisions that other people have to live with?
- How do the needs I have from people I am attracted to differ from the expectations I have of other people?
- What do other people think of my relationship skills?
- What would happen to me if someone I love changes their relationship to me, leaves me or dies?
- Is there anything else I would like to add?

Being determines consciousness! Consciousness determines being!

Experience shows that many people have an unconscious tendency to start by blaming the You for any relationship problems, in which case recriminations are made that stand in the way of a real reconciliation of interests. Background and upbringing are often mentioned as being causes of relationship problems; in these cases the following considerations may help to clear up blockages.

How do inheritance and socialisation/nature and nurture influence my relationship behaviour?

The question as to whether nature or nurture determines character traits or personal abilities is an old argument in the social sciences. Astrological psychology has a synthetic approach to this issue.

Every individual brings his own raw potential with him into this life, which is gradually shaped by his environment. There is a reciprocal action between what we call nature and nurture, the effects of which (among other things the formation of the character structure) can be understood as the interaction of genetic, family background, cultural, politico-social and religious factors.

Environmental adaptations made by our ancestors were passed on to subsequent generations as characteristics embedded in genetic code, while constant changes in living conditions and the development of the consciousness help to modify the genetic make-up.

The phenomenon of "family secrets" crops up again and again in this context. By this I mean events and ways of behaving within a family that over the generations can become principles and specific patterns. (*A historical example is the tragic destiny of the Kennedy clan.*)

However, all it takes is one person whose character is strong enough to break this pattern for a new cycle to begin, with wide-ranging implications for the quality of life of a whole group of people. But the change may equally be for better or for worse.

The eternal battle between "good and evil" is a metaphor for another kind of interaction of forces: making an effort to eliminate anything that stands in the way of good living conditions so the powers with "lower" intentions back down. Every person will be caught in the crossfire between these two forces at some point during their lives and experience it as a crisis or work on growth in consciousness.

Attempts to use competing definitions, such as nature versus nurture, to interpret human behaviour does not really seem to help in the holistic understanding of the causes and effects of developmental crises and showing ways of solving them. It is much more interesting to try to figure out which guidelines and forces the interaction of the developmental factors follows.

The development of our relationship skills is also subject to the conflicting polarity between the unique genetic make-up we are born with and the specific socialising conditions we are born into.

It is important to bear this in mind in the consultation process to aid understanding and acceptance of one's own personality structures in the context of social norms.

The confrontation with early childhood influences, the Family Model, the social network diagram, the interpretation of Moon Nodes or horoscope clicks are only a few of the astrological "techniques" that may help the consultee to discover new strategies for conflict resolution.. If the person learns to take full responsibility for his "ancestral destiny", to free himself from recriminations and influences that restrict development due to the influence of nature or nurture, he will be able to exercise real freedom of choice and creativity.

To achieve this, it may be necessary to break off connections and relationships for a while in order to be able to return to them at a later date on a new footing, once the required development has taken place, based on a clearer insight into and a better understanding of one's own needs.

Difficult relationships are difficult to break out of, as we have chosen the people involved specifically because there is something about them that we have an affinity with in our current developmental stage. If we cannot change this inner affinity, we carry over the theme to the next relationship, in other words, the affinity is more important to us than the person. (*We wonder why our new partner is also an alcoholic, for example.*)

How can I learn from my horoscope and acquire better Relationship Skills?

You can start by taking responsibility for your birth and finding out your exact time of birth. Then look at your horoscope (or get someone whom you trust to do it) and start to explore your spiritual landscape. The symbolism of your life will gradually become apparent to you and you will start to see how it relates to the most important universal human qualities and philosophies. In the process you will also discover that you possess unique strengths and weaknesses.

The discovery of these structures, strengths and weaknesses will provide you with significant psychological, pedagogical or ethical insights. Examining your own chart gives you the possibility of seeing where your potential lies and finding your place in the great scheme of things.

Your Aspect Pattern

If its alignment is predominantly vertical, it means you need to set your own goals and to structure your own life so that you can raise yourself above the "common herd". This may make you unpopular with other people; you may not want to get too close to others or lack the ability to relate to others easily.

If your aspect pattern is horizontal, you may be aware that you make a lot of time for relationships and all kinds of social activity. It is possible that professional qualifications, social career or the realisation of personal visions were neglected in certain phases of your life. *You should learn to interpret your aspect structure as the "circuit diagram of your consciousness".*

Your Ego Planets (Sun, Moon, Saturn)

If they lie on a house cusp, perhaps also on a main axis, you will understand why you are impatient, keen to exert your influence or why other people often avoid or disagree with you.

If they are situated in the centre of the house, in intercepted signs or detached from the aspect pattern, you will learn to accept that you are reliant on people coming to you and that you need time to find your bearings. *You understand that your ego planets represent three different centres of consciousness within you.*

You understand your Tool Planets (Mercury, Venus, Mars, Jupiter). You widen your examination of what you are capable of in terms of perception, abilities and actions and develop your ideas as to how you may search more successfully for this information. You see what kind of relationships you have and why connections may be lacking. *You learn through your tool planets to use a greater range of your energy for your own self-development.*

You let your Spiritual Planets guide you (Uranus, Neptune, Pluto). Their positions in your horoscope reveal the life areas in which you can help to improve the relationship skills of all mankind. You gain more and more inspiration, ideas and creativity and realise that you must structure your own inner world so that others can relate to you! *Your spiritual planets challenge you to go to your limits.*

Study the Path of your Age Point. You realise that there is always a right time to do what has to be done to meet the challenges of your current life phase. *With the help of age progression, you allow your internal clock to determine your external actions.*

You learn the importance of your Moon Node position and your ascendant

You realise that to a certain extent, you are able to give a certain amount of meaning to your own life and start to understand who you really are. You try to be true to yourself while respecting other people. *You try to fill your life with joy and meaning and rise to any challenges you may encounter on this path.*

You discover in your horoscope the abundance of your potential and welcome the open questions it raises as an opportunity to work on yourself and a source of inspiration.

Summary: to a great extent, relationship skills can be acquired by means of consciousness work. We can start by living according to the old saying: "Do as you would be done by" and eventually we will be convinced that we can actually have the kind of fulfilling relationships we want by acting with unwavering integrity and being true to ourselves.

¤ ¤ ¤ ¤ ¤

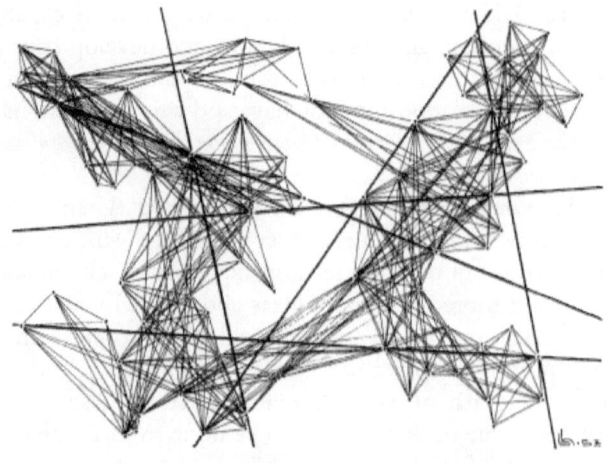

Interwovenness – Dependency
Drawing: Bruno Huber, 22.9.1953

Relationship as a Developmental Process

Click Horoscopes on Three Levels

Louise Huber

First published in AstroLog Issues 100-101, October-December 1997

Sun Sign Comparisons

Classical astrological methods of synastry are almost exclusively limited to the comparison of Sun sign characteristics, making simplistic statements such as: if the Sun is in an air sign and trine [Sun in] another air sign, e.g. Gemini/Libra, then these people will be compatible. The assumption is that a trine connection between elements bodes well for a relationship. The square Signs in the crosses, on the other hand, are considered to be unfavourable. This approach is based on black-and-white thinking and is rarely accurate as individual psychological factors like childhood experiences, traumas, behavioural disturbances, projection of parental themes, working out of ego problems in relationship and so on, are not taken into consideration. So this method is inadequate as a psychological approach to relationships.

House Comparison

In partner comparison in astrological psychology, house positions of planets are compared using a 'click' horoscope. We assume that a relationship is lived and experienced predominantly in the houses. The click horoscope is a new, practical and helpful approach, which reveals both emotional factors and developmental tasks of the couple. The assessment therefore focuses on the search for meaning – we want to know the causes of conflicts and wonder why particular problems exist. All horoscope elements are interpreted from this perspective. In relationship analysis we assume that a romantic relationship offers both parties the best ways of advancing their personal development. Conscious development takes place in life areas, i.e. the houses, so planetary positions in the houses are crucial in the comparison of the partners' horoscopes. Knowledge of the difference between signs and houses is therefore essential.

Difference between Sign and House – Nature and Nurture

The zodiac signs represent nature and the houses represent nurture. Genetic make-up is a code ingrained in our cells and is very hard to change, it allows us to act and react with innate characteristics, often against our better judgment. Conditioning becomes apparent in the twelve houses in the form of childhood influences, habits and attitudes, and is anchored in our consciousness. They soon appear in the daily life of the couple as sources of friction and can be changed. In intimate relationship with a You, we are soon confronted with our needs and emotions, and can get to know ourselves and our partner in depth. The everyday experience of cohabitation brings us face to face with each other's strengths and weaknesses, characteristics and habits, making it a significant learning and discovery process with unimagined opportunities for growth for both parties.

Each can recognise themselves in the other. This process takes place primarily in the twelve houses, where the disparities in behaviour and reactions that we are dealing with are clearly visible, as is the support that nurtures us. If the partners' attitudes or beliefs on a certain topic are too different, they lead to disagreement and conflict.

Learning Processes in the Relationship

From a developmental point of view, we consider a relationship primarily as a learning process. Without relationship to a You, further development is difficult if not impossible, and we run the risk of becoming trapped in our ego-prison. A relationship supports learning and growth, and should therefore not be avoided, but participated in joyfully. The idea that we can solve all our problems in a relationship or marriage and that the partner will make our dreams come true is outdated. As is the notion that women are inferior to men, which was a feature of patriarchal attitudes that are now obsolete. Today, modern intelligent people can take care of themselves. They can make a creative contribution to a relationship in which they take full responsibility for their behaviour. Someone who freely, confidently and lovingly declares himself ready for a constructive relationship will be able to significantly rise above himself and achieve emotional and spiritual maturity.

Click Horoscopes

Comparison of our attitudes, i.e. of our house aspects, immediately reveals whether there is harmony or conflict. It is entirely up to us if we want to change and if so how. Relationship analysis with the click horoscope is therefore very beneficial for anyone who sees a relationship as a conscious developmental task and wants to make it work as well as possible. We will demonstrate how we use click horoscopes with the aid of a case study; they can be created on a computer with suitable software [See Resources at end of book.]

Division into Three Parts

Before starting the interpretation we must make it clear that, for a horoscope interpretation to be psychologically and spiritually valid, it should always be at least three-dimensional. We have risen above mediaeval 'Good and Evil' thinking and now understand the reasons that drive people to do things. We examine their childhood and background to find the causes of their behaviour, and we do not judge. We live in a pluri/multi-dimensional world; a two-dimensional perspective only reveals polarisation that does not give us the whole truth. Our personality also functions predominantly on three levels, physical, mental and emotional. We live out our whole lives on these three levels, including our relationships.

Three Chronological Phases

There are three chronological phases in a relationship, which will be familiar to anyone who consciously experiences and honestly observes their relationship, and they reoccur repeatedly during the course of the relationship.

In the **first phase** we are really lovestruck and see everything through rose-coloured glasses. This is the "honeymoon" period, the symbiotic state of unity.

In the **second phase** we awaken from this state, and conflicts and disagreements start to creep in. We discover things in the partner that we had previously not noticed, which become annoying and get on our nerves. In an attempt to eliminate them, we first point them out to the partner and try to explain the problem. This turns into nagging and criticising. We try to re-educate them until they correspond to our initial image. Unfortunately this nearly always provokes the opposite reaction. The more we try to change the other, the greater the resistance, lack of cooperation and stubbornness we encounter. We resort to new methods, ways of manipulating and ultimatums. But nothing produces the desired result. This second phase often lasts a very long time because many people do not realise that there is also a third possibility.

Only in the **third phase** do we acquire a mature attitude, a clear awareness of reality where we accept the partner as they are with all their weaknesses, and freely decide not to try to change them. This requires us to rise above the polarised attitudes we are used to that lead to conflict and disagreement. Tolerance and work on ourselves are required to reach this stage, but eventually real relationship competence is acquired, where each person possesses a strong, unique ego, can take responsibility for himself and has overcome dependency. Only then are we able to allow the other the freedom he needs for his own personal development.

Crisis Stages in Relationships

1st Stage: Symbiotic Phase
Symbiosis – "rosy" phase – unity – harmony – paradisiacal state – unconscious blind stage – temptation by the snake – awakening and sudden discovery of opposites.

2nd Stage: Conflict Phase
Experience of polarity – discovery of differences – being driven out of paradise – conflict and suffering – anger and rage – growth through learning processes – cultivation of the emotions.

3rd Stage: Tolerance Phase
Rising above polarity – understanding – reconciliation – freedom, acceptance, tolerance, understanding of differences, third way, transformation and forgiveness – new start in human love.

On a still higher level we mature towards unconditional love, where we expect or ask nothing more from the other and love our partner even if they do not correspond to our ideal image.

Paradise and Symbiosis

There is a parallel between this three-phase process and the story of Adam and Eve. They lived in carefree symbiosis in the Garden of Eden, were happy and had everything they needed. When Eve was tempted by the snake to eat the apple from the tree of knowledge, the process of polarisation started. She realised she was naked and was driven from paradise in order to "earn her daily bread by the sweat of her brow." They could only return when they had become knowing and seeing. Only on the third level do they have the opportunity to understand the whole event and eat from the tree of life. These three phases may be summarised as follows.

The Three Stages

Although a relationship always involves two people and is polarised into confrontation between the I and the You, it is worth making the effort to analyse the relationship on three levels as this gives us a greater perspective. Once we have largely understood the first two stages, the third may be understood as a path that is chosen voluntarily and deliberately. Let us try to explain in more detail how it works. In the third stage, we not only adopt a broader perspective, but we see connections and developmental tasks of which we were previously unaware. This allows us to stand back and see things as they really are, and to disengage from polarisation. In a manner of speaking, we take a bird's eye view, we see how the two parties interact and can understand what is going on. We are able to see not only two sides, but many sides of a conflict situation – and this expands our awareness.

Development Objective

From this higher perspective, we can also discover and define the special task, the development objective contained within every relationship. Changes in the aspect patterns (usually a difference of a few houses) between the basic and moon node horoscopes in particular reveal the personal development tasks. As we can establish in the following case study, this is already very helpful, and constitutes a significant step towards increased understanding within the relationship. This is why we recommend that relationships be examined on three levels.

An outline of the systematic astrological treatment of the case study follows.

Information for Relationship Comparison

1. Basic Horoscope comparison   (conscious connection)
(2 basic horoscopes and 1 click horoscope)

Completion in aspect pattern	(balance and trust)
Filling empty spaces	(reliability)
Click points – conjunctions	(access to the inner being)
Click points – oppositions	(dependencies, crises)
Ego planets	(development and change)
Detached planets	(independent and free)

2. Moon Node comparison   (compulsive connection)
(2 moon node horoscopes and 1 click horoscope)

Complementarity of aspect patterns-	(understanding, intimacy)
Filling empty spaces	(unconscious completion)
Click points – conjunctions	(compulsive connection)
Click points – oppositions	(dependency systems)
Ego planets	(old development themes)
Detached planets	(autonomous+misunderstood)

3 Moon node/radix comparison (voluntary connection)
(bridge click horoscopes)

Diagonal relationship between 4 horoscopes
2 radix and 2 moon node

Radix woman to moon node man	(paths to each other)
Radix man to moon node woman	(paths to each other)

Case Study

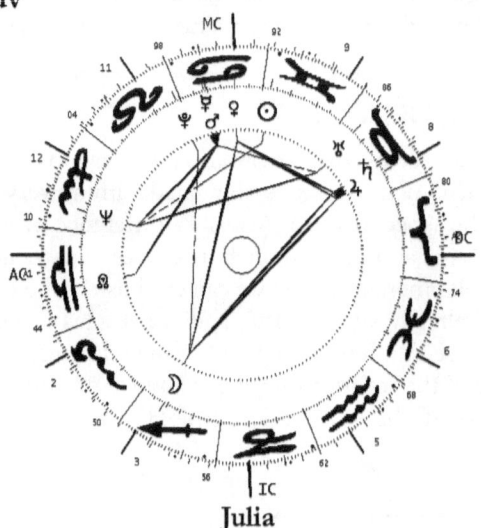

Julia
18.6.1940, 14:30, Düren, Germany

Brief History of the Relationship

Julia married her first husband in 1962 at age 22. Her Age Point (AP) was in opposition to her Pluto. In the 5th house she had three daughters. In 1974, in the 6th house right at the "cosmic fissure" (0° Aries), her first husband died of a heart attack. She suddenly found herself alone with three young children and a business that she had been running for a few years.

In 1975, she met Roland. It was love at first sight. They both had the feeling that they had known each other for a long time.

Marriage: 14th August 1981

External circumstances delayed the marriage. Julia's AP was square Pluto, just into Taurus, where her Saturn/Jupiter conjunction is situated. AP was soon on her Saturn in the 8th house and then came in opposition to the Moon. It was not surprising that difficulties and delays arose, especially where her family were concerned.

His Traumatic Experience

Roland had been married before, but in 1970, after one year of marriage, his wife suddenly left him. She filed for divorce on his birthday. At that time his AP was in opposition to Venus in Scorpio in the 11th house, which is connected to Mercury and Saturn via a linear figure. He was completely unable to understand her behaviour. It took him a long time to recover from this twist of fate. He was traumatised by it and suffered from the constant fear of being abandoned.

Roland
22.12.1943, 07:30, Freiburg i B, Germany

The Marriage of Julia and Roland

Their marriage worked out well; she complemented him and fulfilled his desires. Her Venus right at the top of the chart (at the MC) meant that she made him look great in public. He could show her off as an attractive and intelligent partner. He was proud of her and she wanted to please him. She even managed to obtain her pilot's licence by force of will, overcoming her fear of flying for love. They have known each other for 22 years and have been married for 13.

Between 1988 and 1992, Julia's AP went through Gemini in the 9th house, where her Sun is at the Low Point (LP). She started to be interested in spiritual matters and read a lot. Her three children had already grown up and she had the time to do things that had long interested her. This constituted the start of a phase of development for Julia. Her husband was not interested in spirituality at all and ridiculed everything she did or read.

In 1992, at the transit of the Gemini Sun, on the 9th house LP, she felt a strong urge for freedom and independence, for the big wide world. She had already started upon her spiritual path and made contact with an ashram in India. Almost exactly on the day of the Sun transit, she told her husband about her plan to travel to India, which brought back his old trauma of being abandoned. He reacted violently and shouted at her: "If you want to leave me, you can just pack your bags and go, no woman will ever leave me again!" She just walked away. Later he sent a lawyer to her, so that he was the one to instigate the separation and not her.

In 1994, with her AP at the MC, she moved out. The conflicts were never addressed; they were silent conflicts, slightly subliminal power struggles. He wanted to dominate, to restrict her freedom and prevent her spiritual development. She thought: "I have to get away, I can't stand it much longer." And once she had finally found a nice house, she was able to move out.

They are not yet divorced. They each live their own lives, but a magnetic bond holds them together and their relationship continues. They phone each other every day, often go out for dinner, to the theatre and so on. Once she did not hear from him for a whole week, then suddenly he was back again. They live in the same place. Although he sometimes has other girlfriends, she does not mind, it is not a problem for her. They are happier apart than together, she said "Now he accepts everything, before he sneered at my spiritual ideas, now he listens with interest and even admires me."

1. Basic Horoscope Comparison – Conscious Connection
Complementarity of Aspect Patterns
We start by interpreting the basic charts and comparing aspect patterns. The orientation of Julia's aspect pattern is predominantly vertical, indicating a striving for individuality, whereas Roland's is horizontal, indicating an I-You theme. The graphic structure of both patterns is formed of triangles and lines, indicating the same motivation. Both contain all three colours, indicating the willingness to develop. As far as inner motivation is concerned, there is resonance, a common objective.

Filling up Empty Spaces
The lower part of Roland's chart is almost empty; in Julia's the Moon is a tension ruler on the 3rd house cusp, a place that is empty in his chart. Her Gemini Sun is at the top in the 9th house, his Sagittarius Sun in the 1st house with opposition to Saturn on the I-You axis. This brings her above-mentioned striving for individuality into conflict with his striving for the You.

Click Points – Conjunctions
Access to the inner being
The click horoscope shows the projection of one horoscope onto the other. The husband's planets are situated in the outer planet ring and the wife's in the inner one. There are two click points, the conjunctions and the oppositions. We will start by dealing with the conjunctions.

In the 1st house, we see immediately that Julia's Moon Nodes click on Roland's Sun-Saturn opposition. That is a meaningful click point and a direct access to the partner's inner being.

Julia and Roland Radix Clicks

Moon Node Click Points

Moon Node relationships frequently indicate great intimacy, and the people involved feel that they have already known each other before. Esoterically, this is an "old" relationship, i.e. the people involved were already linked in a previous life, irrespective of which role they had at the time. It is not important whether the Moon Node touches one of the partner's planets in the radix, in the moon node chart or even in the sign. Most people experience a feeling of intimacy when they meet, and immediately say: "I felt as though we had already known each other for a long time." In Julia and Roland's case, this inner intimacy existed right from the start. She saw him and knew that he was Mr Right!

Conversely, his Moon Node/Pluto conjunction in the 8th house lies on her Uranus. With two spiritual planets involved, we call it a "spiritual click", which nearly always has evolutionary implications, i.e. it is significant in the spiritual development process. If Pluto is involved, the opportunities for growth are intensified many times over, meaning that crises or power struggles are inevitable. The 8th house in particular requires a transformation in Roland's consciousness from materialistic to spiritual. Such crises must be faced, as Pluto's influence is almost impossible to avoid. In our case, its position in the 8th house indicates the fundamental nature of the transformation and motivation change.

Ego Planets (Sun, Moon, Saturn)

In the experiences of every relationship the ego has an important role to play. We must start by ascertaining whether the basic chart already contains ego problems, i.e. strengths and weaknesses of the ego planets and how each person copes with them. Ego problems are often delegated to the partner. For example, if someone has a mother problem, they lack self-confidence and need support, approval and security from their partner. They cleverly avoid taking any responsibility. Likewise, a woman looking for a father-figure in her partner allows herself to be guided and led, so her personality does not evolve. We usually see such transferences when there are click points of the ego planets, which represent the threefold personality. Especially if these planets are unaspected in the basic chart, the partner usually "clicks" with it and must then take some responsibility for the other partner.

In our case study, the Sun is clicked twice, as are Moon and Saturn, so all three ego planets participate in the relationship. They are important components and strengthen the relationship.

2/8 Possession Axis

The next click point is visible in the 2nd house. Roland's Mercury is in opposition to Julia's Saturn/Jupiter. This activates the possession axis in this relationship. Because Julia's Saturn is involved, security motives, also of a calculating nature, could play a role. Her Saturn/Jupiter conjunction lies on the 8th house cusp in Taurus, which indicates a special ability to get what one needs in life. The opposition to his Mercury shows a certain dependency, she can influence and charm him. In times of crisis, misunderstandings may also occur, hence his behaviour in the separation crisis, which he was unable and unwilling to understand.

The husband's **Moon** (feeling self) clicks with the wife's Mars/Mercury conjunction in the 10th house. There is therefore already an understanding both on emotional and verbal levels, although as well as vitality, Mars also indicates arguments.

Sun/Neptune connections nearly always indicate a happy experience of love. Julia's Sun is situated on his Neptune position. Neptune as the spiritual higher model of love pervades all levels. Love remains through thick and thin. With nearly all Neptune click points, there is always the hope that love will conquer all.

Opposition Click Points

There are four opposition click points in the basic charts. This is an indication of dependency systems that bind a couple together. If one of them wants to leave the union, a crisis is triggered in these planets, in which they are blown out of proportion to become insurmountable bogeymen. The bond that used to work so well becomes dysfunctional. In the conflict phase the planets involved provide a defensive arsenal that explodes into reproaches, accusations, allegations etc. On this polarised level, conciliation or compromise are impossible in times of crisis.

In reality though, the oppositions are a kind of guarantee of stability, indicating a steady, ongoing mutual support which is beneficial for both parties. They create a well-functioning role game like a see-saw, which swings up and down to the rhythm of life and is successfully used for the achievement of common objectives.

3/9 Thinking Axis
There is another opposition involving ego planets, between Julia's Moon and his Jupiter on the 3/9 axis. Moon/Jupiter connections are nearly always a sign of a profound mutual trust. We just know that our partner wants what is best for us. That is, of course, a particularly auspicious foundation for the continuity of a relationship.

6/12 Existence Axis
In the basic click chart, we also see an opposition between the spiritual planets Neptune and Uranus/Mars. Julia's Neptune is rejected by Roland's Mars in the crisis. This involves the 6/12 axis. Existential issues become the touchstone; he thought he could stop her from pursuing her spiritual quest, if existential problems were to arise. But he was wrong; she did not back down.

2. Moon Node Comparison – Compulsive Connection
What does the Moon Node Level tell us?
The moon node horoscope (MNH) essentially reveals the repressed side of the personality. Everything that has not been processed consciously sinks into the unconscious. This often includes early childhood influences or traumas, which can appear in the first quadrant of the basic horoscope, but can also include experiences from past lives. From the point of view of depth psychology, in the MNH we can see the shadow personality, that part of ourselves that Freud called the Id. This Id reacts almost exclusively without our active involvement. We often do things that we do not want to do at all; we are at the mercy of inner compulsion and do not understand why we act, talk or think as we do. This can sometimes have disastrous consequences in relationships.

From an esoteric point of view, the MNH is the reflection of experiences accumulated over many incarnations. It shows our potential, what we have already learnt and achieved. The MNH reveals the accumulation of all life experiences from a long chain of incarnation. The developmental task found by comparing the moon node and basic horoscopes is informative, and can explain many learning processes in a relationship.

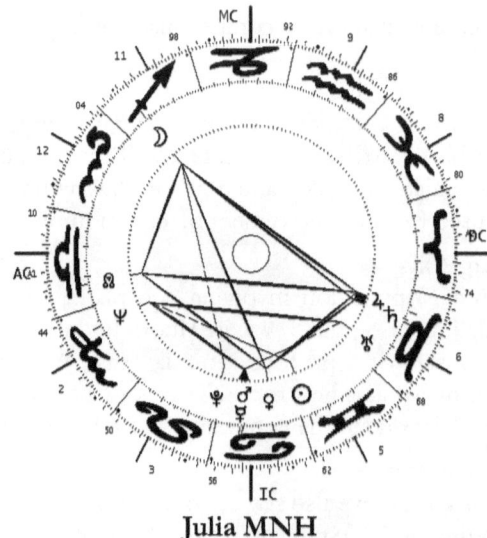

Julia MNH

It is obvious that the comparison of the two MNHs reveals the karmic roots of a relationship. Here can be found deep inner relatedness, dependencies, commonalities and old conflicts that have not yet been overcome and which penetrate conscious existence. Only when we have faced and consciously processed them do these compulsions to act unconsciously or uncontrollably disappear. You can read more on this in the book *Moon Node Astrology*.

Case Study of the Moon Node Level

In Julia's MNH we immediately see that the aspect pattern occupies the bottom part of the chart, while Roland's mainly occupies the top part, indicating that they unconsciously complement each other, have an instinctive, unspoken understanding and a profound intimacy. In order to discover the karmic connections of this relationship, we must first take a look at the developmental task in the comparison of each partner's moon node and basic charts.

The Wife

The fact that Julia's aspect pattern occupies the bottom of the chart indicates an upwards movement. A 4th house Sun must become a 9th house Sun. In other words, her own reasoning releases her from the conventional thinking and behaviour of the collective and takes misunderstandings, loneliness and even separation in its stride in order to reach the stage where she can think for herself in the 9th house. This is where her spiritual development, predominantly in this incarnation, is concentrated. At her Sun transit, she also started to gain independence and made the journey to India. The examination

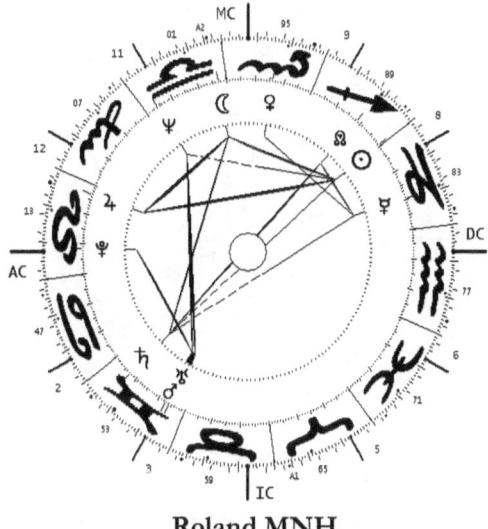

Roland MNH

of every single ego planet that requires developmental changes would go beyond the scope of this article.

The Husband

The Sun/Saturn opposition in Roland's basic chart moves to the 2/8 axis in the MNH, which indicates an issue with possession-loss, which in this life (basic) has shifted to the I-You axis. This indicates a deep-seated fear of loss and the associated possessiveness with regard to his partner that so affects this relationship. In reality, the developmental step from MNH to basic chart was responsible for the whole separation crisis. To understand this connection is also to understand and accept the crisis. It becomes a meaningful and life-enriching experience that is in line with the evolutionary plan. The point of the crisis is ultimately transformation and liberation from old compulsive behaviour patterns. In other words: it aids development and frees one from ancient karma. Compulsive behaviour patterns and karma are terms from different fields, but basically refer to the same thing.

Conjunction Click in the MNH

As Julia's Moon is the only planet in the top part of her MNH, that is also the only click point with his Neptune after the 11th house cusp. His Neptune in the radix already clicked with her Sun, now in the MNH it clicks with her Moon. A dual Neptune love is revealed here. That is a stable foundation for the continued existence of their love, a deep feeling of belongingness which will not disappear. This also characterises the root of their relationship; it will never break.

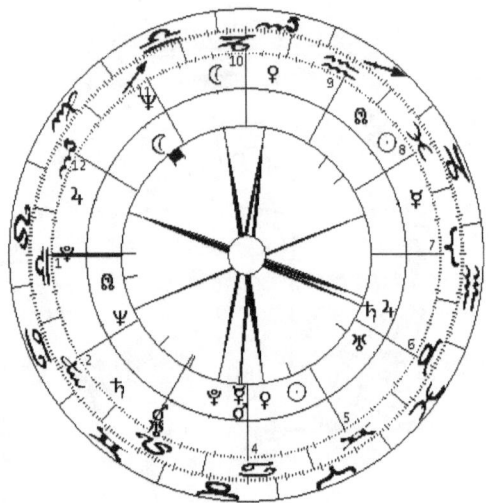

Julia and Roland MNH Clicks

Opposition Clicks in the MNH

Oppositions here are usually unconscious dependency systems, or automatisms that function instinctively. In the 1st house Julia's Neptune is opposite his Mercury in the 7th, which activates the I-You level. Julia's Neptune-inspired impulse indicates she wants to bring him onto the spiritual path. But in crises this opposition will initially result in misunderstandings, as we saw in the basic chart. In the next opposition her Pluto and Mercury/Mars at the bottom target his 9th house Venus. Venus in the husband's horoscope is normally the target planet for the opposite sex. He therefore has an unconscious image of what a woman should be in his MNH.

In this opposition, he will have to change this image, and this is what both the sign Scorpio and the planet Pluto aim for. Conversely, Julia's Venus is opposite his Moon in the 10th house. Venus/Moon relationships are usually easy to tolerate, they are good for each other, feel good together and are attracted to each other. The change in his vision of what a woman should be takes place on an unconscious level.

However, there is another ego contact on the MNH level: an opposition to his Jupiter from her Saturn/Jupiter on the existence axis 6/12. Two Jupiters together guarantee a mutual trust that lasts through any crisis, and also a sense of justice. It makes them very fond of each other and they trust each other on both material and spiritual levels. Only the Suns in the MNH have no connection to each other, but even the not-aspected ego planets are important here, either making one feel free or lonely. But as we are talking about the

Sun here, it is not so bad – this planet is after all oriented towards autonomy, independence and self-sufficiency. The Sun self remains untouched on the MNH level and can develop in peace.

3. Moon Node-Radix Comparison – Voluntary Connection

The so-called bridge click allows the discovery of paths between the partners, who can choose to take them in a crisis or not, depending on their state of consciousness. A bridge indicates a conscious decision to make peace. This involves voluntary renunciation of revenge measures. An act of will is necessary in order to forget and forgive previous insults, unfairness and differences. The fight is over, and weapons lain to rest. What was done before no longer matters, one disengages completely from it and liberates oneself. Only once this has been done can the two partners find each other again.

Bridge Click Horoscope – Radix Julia to MNH Roland

Bridges can be found at the click points (conjunctions and oppositions) between planets in the basic horoscope of one partner to those in the MNH of the other and vice versa. In Julia's MNH her Moon Node is in the 1st house and in Roland's basic horoscope, his Sun is in the same place. That gives a bridge between this Sun and Moon Node with a simultaneous opposition to Saturn. It is the same theme that we found before in the basic chart comparison. When the same topic reoccurs in the bridge click, it can be called a "stable bridge", which affords many possibilities for access. This is confirmation of both the fact that this relationship is already very long-standing and also that the third level may be reached.

Consider the bridge click chart [next page] between Julia's basic chart and Roland's MNH. There are five bridges that we will discuss separately.

The first bridge is on the possession axis 2/8 between his Saturn and her Uranus. The opposition on this axis is already present in Roland's MNH; the issue involved is therefore his possessiveness. Now her Uranus triggers this old behaviour pattern. It may have been that in past lives he wanted to tie down or buy a wife with money, security and status. In this life, this possessiveness is moved to the I-You axis (see his radix), where the object of his possessiveness is a You who will not be bought and who dares to resist. The experience of painful separation and being abandoned allows him to change this misguided behaviour. Eventually he learns that one person actually has no right to possess another.

The second bridge is a conjunction with her Moon and his Mars/Uranus in the 3rd house. The 3rd house is usually concerned with mutual understanding, conversations, sometimes also arguments,

**Bridge Click
Julia basic to Roland MNH**

especially if Mars is involved. Her Moon is stressed here (also the tension ruler in her basic chart). As a bridge, this means that he must expand his mind to embrace spiritual connections. Finally, in his chart the three spiritual planets are connected to each other in a blue Talent triangle, which means that his wife will blossom emotionally, confide in him and go on spiritual journeys with him (Moon in Sagittarius).

The third bridge does not appear until the 8th house, the house of society and transformation. Her Saturn/Jupiter conjunction already indicates a special ability to play her assigned role in the relationship well. The bridge is made with his Sun, in the 8th house of the MNH. Her behaviour fits well with the importance he unconsciously attaches to status. He is proud of her, he can show her off and she is accepted socially. This bridge concerns the behavioural role that is important in the aspiration for status.

The fourth bridge is at the top of the charts in the 9th house, where his Venus clicks with her Sun. The harmony-seeking Venus basically wants to adapt here, but this is not so easy for a Scorpio Venus, and she remains in a waiting position, which apparently suits her Gemini Sun. They enjoy each other's company on the 9th house level; the occasional meetings are fun for both of them. They use their freedom to take holidays together.

The fifth bridge is in the 10th house, where his Moon clicks with her Mars/Mercury. This is another bridge where common sense must prevail and arguments are avoided, but it means that problems are never talked through. This tendency is intensified by his Libra Moon, which avoids conflict and may be too willing to compromise.

The sixth bridge is in the 12th house. Her Neptune is in the same place as his Jupiter. Another Neptune bridge indicates that their love will last, even if only in secret. Jupiter also allows them to experience strong affection and sensual pleasure.

Bridge Click Horoscope – Roland's Radix to Julia's MNH

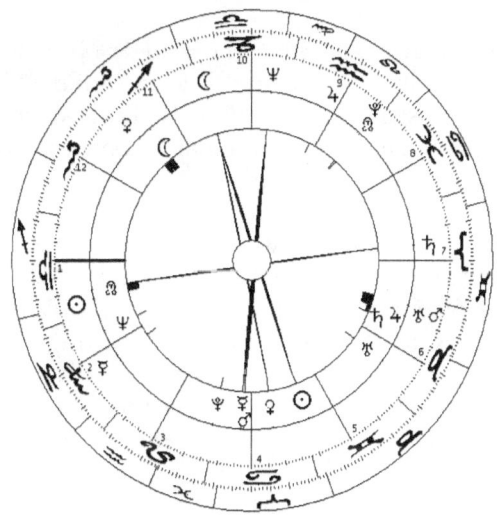

**Bridge click
Julia MNH to Roland basic**

We see the first bridge right after the AC. Roland's radix Sun clicks with Julia's MNH Moon Node. These are the same planets that were already connected in their radix chart comparison. The fact that this is a repeated theme means that it is a stable bridge, indicating a path that is established and always accessible. It involves not only the Moon Node connection, but also his Saturn-Sun opposition, as before.

The second bridge is just before the IC. Her Mercury/Mars is opposed by his Neptune. In the bridge click, oppositions do not necessarily denote differences or conflicts. It is rather that the tension means that taking this path involves a challenge; one is forced to make an effort and cannot avoid it. Therefore his Neptune (ideal love) must accept her adventures. Out of true love, he eventually accepts her escape from the relationship, transforming his own trauma of the fear of loss in the process.

The third bridge is on the individual 4/10 axis. In the 4th house her MNH Venus and Sun are in opposition to his radix Moon in the 10th house. This again involves ego planets of both partners. It is therefore a great challenge to free oneself from dependency on the family and groupthink and attain the satisfaction of individual freedom. The willingness is there. As her AP reached the MC and Venus, she found a nice house that met her needs and became her new home. The bridge also reveals opportunities to reconcile her Moon needs in the 10th house. He ultimately enjoyed her beautiful home on his occasional visits, which meant something special to both of them.

The fourth bridge is in the 6th house. Her MNH Saturn/Jupiter clicks with his radix Mars/Uranus. Bridges in the 6th house nearly always involve existential themes. One is also ready to compensate for mistakes, agree rationally on a common consensus and try to find solutions that benefit both parties.

The fifth bridge does not occur until the 11th house, where his Venus clicks with her Moon. We already found a bridge where his Venus clicks with her Sun. This time it is with her Moon, which also clicked in the other bridge with his Mars, and now Venus is involved. Mars and Venus are the two libido planets, and they must also be considered in a relationship. Where there is a relationship between Mars and Venus, there is also sexual attraction. His Venus can adapt to the needs of her Moon. In the 11th house, one is "free from the compulsive agitation of the 5th house" (Thomas Ring), as here an ethical, friendly, benevolent Venus-Moon bridge prevails. Such bridges are relatively easy to cross; the nobility and goodness of the 11th house is fully felt in their appreciation of each other.

By using the three levels in this way, we were able to see that this couple actually has a good, stable relationship. The existing problems were acknowledged and they were able to grow out of the compulsions and to deliberately eliminate misunderstandings. This relationship will certainly work on all three levels and last for a long time in the third stage, which can usually not be fully experienced without maturity.

◻ ◻ ◻ ◻ ◻

A Life Not Worth Living

Verena Bieri

First published in Astrolog Issue 68, June 1992

For a few years now I have been working with handicapped children. Recently I overheard a snippet of conversation that really made me think. I heard an obviously handicapped woman say: "I'm glad that I was born 35 years ago, today I probably would not have been born." It is true that increasingly sophisticated methods are used, pre-natal diagnosis is increasingly refined in order to detect any possible anomalies as soon as possible. The call for the elimination of worthless lives is greater and greater; in my opinion we now find ourselves on a very dangerous path. A few weeks ago, the most-read newspaper in Switzerland featured an article by Professor Singer, a bio-ethicist, advocating that the most severely-handicapped babies be killed. In our city there is currently a perfidious advertisement for gene manipulation. Rigorous spending cuts in public services also indicate that, in the longer term, special schools or homes for the handicapped are not a priority.

I heard the above-mentioned woman also say that people often looked at her strangely, as though she ought to feel guilty even to be alive. She actually coped with her life completely independently, without external help, and led a good, fulfilled life.

I have observed many times that, despite their problems, handicapped children have a beneficial effect on their family. That is why I would like to use two horoscopes (mother/daughter) to elaborate a little on the valuable components of such a relationship. I would like to say in advance that for me every relationship has something mysterious about it that ultimately cannot be explained. I believe that the intuition of a kind of secret, a power, an acting god or whatever we want to call it, is extremely important.

Is it not mankind's responsibility to use our technical progress for the preservation of life, not for its destruction?

Death and Rebirth Process of a Scorpio
The Mother's Story

Elspeth Radix Chart

Elspeth was born into a family as the third and youngest daughter, and this is her experience.

Her father was a patriarch who repressed the mother and the whole family and thought of nothing but his business. He had built it up himself and it went from strength to strength. (Scorpio Sun opposite Jupiter [unconscious strong ambition], 6th house mutable area; from which comes the Uranus/Sun trine that gives the image of a cold, headstrong man.) Her mother, who worked in the business, was completely overwhelmed. She was often ill and had migraines. (The Saturn/Neptune conjunction in Libra in the 6th house indicates the serving sacrificial role of the mother; in the house chart this conjunction is missing.) The grandmother often looked after her sisters, but she had no room for Elspeth, so her mother had to take her to work. Elspeth describes how she could find no protection within her family. She was often beaten and early on experienced feelings of abandonment and loneliness. (Pluto in 4th house, intercepted, is an indication of harsh family conditions that are not visible from the outside.) The Moon has a weak trine to Saturn (maternal bond) and shows that Elspeth's mother was strict with her. She also always had to be happy (Gemini Moon, 2nd house).

There was one person she loved and admired very much: her father's brother. Then, out of the blue he shot four people. He went to prison and Elspeth has not seen him since (AP transit Uranus).

In the family this incident was brushed under the carpet, not to be spoken of (unaspected Mercury: no discussion of people's personal affairs).

Elspeth had problems at school, nobody cared about her, or whether she had done her homework or not. After school she went to French-speaking Switzerland, but was soon brought home as she had attracted attention due to drug abuse (AP square Saturn). She then worked with her father in the family business, then as a waitress in a tea-room etc. She was considered to be unsuited to follow her chosen career of children's nurse.

She married at age 19, and after two years gave birth to a healthy son (AP quincunx Mars). A severely handicapped child named Muriel came into the world a year later (AP Pluto transit). This was the start of a difficult time for Elspeth. Her marriage hit a rough patch. She could not talk to her husband about her feelings. He plunged himself into work, went to Evening Technical College and was hard for his family to reach. In 1980 (intersection of AP with Moon Node AP), she attempted suicide and went to hospital. She had a difficult time there and underwent a huge transformation. A year later she divorced. In the meantime, Elspeth had gained so much strength that she was able to take the two children with her and look after them by herself. The theme of serving and looking after others was a constant feature. This is not surprising given her strong 6th house presence (two ego planets). Admittedly the 6th house is not only connected with work, but also with illness and health. Elspeth, who originally wanted to be a children's nurse, now had to look after a severely handicapped child.

Elspeth House Chart

At the time of the AP transit of Saturn/Neptune, Muriel also came down with juvenile arthritis, and her mother's strongly aspected Saturn was further burdened.

Elspeth spent a year alone with both children until at the AP transit of the Sun she fell in love with a man and moved in with him.

Today, her AP is directly over the unaspected Mercury (7th house, Sagittarius). She tells me that the relationship with her boyfriend will not last much longer. Muriel, the handicapped daughter, went away to school and in two years will be moved to a protected living group. Her son is a teacher. Elspeth senses that she will be left alone once again. She is currently preoccupied by thoughts of fulfilment at work, studying again and financial independence.

In the house chart, the unaspected Mercury is aspected with a sextile from Mars and a trine from Uranus; at the same time, the opposition Mars/Uranus is activated on the thinking axis and also receives a quincunx. Elspeth has already learned a lot and will certainly continue to learn more in future. She strikes me as being very mature and I am convinced that she will also clear this new hurdle. The strongly-positioned Venus will surely help her. Let us consider the Moon Node in the 10th house (Aquarius, LP, intercepted), which indeed speaks of spiritual growth and prompts the individuality to develop, so we see that Elspeth is now at an important point in her life.

The Story of the Daughter Muriel

Muriel was born 16 years ago after a pregnancy with no particular complications. Her mother described that during the birth she noticed from the reactions of nurses and doctors that something was wrong. At that time ultrasound scans were only carried out if there were problems during the pregnancy. Muriel was born with hydrocephaly and spina bifida. The mother did not even see her baby after she was born; she was taken away immediately. During her first year of life, Muriel was always in hospital and had several operations. The mother visited her nearly every day. Now, after many operations, she can walk with crutches but is usually in a wheelchair. Her bladder is paralysed and must be catheterised. She has a mental age of six.

Muriel has turned into a little ray of sunshine. She suffered all the physical hardships without ever once complaining. She is nearly always beaming, happy and undemanding. As long as she knows someone is looking after her, she is happy. She is the favourite of whoever is looking after her, be it in the hospital or the special school.

At age 8 she developed a new problem, juvenile arthritis. This is a very painful illness, but even this she bears stoically.

Muriel never asks for anything, but if given something she is very happy. The father has very little to do with his daughter. She is always

Muriel Radix Chart

glad to see him when he does occasionally visit, but she never asks about him. The relationship with her mother is very close. She says that Muriel is love itself and gives a lot to those around her despite living in a handicapped body.

Astrological Treatment

By itself, the horoscope never indicates an illness or handicap because the constellations can work on quite different levels.

Muriel's Saturn is in a Learning triangle with Uranus and Mars and only connected with the other figures by Uranus. It is only red and green, and is therefore a sensitive point; there is a great weight stuck right on the cusp of the 2nd house. Obviously, an inner learning process is taking place, which probably enables an inner transformation (Mars after LP, 12th house, double water).

Saturn's great importance only becomes clear in the house chart. The three squares with Sun, Moon and Uranus are an indication of the pain Muriel must undergo. The Learning triangle disappears in the house chart though, which means that what she has learnt from this handicap is barely visible from the outside.

We can only guess at which profound scorpionic processes are underway there, and this also includes the effect this child has had on her mother's life. She describes how her world, a perfect world, fell apart when Muriel was born. She had a brutal confrontation with the world, as she put it. Accepting the task of caring for her involved a lot of hard work on herself, but with time, it actually gave her self-confidence. Any compliments she received did her good. However, the fear of abandonment remained, as Elspeth received no support

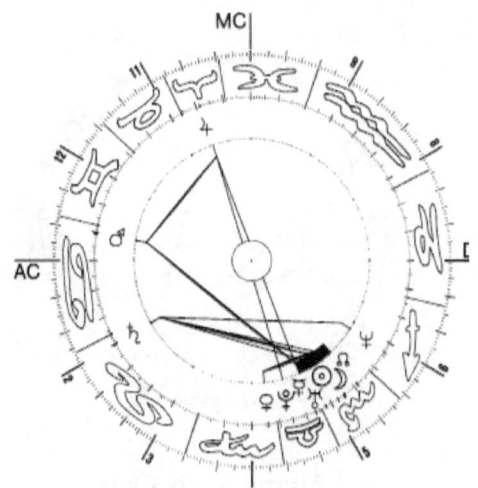

Muriel House Chart

from her partner or parents. The grandmother has never once pushed Muriel in her wheelchair, let alone looked after her.

On the other hand, one could also ask how many people could act out their Helper Syndrome in looking after Muriel? Caring for and looking after such an undemanding, happy ray of sunshine is really one of the more enjoyable tasks of the caring profession.

In the radix, Muriel's Sun is connected to the three spiritual planets, as is the mother's Sun. This indicates a secret spiritual transformation process.

Apart from that, Muriel "enjoys" her life in her way, although she has to overcome educational, relationship and existential problems (Sun in 5th house). She is well cared for and everything is done to make her life worth living (Venus, 4th house Virgo). The fact that she only has the mental age of a child can also be seen as a relief.

Click Points between Mother and Daughter

In the radix, Muriel's Mars (12th house Cancer) has a click point with her mother's Jupiter (Taurus, 12th house). Muriel's restricted and dependent state in this life really makes sense with her mother's strong Jupiter aspect. It represents a liberating help for Muriel and a growth process for her mother, in which Muriel helps her to find meaning.

It is interesting that in the radix, the mother's Moon Node forms a click-point with the daughter's Jupiter (10th house), and here too a profound and unshakeable belief in the wisdom and meaning of life is formed. Both are in an intercepted sign, denoting an inner mission.

The mother's Pluto clicks with the daughter's Mercury in the 4th house. I think that the daughter expresses Elspeth's harsh childhood

Elspeth Radix Chart    **Muriel Radix Chart**

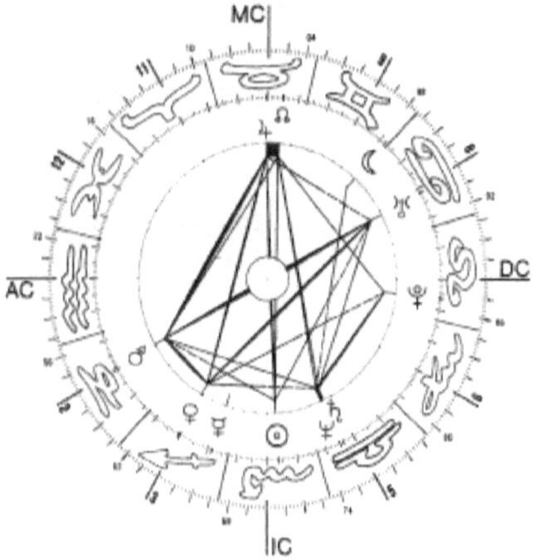

Elspeth Moon Node Chart    **Muriel Moon Node Chart**

experience, as though the handicapped Muriel were giving voice to her inner, injured child.

Elspeth's MN Saturn clicks exactly with Muriel's radix Sun/Moon conjunction in Scorpio, which indicates an inner affinity, as does the Venus/Venus click in the Moon Node charts.

Moon Node-Radix Comparison

Finally, I would like to compare the main planets in the moon node chart with those in the radix.

Mother Elspeth

In Elspeth's moon node chart, the 4th house contains Sun and Saturn. The theme of the family here appears to be an old story. In the radix both ego planets are in the 6th house (existence axis), and both in an Achievement triangle. Is Elspeth being called upon to take charge of her own life and free herself from external conditioning?

In the moon node chart, the Moon is at the Low Point of the 8th house and it shifts to the 2nd house in the radix. Is Elspeth familiar with the feeling of being under pressure due to being judged by society? Is the shift of the Moon into the 2nd house a challenge to search for spiritual reserves within herself?

Daughter Muriel

In Muriel's moon node chart, the Sun and Moon are in the 1st house. In the radix, this conjunction moves to the 5th house. Has Muriel perhaps in the past been too self-sufficient, so that now in contrast she must be dependent on others?

Saturn in the moon node chart at the LP of the family house implies that Muriel knows the symbolic figure of the mother and the experience of belonging, but perhaps also hardships and restrictions in the family domain.

In the radix, this Saturn is at the cusp of the 2nd house in a Learning triangle with Mars and Uranus. The inner learning processes that take place there must remain secret.

Conclusion

In my opinion, a spiritual conception of the life tasks of these two people is revealed in their horoscopes. Elspeth and Muriel appear to have been connected for a certain period on their developmental paths in order to help each other.

Ultimately, every human soul must take responsibility for itself. If this can be acknowledged and accepted, even difficult tasks can be a source of inspiration and happiness.

¤ ¤ ¤ ¤ ¤

The Transformation of the Heroine – Mother-Daughter Relationships

Disengagement from Emotional Dependence and Inner Integration

Using the Example of Snow White

Dr. Reinhard Müller

First published in AstroLog Issue 150, March 2006

Why do women sometimes find the process of disengagement from their mothers so difficult? Why do they sometimes struggle so long to acquire their own identity, without the unconscious and subtle influence of their mother's internalised expectations of them? Why is the mother with her value judgements, expectations, attributions and restrictions of the daughter – even when no longer directly physical – almost constantly present in women's psyches? And why do women whose fathers left home when they were very young, due to separation or divorce, experience in their forties a second inner disengagement from the mother that involves considerable conflict? And finally, why is the subtle competition between women so characteristic of many personal and professional situations?

Mother-daughter relationships are often characterised by a great ambivalence between dependence and autonomy, closeness/symbiosis and separation, love and hate. On the one hand there is a close emotional, almost symbiotic bond, which is all the stronger if the father is absent (in the case of separation and divorce, and also emotional absence). Yet on the other hand, this is precisely what complicates the daughter's emotional disengagement process, her liberation into independence and therefore also the formation of her individuality and self-awareness. Through subtle emotional feminine enmeshment a bond has developed that often cannot be modified and dissolved by an simple process of disengagement alone. The daughter, in particular, harbours deeper emotional structures that still indicate a strong internal maternal bond.

For the female psychotherapist Hendrike C. Halberstadt-Freud, it is natural that the daughter only disengages partially from the mother (1). This rather permeable boundary between mother and daughter creates a "symbiotic illusion" (2) that not only influences the internal mother image but which causes a distinct ambivalence between autonomy and inner dependence and bonding in the disengagement process. The symbiotic illusion *"describes a silent pact between mother and child in which the child sacrifices their independence and receives the mother's love in return. This narcissistic bond... restricts the disengagement and individuation of the child. Every attempt at independence is quickly perceived as an act of aggression that threatens the desired symbiotic merging"* (3), both in the projection of the mother and of the daughter. All negative feelings are "buried" in the subconscious for the sake of this idea of togetherness. If the daughter longs to merge symbiotically with the mother, while simultaneously experiencing the desire for separation, the consequence will be feelings of hate and aggression towards the mother:

> *"Instead of developing freely, mother and daughter solidify into a mirror for each other. Such a daughter remains within the mother's sphere of influence, becomes symbolically a part of her body and her soul. Instead of fulfilling her own desires, she aspires to fulfil her mother's. Hidden resentment will be the result."* (4)

This restriction of the free development of personal identity and individuality gives rise to a state of anxiety; the feeling that one is "trapped" by one's mother, masochism, depression or the hopeless longing for love. (5)

Mothers often find it difficult to truly give their daughters the freedom to become independent.

> *"Motherly love involves the separation of two people who used to be one... the mother must not only suffer the disengagement of the child, she must even want it and encourage it. This phase of motherly love is a difficult one that requires selflessness and the ability to give everything and want nothing but the happiness of the beloved child."* (6)

However, this is often replaced by double-bind messages that confront the maturing daughter's desire for independence with the subtle directive to remain in the dependent role. The fear of confronting one's own shadow and the indirect reflection of one's own inadequacies by the daughter's development give rise to all kinds of defensive mechanisms. One of them is envy: envy of the developing independence and size of the daughter on the part of the mother is quite fundamentally linked to her feelings of self-esteem:

> *The sense of our identity and our self-esteem are therefore connected... how far we have succeeded in achieving age-appropriate autonomy and ability to form attachments."* (7)

According to Erich Fromm, envy is connected to a lack of self-love (8). Envy is linked to the defence against a personal attack that would deny us part of our individual and free personality development, which we henceforth deny ourselves by means of internalised self-restricting beliefs. The self-anger caused by this lack is projected onto others who manifest precisely that which we ourselves lack and who make us feel inadequate. On the other hand, the envy-arouser, here the daughter, experiences unconscious (introjected) feelings of guilt (9) due to her opportunity for positive development and therefore tries to keep herself small, to reverse her actual inner development (10). This leads to "atonement strategies" in the form of an excessive willingness to help, the acceptance of burdens and the righting of "wrongs".

In an attempt to defend her theme, the envier not only tries to project onto her counterpart but to put manipulative pressure on her to behave according to the projection ("projective identification") (11).

Fairy tales graphically illustrate these unconscious mechanisms and role games in human relationships using symbolic language. They ostensibly deal with external conflicts with other people (here: mother/daughter relationship), but these are always mirrors of the unconscious inner relationships in the psyche, i.e. partially conflicting inner persons within the personality.

The universally known fairy tale Snow White clearly demonstrates the thematic of the mother-daughter relationship. The comments below can be applied directly to the mother-daughter thematic, but also to our inner mother image and the inner people connected to and to some extent conflicting with it. Snow White can be divided into the following stages (12).

1st Phase: Three Drops of Blood

It is the middle of winter. A Queen sits sewing before a window that has a frame of black ebony. Suddenly she pricks her finger with the needle and three drops of blood fall into the snow. She wishes for a child who is as red as blood and as black as ebony.

The tale begins with the image of a solitary woman, who is lost in self-contemplation and feels sad and lonely. The absence of her husband (or her inner father) gives her a feeling of emptiness and she desires a child to fill it. Her own inner wishes and longings are projected onto the future child. She is the depressive personality type according to Riemann (13), who is excessively dependent on the You and orients themselves completely according to their needs. The inner drive for this is the fear of insecurity and loneliness due to the loss of the You. The black frame represents this rather pessimistic worldview. The blood symbolises the need for vitality and lifeflow. As far as the internalised pattern of the daughter is concerned, this can also mean the attitude "I don't want to grow up, I want to remain a protected and dependent child! But I lack the strength (i.e. the inner father) to confidently take control of my destiny. That is why I prefer to remain small and suffer but am unable to see the cause of my suffering."

2nd Phase: Birth of the Child and Death of the King

With the birth of the child or, if we treat this aspect as the emergence of the inner child (which also has an important role to play in the adult), the death and rebirth processes of the previous personality begin. The previous self-image, which did after all contain a feeling of low self-esteem, is called into question. The mask (persona) of being a suffering, benevolent person who life has passed by falls, the repressed shadow themes become quite apparent from the next phase onwards.

3rd Phase: Appearance of the stepmother

...who constantly checks her beauty in the mirror.

Taboo feelings of hate, envy, jealousy and anger emerge as the daughter's existence calls into question the mother's self-image, which requires constant positive affirmation due to her depressive and negative attitude, thereby confronting her with the shadow of her own feelings.

4th Phase: Hate, envy and pride of the stepmother

...towards Snow White, when the mirror tells her that Snow White is the fairest of them all.

The mother-daughter conflict erupts when the Snow White girl becomes a young woman: there is jealousy and envy, and the mother feels inferior and unlovable and compares herself with her daughter. She is no longer able to identify with the desired child. The mother has to confront the ageing process and her own mortality and the feeling that her own personality is not fully developed, i.e. that she has "achieved nothing".

5th Phase: Attempt to have Snow White killed

...by a hunter in the forest; the hunter lets Snow White go and brings the lungs and liver of an animal back as proof instead of hers.

The mother puts Snow White down in order to assert her role and to maintain her self-esteem and in the process restricts her personal growth (the liver represents Jupiter/Sagittarius) and in this role fixation would like to bond with her in her small state: she takes away the air that she breathes, her possibility of having her own new experiences in life (the lungs = Mercury/Gemini). Emotionally the liver also stands for hidden passive aggression, which arises when personal growth cannot take the form of self-confident action (inner, accumulated anger against oneself and in the external projection against the mother). The liver is an organ of detoxification, but in the case of unresolved problems it can also indicate auto-aggressive self-poisoning with an other-determined identity (= utilisation and processing of externally supplied nutrition which can also be emotional).

At the same time, Snow White's transformation process begins, a process of emerging from a state of smallness, bondage and dependence and maturing towards her own experiences and inner freedom. The heroine's journey of disengagement begins.

Incidentally, in ancient cultures there existed rites of initiation, in which young girls were initiated into the secrets of the sexually mature woman, they were an introduction to feminine knowledge and wisdom (14). The theme is the determination of destiny by the initiation into independence.

6th Phase: Loneliness, Snow White in the Forest

Loneliness as a feature of the heroine's journey, as a necessary stage just before the breakthrough. Need to confront one's fears and anxieties. The experience of one's fears as means of transformation. Transformation phase in puberty. The missing, absent or unapproachable father during puberty: longing for closeness and affection, but at the same time fear of the mother's anger. The gap of the absent father cannot be filled in the maturing process.

7th Phase: Encounter with the Seven Dwarfs

Snow White takes refuge in a world of small children from ideas of compulsive hierarchy, endless feelings of guilt and antisexual contact taboos in order to avoid be devoured by the evil step mother.

- She shrinks her life aspirations to "dwarf size": "whoever bothers too much with the small things usually cannot deal with the big things." Snow White therefore remains stuck at the threshold of womanhood.
- Snow White suffers from a negative mother complex, combined with a fear of life and low self-esteem (great feelings of guilt). She feels unprotected in the great big forest and in the world; the dwarfs' cottage feels small and restricting. Feeling of being defencelessly at the mercy of an overpowering fate.
- Feelings of guilt towards the mother, growing up.

8th Phase: Further Attempts by Step Mother to kill Snow White

In this phase, the disengagement process in well under way. She is strongly torn between the search for individuation and her emotional dependency on her mother. The disengagement from the mother actually involves a death and rebirth process. The fact that this is a shadow initiation with the goal of emotional transformation towards individuality and dependence is also indicated by the following symbolism:

- The queen questions the mirror seven times. Seven is a spiritual number. In astrology, the 7th harmonic is connected with self-limiting beliefs, which distort our perception of the world, but at the same time express our inner wishes and our inner reality (15). However, it also gives her the opportunity to develop her own creative potential through her inner zeal (16). The division of the zodiac circle into seven gives the septile aspect (51°26'), which is interpreted as the Saturnine process of giving shape to inner visions.

Snow White is confronted with her shadow themes, i.e. the obstacles on her journey to individuation, in three steps:

a) thwarting of her own femininity (the corset that squeezes the air out of her when laced up)

b) combing her hair with the poisoned comb: the hair is a symbol of freedom , strength and glamour (17), and represent aspirations and personal beauty. The poisoned comb would be the struggling with outside influences that hinder the development of personal freedom and growth.

c) The poisoned apple poisons the soul. In mythology, the pomegranate symbolises a Plutonic possession, the experience of and dwelling in the shadow themes (c.f. also the myth of Persephone), but also the obsession with previous, development-inhibiting patterns. However, the apple is also the symbol of fertility (also spiritual) and of sexual maturity (18).

9th Phase: Snow White's Death and the Glass Coffin

The glass coffin means that Snow White perceives the world as though from behind glass and walls herself in behind it.

This is the psychological image for a woman who allows herself to be belittled by the mother, distanced from her feelings and lives an emotionless life. She is dead inside, desperate, totally alone.

> *"Being seen as something that one knows very well one is not – this is exactly what it means to live as 'beautiful corpse' under 'glass'... The fear of falling into the void due to no longer being controlled by the mother is much too great."*

10th Phase: The Prince as a Rider

Snow White's spitting out the apple symbolises her disengagement from the mother. She discovers her inner father, which is linked to the themes of self-confidence, creative self-expression, and with the courage and strength to go out into the world.

11th Phase: Marriage to the Prince; Death of the Step Mother

By living out her inner father, and integrating it into her personality development, the shadow themes, which are connected to her belittlement, can also be redeemed.

> *"Snow White's Mother ... must dance herself to death in red-hot shoes, an image for the fact that these structures that the envy projections wear must be transformed in a blazing passion for life so that the envy within her collapses"* (20). *"Only then can the passion between mother and daughter turn into friendship"* (21). Astrologically, the heroine journey of Snow White into independence is connected with Moon/Pluto themes:

Moon-Pluto themes above all indicate emotional entanglements in the context of the mother-theme, as expressed predominantly by subtle manipulation through "smother love" and protection, connected to a strong need for symbiosis on the part of the mother, with simultaneous control of every step towards independence on the part of the daughter. One often finds a strong mother connection or mother fixation. The child finds itself symbolically "in the stranglehold of the mother" (22). The manipulation by the mother is often very subtle. Through the emotional dependency that this produces in the mother (23), the true inner nature cannot be expressed. The mother, who is herself repressed in the first place, expects deference from the child. She projects conscious or unconscious feelings of guilt onto the child if it does not behave as she wants. The mechanism: reward if expectations are fulfilled, otherwise the withdrawal of affection.

People with Moon-Pluto themes have therefore often experienced a symbiosis with their mother – at the expense of the development of their own feelings. They were "brought" to behave in a certain way, without them really noticing. Only gradually did they start to realise the dependency, at least in the form of emotional resistance. However, this one-sided secret relationship contract engraved itself as a relationship pattern: *"I give you affection, love and care and you are my special one only if you do just what I secretly expect of you."* This may take the form that we must always be there for others in order to be loved, which is what we want so badly. In this way, we simultaneously give and control the affection we desire.

> *"The aspect characterises a person who responds with emotions and physical reactions to their environment although the causes for their reactions remain obscure. In order to compensate for this, the person thinks he must always have his emotional reactions under control. That is why he must keep his feelings to himself and just make sure that as little as possible happens in his environment that could surprise him or could allow the control of his family to be lost"* (24).

Moon/Pluto themes are all about *"reformulating one's behaviour and self-image"* (25). The important thing is to support emotional self-sufficiency and security in oneself and others. Freedom, self-assurance and the lack of expectations of others are also themes, as are confidence in the flow of life, openness and mindfulness. It is all about developing inner self-protection that enables the authentic and free expression of one's feelings.

'Snow White syndrome', i.e. a subtle symbiotic relationship between mother and daughter (at least as a behaviour pattern internalised by the daughter) along with simultaneous restriction of autonomy, are primarily visible in the horoscope in the Moon/Pluto aspects in the horoscope of the daughter or also in the synastry between mother and daughter. It indicates that a transformation process of one's inner emotional world is necessary in order to be free from family pressures and dependencies and above all to be free from feelings of guilt, hate and revenge (26). By recognising and changing these emotional mechanisms and accepting the mother's neediness and suffering, both a reconciliation with the mother and also an "inner reconciliation with oneself" can be achieved, in the sense that we start to take responsibility for our personal development in the here and now from a position of inner freedom and relatedness to our own spiritual learning task. Pluto's transformation crises are connected to emotions that sometimes trigger a combination of narcissistic overestimation of one's own capabilities and depressive feelings of inferiority and "worthlessness" due to old traumas. The purpose of the transformation process is to probe more deeply into the inner self and to discover its motivations (27).

Bibliography:

1-5) **Hendrika C. Halberstadt-Freud:** *Elektra versus Ödipus. Das Drama der Mutter-Tochter-Beziehung*
6) **Erich Fromm:** *Die Kunst des Liebens*
7) **Verena Kast:** *Neid und Eifersucht*
8) **Erich Fromm:** *The Fear of Freedom*
9) Introjection means that out of the desire for symbiosis with another person, that I absorb an unloved part of the other, which I actually don't like. Usually this is a development-inhibiting characteristic.
10, 11, 20) **Verena Kast:** *Neid und Eifersucht*
12) **Matthias Jung:** *Schneewittchen. Der Mutter-Tochter-Konflikt*
13) **Fritz Riemann:** *Grundformen der Angst*
14) **Angela Siefert/Theodor Siefert:** *Wie verletzte Gefühle heilen können. Schneewittchen*
15) **Michael Harding/Charles Harvey:** *Working with Astrology*
16) **David Hamblin:** *Harmonic Charts*
17) **Rüdiger Dahlke:** *Krankheit als Symbol*
18) **Günther Harnisch:** *Das grosse Traumlexicon*
19) **Eugen Drewermann:** *Schneewittchen/Die zwei Brüder*
21) **Matthias Jung:** *Schneewittchen*
22, 23, 26) **Öhlschlager Rainer:** *Stichworte zur Horoskopdeutung*
24) **Betty Lundsted:** *Astrologische Aspekte*
25) **Jeff Green:** *Pluto*
27) **Bruno und Louise Huber:** *The Planets and their Psychological Meaning.*

❑ ❑ ❑ ❑ ❑

Snow White

The Fairy Tale of Close Moon-Saturn Connections

Ruth Schmidhauser

First published in AstroLog Issue 152, July 2006

The previous article "The Transformation of the Heroine" provoked a lot of reaction and comment. AstroLog 152 included this article written by Ruth Schmidhauser from a woman's perspective.

The Fairy Tale of "Snow White"

Once upon a time in the middle of winter, when the snowflakes fell like feathers from the sky, a Queen sat sewing at her window, which was framed in black ebony. As she sewed and looked out at the snow, she stuck a needle in her finger and three drops of blood fell into the snow. And because the red looked so pretty in the white snow, she thought to herself: "If only I had a child as white as snow, as red as blood and as black as the wood in the frame." Soon she had a little daughter who was as white as snow, as red as blood and her hair was as black as ebony, and for this reason was called Snow White. As the child was born, the Queen died.

Although she was a Queen, she corresponded to society's ideal female image, i.e. she was unable to access her feminine powers. As she saw no possibility for her own self-actualisation, she wished for a child in the colours of the goddess; i.e. a child that, unlike herself, could find fulfilment by fully developing her feminine powers.

The three goddesses symbolise the three aspects of the feminine powers and they were worshipped in all matriarchal cultures, albeit under different names. Marko Pogacnik, for example, has described in various books how these goddesses even continued to be worshipped in the Christian church as the white, red and black Madonnas:

> The white goddess embodies youth, virginity and purity.
>
> The red goddess embodies the fully-blossomed, sensual, lively, fertile woman.
>
> The black goddess embodies age and transformation, as well as the devouring and regenerating goddess.

The Queen in the fairy tale was not able to teach her child about the feminine powers, as she died in childbirth. The beginning of this fairy tale can also be seen as the weakened femininity making space for the new. Snow White was set the difficult task of redeeming the primal, repressed feminine powers that are known to us from the goddesses of ancient cultures and their priestesses, for example the Egyptian goddess Isis.

Even if Snow White is blessed with the talents of the goddesses, she can only access her primal feminine powers by overcoming a terrible fate, and so her life's journey begins with the loss of her mother.

Every child loves their parents unconditionally. A mother's death in childbirth gives the child a heavy burden of guilt as well as a terrible sense of loss. It would be better to be dead oneself than to feel responsible for the death of one's mother. The child's perceived guilt buries itself deep in the unconscious and determines the child's destiny.

The tendency to feel guilty, even to the point of denying oneself the right to live, is mainly found in Saturn-Moon aspects in the horoscope, especially in conjunctions and trines.

After a year had passed, the King found himself another wife. She was a beautiful woman, but she was proud and haughty and could not stand that anyone should surpass her in beauty. She had a magical mirror and when she stood in front of it and looked into it, she said: "Mirror, mirror on the wall, who is the fairest of them all?"

And the mirror answered: "Oh Queen, you are the fairest of them all."

This satisfied her, for she knew that the mirror told the truth.

However, Snow White was growing up and was becoming more and more beautiful, and when she was seven years old, she was as beautiful as the day, and more beautiful even than the Queen. Once, when she asked her mirror: "Mirror, mirror on the wall, who is the fairest of them all?"

It replied to her: "Oh Queen, thou art fairer than all who are here, but Snow White is a thousand times more beautiful than you."

The Queen was horrified at this and turned yellow and green with envy. Thenceforth, whenever she saw Snow White, her heart heaved in her chest, she hated the girl so. And envy and pride grew like a weed in her heart, taller and taller, so that day and night she had no peace.

Snow White's stepmother embodies a woman who only lives for external appearances, and who, as far as astrological psychology is concerned, is trapped in the houses (patterns). This stepmother is only interested in her external beauty; she has no feelings for herself nor for other people. To compensate for her missing life content, she nourishes and cherishes her cold beauty, which is nevertheless eclipsed by Snow White's purity, as embodied by the white goddess.

Snow White is very affected by the death of her mother and wants to atone for her guilt and allows herself only to show her virtuous side; this is the only way she can grant herself the right to live, hence her manifestation of the purity of the white goddess in the form of external beauty. At the same time, the stepmother could also be seen as Snow White's shadow side, which she must confront at some stage during her life. The stepmother therefore also brings aspects of the black goddess into Snow White's young life.

> *She called a huntsman, and said: "Take the child away into the forest. I will no longer have her in my sight. Kill her, and bring me back her lungs and liver as a token."*

The stepmother cannot stand to see her shadow in Snow White, for Snow White embodies that which she perhaps would like to have been but could not be, for she was and is trapped in her role in society, and is forced to take refuge in compensation. The shadows of Snow White and her stepmother reflect each other, which is why there is a magical attraction between them and they find it hard to tolerate each other.

> *The huntsman obeyed, and took her away but when he had drawn his knife, and was about to pierce Snow White's innocent heart, she began to weep, and said: "Ah dear huntsman, leave me my life. I will run away into the wild forest, and never come home again." As she was so beautiful the huntsman had pity on her and said: "Run away, then, you poor child." The wild beasts will soon have devoured you, thought he, and yet it seemed as if a stone had been rolled from his heart since it was no longer needful for him to kill her. And as a young bear just then came running by he stabbed it, and cut out its lung and liver and took them to the queen as proof that the child was dead. The cook had to salt them, and the wicked queen ate them, and thought she had eaten the lungs and liver of Snow White.*

By eating Snow White's lungs and liver, the stepmother symbolically tries to acquire the qualities that she herself lacks. She also assumes that their power will rid her of the confrontation with her missing life content and purity that she finds so unbearable.

But now the poor child was all alone in the great forest, and so terrified that she looked at all the leaves on the trees, and did not know what to do. Then she began to run, and ran over sharp stones and through thorns, and the wild beasts ran past her, but did her no harm. She ran as long as her feet would go until it was almost evening, then she saw a little cottage and went into it to rest herself. Everything in the cottage was small, but neater and cleaner than can be told. There was a table on which was a white cover, and seven little plates, and on each plate a little spoon, moreover, there were seven little knives and forks, and seven little mugs. Against the wall stood seven little beds side by side, and covered with snow white counterpanes. Snow White was so hungry and thirsty that she ate some vegetables and bread from each plate and drank a drop of wine out of each mug, for she did not wish to take all from one only. Then, as she was so tired, she laid herself down on one of the little beds, but none of them suited her, one was too long, another too short, but at last she found that the seventh one was right, and so she remained in it, said a prayer and went to sleep.

In the great forest, Snow White is forced to face her fear. Astrologically, it could be seen as a Plutonic transformation, in which she loses her childhood and is forced to take a leap towards personal responsibility. Running makes her feel better: activity and movement give her strength and help to prevent her from becoming rigid with fear, even though the thorns may hurt her. This pain allows her to be aware of her body (Saturn), which strengthens her instinct for survival and her will to live.

As she is beautiful and pure and led by the white goddess, she is not vulnerable: the hunter does not have the heart to kill her, and actually gives her new life. She therefore has a greater right to live than before, and even begged him not to kill her. Because of her purity, she is protected by the white goddess and the wild animals do not harm her either.

By chance, she finally finds refuge in the house of the seven dwarfs. The number seven must make us sit up and take notice: Snow White is seven years old and goes to the seven dwarfs. In astrology, we are familiar with the seven classical planets, and therefore at the age of seven, Snow White has completed the first stage of her life and is ready for the first initiation, the Saturn initiation. For this, she must look death in the face and confront her fear so that she can finally reach a place that is appropriate for her new stage of development: the seven dwarfs' cottage.

When it was quite dark the owners of the cottage came back. They were seven dwarfs who dug and delved in the mountains for gold. They lit their seven candles, and as it was now light within the cottage they saw that someone had been there, for everything was not in the same order in which they had left it. The first said: "Who has been sitting on my chair?" The second: "Who has been eating off my plate?" The third: "Who has been taking some of my bread?" The fourth: "Who has been eating my vegetables?" The fifth:  "Who has been using my fork?" The sixth: "Who has been cutting with my knife?" The seventh: "Who has been drinking out of my mug?" Then the first looked round and saw that there was a little hollow on his bed, and he said: "Who has been getting into my bed?" The others came up and each called out: "Somebody has been lying in my bed too." But the seventh when he looked at his bed saw little Snow White, who was lying fast asleep on it. And he called the others, who came running up, and they cried out with astonishment, and brought their seven little candles and let the light fall on Snow White. "Oh, heavens, oh, heavens", they cried, "What a lovely child." And they were so glad that they did not wake her up, but let her sleep on in the bed. And the seventh dwarf slept with his companions, one hour with each, and so passed the night. When it was morning little Snow White awoke, and was frightened when she saw the seven dwarfs. But they were friendly and asked her what her name was. "My name is Snow White" she answered. "How have you come to our house?" asked the dwarfs. Then she told them that her stepmother had wished to have her killed, but that the huntsman had spared her life, and that she had run for the whole day, until at last she had found their cottage. The dwarfs said: "if you will take care of our house, cook, make the beds, wash, sew and knit, and if you will keep everything neat and clean you can stay with us and you shall want for nothing." "Yes", said Snow White "With all my heart." And she stayed with them. She kept the house in order for them. In the mornings they went to the mountains and looked for copper and gold, in the evenings they came back, and then their supper had to be ready. The girl was alone the whole day, so the good dwarfs warned her and said, beware of your stepmother, she will soon know that you are here, be sure to let no one come in.

Snow White has come to a Saturnine place of purity and order. Every change she makes is noticed. However, she is accepted with warmth and joy and the dwarfs even make sure that her sleep is not disturbed. Snow White's Saturn lesson ends here, where the dwarfs teach her to control matter by keeping everything tidy. In the process, she experiences real goodwill and genuine affection for the first time in her life, a great psychological support, but still a mother's love is lacking.

If she had not been set tasks, she could not have stayed. The perceived guilt that still exists deep in her unconscious requires that her right to exist be conditional, which the dwarfs seem to have understood. At the same time, she has also much to learn on the emotional level as she is left alone all day long. The dwarfs' anxiety means that they are aware of the difficulty of this task.

> *But the Queen, believing that she had eaten Snow White's lungs and liver, could not but think that she was again the first and most beautiful of all, and she went to her mirror and said: "Mirror, mirror on the wall, who in this land is the fairest of all?"*
>
> *And the mirror answered: "Oh, Queen, thou art fairest of all I see, but over the hills, where the seven dwarfs dwell, Snow White is still alive and well, and none is so fair as she."*
>
> *Then she was astounded, for she knew that the mirror never lied, and she knew that the huntsman had betrayed her, and that Snow White was still alive.*
>
> *And so she thought and thought again how she might kill her, for so long as she was not the fairest in the whole land, envy let her have no rest. And when she had at last thought of something to do, she painted her face, and dressed herself like an old pedlar woman, and no one would have recognised her. In this disguise she went over the seven mountains to the seven dwarfs, and knocked at the door and cried: "Pretty things to sell, very cheap, very cheap." Little Snow White looked out of the window and called out: "Good-day my good woman, what have you to sell?" "Good things, pretty things", she answered, "Stay-laces of all colours", and she pulled out one which was woven of bright-coloured silk. "I may let the worthy old woman in," thought Snow White, and she unbolted the door and bought the pretty laces. "Child", said the old woman, "What a fright you look, come, I will lace you properly for once." Snow-White was not suspicious, but stood before her, and let herself be laced with the new laces. But the old woman laced so quickly and so tightly that Snow White lost her breath and fell down as if dead. "Now I am the most beautiful", said the Queen to herself, and ran away.*
>
> *Not long afterwards, in the evening, the seven dwarfs came home, but how shocked they were when they saw their dear little Snow White lying on the ground, and that she neither stirred nor moved, and seemed to be dead. They*

lifted her up, and, as they saw that she was laced too tightly, they cut the laces, then she began to breathe a little, and after a while came to life again. When the dwarfs heard what had happened they said: "The old pedlar woman was none other than the wicked Queen, take care and let no one come in when we are not with you."

Snow White already masters the Saturn level well after her first initiation; she keeps the dwarfs' cottage tidy. The next great learning task tests her emotional level, her psyche. Great inner strength is required to be able to be alone all day, and to resist such a colourful temptation, but Snow White lacks this. Like a typical girl, her head is turned by bright colours and she wanted to have these laces.

She tells herself that the woman is harmless and ignores her inner sense of foreboding. Snow White has let herself be tempted; her unfulfilled desires are stronger than her willpower, which nearly led to her death.

At the same time, we can also see this scene as the playing out of Snow White's unconscious. Her perceived guilt demands its due, but Snow White is getting on very well at the dwarfs' cottage. Snow White's shadow turns up in the person of the step mother and Snow White, who is not yet able to look at her shadow, is devoured by her.

Were she already able to look at her shadow, she would not have been so trusting, and would have become suspicious when she saw the old pedlar-woman and wondered what she was doing so deep in the forest at the dwarfs' cottage.

The well-meaning dwarfs save her and give her a maternal warning against further temptations, knowing full well how hard that must be for Snow White.

> But the wicked woman when she had reached home went in front of the mirror and asked: "Mirror, mirror, on the wall, who in this land is the fairest of all?" It answered as before: "Oh, Queen, thou art fairest of all I see, but over the hills, where the seven dwarfs dwell, Snow White is still alive and well, and none is so fair as she."
>
> When she heard that, all her blood rushed to her heart with fear, for she saw plainly that little Snow White was again alive. But now, she said, I will think of something that shall really put an end to you. And by the help of witchcraft, which she understood, she made a poisonous comb. Then she

disguised herself and took the shape of another old woman. So she went over the seven mountains to the seven dwarfs, knocked at the door, and cried, "Good things to sell, cheap, cheap." Snow White looked out and said: "Go away, I cannot let anyone come in." "I suppose you can look," said the old woman, and pulled the poisonous comb out and held it up. It pleased the girl so well that she let herself be beguiled, and opened the door. When they had made a bargain the old woman said: "Now I will comb you properly for once." Poor little Snow White had no suspicion, and let the old woman do as she pleased, but hardly had she put the comb in her hair, than the poison in it took effect, and the girl fell down senseless. "You paragon of beauty," said the wicked woman, "You are done for now," and she went away.

But fortunately it was almost evening, when the seven dwarfs came home. When they saw Snow White lying as if dead upon the ground they at once suspected the stepmother, and they looked and found the poisoned comb. Scarcely had they taken it out when Snow White came to herself, and told them what had happened. Then they warned her once more to be upon her guard and to open the door to no one.

Once again, Snow White had not been strong enough to withstand the great temptation. Once again, her shadow had got the better of her and she nearly died as a result. Again, the dwarfs' genuine devotion to her saved her life. This must have further reduced the power of her perceived guilt. The fact that only her "light" side lives with the dwarfs explains why she is so easily led astray and why her stepmother has so much power over her. The stepmother's understanding of witchcraft tells us how cunning the repressed parts of our personality can be, something that is also recognised in psychosynthesis as the phenomenon of partial personalities.

Snow White's ego parts have therefore determined events and she could not transform them until now. Because as a child, she was previously not in a position to realise her wishes, she has not learned how to deal with them. She went without due to circumstances and not to her power of resistance.

From an astrological point of view, this means that Snow White still finds herself in the lunar emotional dependency on Saturn, which is also illustrated by her innocence. Her mind is still childlike; it has not yet reached the second initiation.

The Queen, at home, went in front of the mirror and said: "Mirror, mirror on the wall, who in this land is the fairest of all?" Then it answered as before: "Oh, Queen, thou art fairest of all I see, but over the hills, where the seven dwarfs dwell, Snow White is still alive and well, and none is so fair as she."

When she heard the mirror say these words, she trembled and shook with rage. "Snow White shall die," she cried, "even if it costs me my life."

Thereupon she went into a quite secret, lonely room, where no one ever came, and there she made a very poisonous apple. Outside it looked pretty, white with a red cheek, so that everyone who saw it longed for it, but whoever ate a piece of it must surely die.

When the apple was ready she painted her face, and dressed herself up as a farmer's wife, and so she went over the seven mountains to the seven dwarfs. She knocked at the door. Snow White put her head out of the window and said: "I cannot let anyone in, the seven dwarfs have forbidden me." "It is all the same to me," answered the woman, "I shall soon get rid of my apples. There, I will give you one."

"No", said Snow White, "I dare not take anything." "Are you afraid it is poisoned?" asked the old woman, "Look, I will cut the apple in two pieces, you eat the red cheek, and I will eat the white." The apple was so cunningly made that only the red cheek was poisoned. Snow White longed for the fine apple, and when she saw that the woman ate part of it she could resist no longer, and stretched out her hand and took the poisonous half. But hardly had she a bit of it in her mouth than she fell down dead. Then the queen looked at her with a dreadful look, and laughed aloud and said, "White as snow, red as blood, black as ebony-wood, this time the dwarfs cannot wake you up again."

And when she asked of the mirror at home: "Mirror, mirror, on the wall, who in this land is the fairest of all?"

And it answered at last: "Oh, Queen, in this land thou art fairest of all." Then her envious heart had rest, so far as an envious heart can have rest.

Because Snow White is unable to resist the ever greater temptation the third time either, she must die. She is poisoned by her own shadow/her stepmother.

As she still has not reached emotional maturity after three chances, her destiny takes over. Her deep seated perceived guilt may also have been to blame. On a very deep level, Snow White's death has brought her closer to her mother. The pull towards death was stronger than the urge to live, another indication of a Moon-Saturn aspect.

Bert Hellinger describes in different books the deep loyalty that children have towards their parents and also how hard it is to rise above the parents' destiny. An additional complication is that her father is never mentioned and he apparently never supported his child. This must have unconsciously reinforced Snow White's belief that she had no right to life and so her death was an inevitable outcome.

> When they came home in the evening, the dwarfs found Snow White lying upon the ground. She breathed no longer and was dead. They lifted her up, looked to see whether they could find anything poisonous, unlaced her, combed her hair, washed her with water and wine, but it was all of no use, the poor child was dead, and remained dead. They laid her upon a bier, and all seven of them sat round it and wept for her, and wept three days long.

> Then they were going to bury her, but she still looked as if she were living, and still had her pretty red cheeks. They said: "We could not bury her in the dark ground," and they had a transparent coffin of glass made, so that she could be seen from all sides, and they laid her in it, and wrote her name upon it in golden letters, and that she was a king's daughter. Then they put the coffin out upon the mountain, and one of them always stayed by it and watched it. And birds came too, and wept for Snow White, first an owl, then a raven, and last a dove.

> Snow White lay a long, long time in the coffin, and she did not change, but looked as if she were asleep, for she was as white as snow, as red as blood, and her hair was as black as ebony.

Although Snow White is dead, her body does not decompose, and even her rosy cheeks remain, in a reminder of Sleeping Beauty's hundred-year sleep. Snow White lies in her coffin like a caterpillar in a cocoon. Although she appears to be dead, a transformation must take place within her through which she can overcome death in order to finally receive the right to live. That is the way the black goddess works. Everything that is role-related must die through her, to make way for the birth of what is intrinsic. Snow White's death symbolises the inner reunification with her mother. In this way, she can overcome the power of her unconscious influence, her perceived guilt at the death of her mother that prevents her from accepting the dwarfs' devotion. The dwarfs' love turned out to be a caring, unconditional, maternal love that Snow White had never known before and which opened up the way to an inner reunification with her mother.

Even when she was lying in the coffin, the love of the dwarfs, who kept an unbroken watch over her, opened up a way back to life. The fact that her coffin lay on the mountain symbolises Snow Whites proximity to the cosmic forces, and that even the animals mourn symbolises how deeply connected Snow White is to mother earth. Borne by the sky and by the earth, on the mountain in the glassy coffin, upon which her name and status are written in gold letters, always watched over by a dwarf, she matures into a woman, and matures into her name and her royal status.

In our lives too, Moon-Saturn aspects lead to feelings of guilt, childlike dependency and the death of the corruptible ego that considers others too much and loses itself in the process.

> *It happened, however, that a king's son came into the forest, and went to the dwarfs' house to spend the night. He saw the coffin on the mountain, and the beautiful Snow White within it, and read what was written upon it in golden letters. Then he said to the dwarfs: "Let me have the coffin, I will give you whatever you want for it." But the dwarfs answered: "We will not part with it for all the gold in the world." Then he said, "Let me have it as a gift, for I cannot live without seeing Snow White. I will honour and prize her as my dearest possession." As he spoke in this way the good dwarfs took pity upon him, and gave him the coffin.*

> *And now the king's son had it carried away by his servants on their shoulders. And it happened that they stumbled over a tree-stump, and with the shock the poisonous piece of apple which Snow White had bitten off came out of her throat. And before long she opened her eyes, lifted up the lid of the coffin, sat up, and was once more alive. "Oh, heavens, where am I?" she cried. The king's son, full of joy, said: "You are with me." He told her what had happened, and said, "I love you more than everything in the world, come with me to my father's palace, you shall be my wife."*

> *Snow White was willing, and went with him, and their wedding was held with great pomp and splendour.*

When the time is right, a prince is drawn to this place. The dwarfs give Snow White away like a mother, for they sense that the prince's love is genuine and feel the force of destiny. In Snow White he has found his anima, and the shock (also an emotional one) enables Snow White to expel the poisoned apple. The stepmother's poison is no longer effective; Snow White opens up her heart in love to her prince and rides with him into the period of the red goddess. Now ready for marriage, Snow White is in the prime of her life. She has now been through the second initiation and therefore embodies the power of the red goddess: liveliness, sensuality, fertility and devotion.

> *But Snow White's wicked stepmother was also invited to the feast. When she had dressed in beautiful clothes she went to the mirror, and asked: "Mirror, mirror on the wall, who in this land is the fairest of all?" The mirror answered: "Oh, Queen, of all here the fairest art thou, but the young queen is a thousand times fairer now".*

Then the wicked woman uttered a curse, and was so wretched, so utterly wretched that she knew not what to do. At first she would not go to the wedding at all, but she had no peace, and had to go to see the young queen. When she went in she recognised Snow White, she was rooted to the spot with rage and fear. But iron slippers had already been put upon the fire, and they were brought in with tongs, and set before her. Then she was forced to put on the red-hot shoes, and dance until she dropped down dead.

The stepmother, Snow White's shadow, has lost her power as Snow White has blossomed. The insecurity and fear that she had previously hidden under her wickedness are now apparent.

At the same time, the stepmother's weakness tells us that Snow White has recognised her shadow, which corresponds to the third initiation. Snow White is now the fully-blossomed woman who is completely alive and can experience both her light and her shadow sides.

The dance of the stepmother in the red hot shoes symbolises both the transformation of the shadow qualities and their integration. With the stepmother's death, Snow White has become the archetypal woman who can be a real partner for her husband, unlike her mother and stepmother.

The fairytale "Snow White" shows us the way out of the guilt and dependency of the Moon-Saturn aspects into a responsible, active life, i.e. into the life of an adult.

The stronger the Moon-Saturn aspect (conjunction, trine), the greater the similarities with Snow White, even if on a largely unconscious level.

◻ ◻ ◻ ◻ ◻

Part 4: Health and Therapies

The articles in this part of the book are all concerned with the use of astrological psychology in the context of health issues and alternative therapies.

The first four articles particularly relate to health:

The Language of the Body, by Bruno Huber
   An outline of medical astrology and its links with the house system.

I am my own Doctor, by Louise Huber
   A comprehensive assessment of the causes of illness and various aspects of its reflection in the horoscope.

When the Psyche makes the Body Ill, by Agnes Hauser
   A real example of psychosomatic illness and its reflection in the horoscope.

When the Sweet Things in Life make us Ill, by Birgit Braun
   Presents common themes in the horoscopes of five diabetes sufferers.

The final two articles relate astrological psychology to the approaches of Tarot and Bach Flower Remedies.

The Tarot and Astrological Psychology, by Ruth Schmidhauser
   Draws out correspondences between the Tarot, particularly the trump cards, and astrological psychology.

Images of Man, by Christian U. Vogel
   Relates the journey through the astrological houses and signs to the 7 groupings and 37 essences of the Bach Flower Remedies.

The Language of the Body

Man on the House Axes

Bruno Huber

First published in AstroLog Issue 115, April 2000

This lecture, given by Bruno Huber in 1983, is still relevant today. Bruno later went into more detail in a course on "Medical Astrology". This lecture laid the foundations for this later work. As well as being of interest, this gives us food for thought and stimulates us to perform our own research.

I would like to start by highlighting some principles, based on functional reality, that improve our understanding of how the body can express itself with its different components. For example, if I make expressive movements with my shoulders, I am saying something different than if I express myself with my hands. Hands and arms are important tools of body language. We use our hands to reinforce and influence. Feelings can be expressed easily with the hands and arms. We are often unaware that body language is just as important as spoken language, actually even more so. Man is the only living creature to walk upright. Everything is aligned around the body axis, the spine. At the top is the head, with which we think and speak; at the bottom are the feet on which we stand. Feet are what ground us, they are in contact with the earth. The head on the other hand is normally raised above the earth. These are not just theoretical statements, but organic realities. The body parts in between have various functions in our overall mental balance, and we need to know more about them.

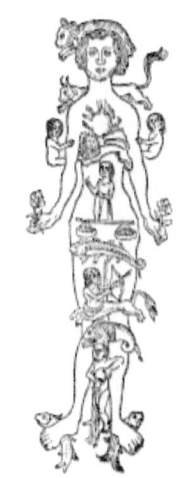

Attribution of Parts of the Body to Signs of the Zodiac

Astrological books that attribute the parts of the body to the signs of the zodiac follow the classical model. Most people are familiar with these associations, and images of them are common.

Aries is associated with the head, Taurus with the neck, Gemini with shoulders, arms and lungs. Cancer is associated with the chest, breasts and stomach, Leo the heart. Virgo rules the abdomen and digestive system, and the pelvic area with Libra. Scorpio rules the reproductive system, Sagittarius the thighs, the knee is associated with Capricorn, the lower leg with Aquarius and the feet with Pisces. This ancient attribution is impossible to date, and its roots are unknown. In the Middle Ages it was used extensively in medical astrology.

Medieval astrological books, particularly those on the subject of health, use this attribution as their basis of thought. In the Middle Ages people still believed in 'humorism', the theory of the humours, which is connected with the four temperaments. We cannot really take this attribution seriously today, especially not when it comes to medical diagnosis. Also its division of body parts and associated organs is a tricky subject, which remains unsatisfactory in the light of current medical knowledge. Modern medical astrology is still trying to work with it, and there is even an attempt to further refine it by attributing individual sign degrees to different parts of the body, e.g. the head/nose/tip of the nose, or quite specific muscles in a specific part of the arm. I consider this to be speculative, if one looks into it, 60-70% of cases do not back it up; it is therefore not a reliable system. This is also because the attribution is actually very superficial. The body is interpreted according to outward appearance. We can therefore assume that the associations with the heart and lungs etc. were later additions and are not original. The original attributions only involved the parts of the body that were visible from the outside. In my opinion this is not a satisfactory approach.

Attribution of Parts of the Body to the House System

A different attribution can be made to the house system. This may be new to you, you will find it at the most mentioned in passing in books.

We place man in the house system and initially assume that the person is standing inside their horoscope; we see them from behind, with their back to us and facing southwards. The horoscope is also oriented towards the south on the northern hemisphere. Let us imagine the famous drawing by Leonardo da Vinci, where a man stands with two arms positioned inside both a circle and a square. Leonardo must have known more about astrology than he lets on in his famous *Last Supper*, which shows knowledge of the signs.

The drawing demonstrates a depth of understanding of medical astrology. If we apply the house system to this circle, we have a clear attribution of the area of the chart to the human body. We can even be more precise and say that the IC/MC line is the spine, the key human function that allows us to stand up straight. It is obvious to look for the spine in the vertical. It is even called the spinal axis in some books.

4/10 Axis

If a horoscope shows tensions, e.g. one or more oppositions in this meridian axis, this person has a tendency to suffer from back problems. If he has bad posture, or finds himself in a psychosomatic pressure situation, this postural disorder may be communicated to the spine.

Now there are different types of back problem, which have three basic causes: the first being quite classical, where the problem is caused by the person's posture. According to our observations, the oppositions are fairly concentrated on the meridian axis, i.e. almost on the 4/10 cusp. This indicates the upright vertical posture. If something is wrong on this axis, the result may be a back problem. If the person has had bad posture for a long time, if he has had to bow and scrape for any length of time, or has a subordinate position, he will have a tendency to this kind of postural disorder. The spinal line may be bent over and forward at the top, which over time can lead to a kind of hunchback posture; in extreme cases even to a real hump. There are also disorders in the middle section where one part is too straight, which comes from a stiff posture. This person has always been told to stand up straight, so they have genuinely extended their spine, leading to a rigid posture.

Question: What if there is a concentration of planets in the 10th house?

Answer: I have just mentioned opposition tensions on the 4/10 axis, where the effect is most obvious and affects the whole axis. Concentrations in the 4th or 10th houses with no opposing tensions may cause back problems, but only if close to the MC or IC.

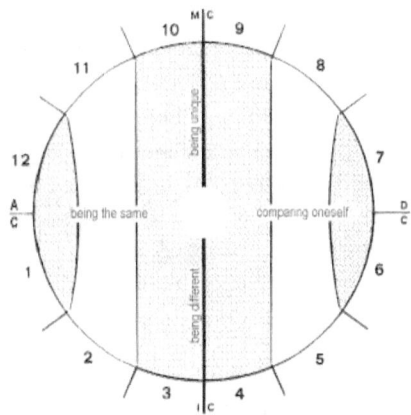

The 3/9 and 5/11 axes

There are also other causes. There are two more vertical axes, 3/9 and 5/11, which are concerned with the theme of upright posture and which can also be expressed in the form of back problems. I call 5/11 the heart axis and 3/9 the axis of the central nervous system. These together condition the posture directly controlled by the spine. There are movements that develop from the vertical posture. For example, if giving a massage, one never massages the spine directly but the muscles to the right and left. The state of these muscles is closely connected to the state of the heart. For example, if postural tensions occur connected with coping with life, and especially coping with relationships, these muscles can contract, leading to heart problems. Heart attacks are associated with these axes, and can often be traced back to postural problems. The tendency to hypertension and hyperactivity can only be expressed in a fire-air axis. In this case, where the heart is affected, it is the heart axis 5/11.

However, there are also movement disorders caused by coordination problems, which usually occur on the 3/9 axis. Nervous control of physical posture and the body's possible movements are regulated on the 3/9 axis.

The Will Axes

The 3/9, 4/10 and 5/11 axes can be grouped under the heading: will axes. This is the space in which the personal will moves, in which one can want, adopt a certain attitude and carry out certain actions. All conscious processes are reflected in these axes. The meridian axis represents the actual spine and is primarily responsible for basic physical posture. The axes 3/9 and 5/11 then show the two sides of the postural influence. The Heart Axis and the Nerve Axis in this area represent will potential that finds direct expression in physical posture, physical activity and above all in body language.

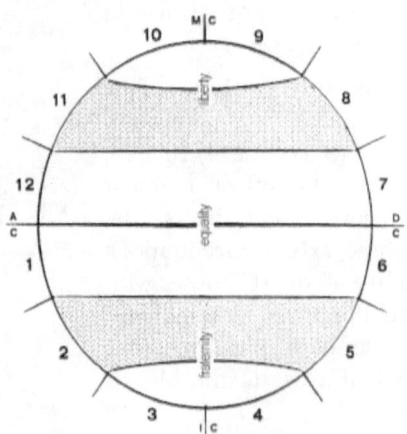

In the layer diagram we can picture the head at the top. It is the coordinator, and the place from which we control our lives. Then in the fixed houses 8 and 11 we have the shoulders, also including the neck and part of the chest. If you want to say something with your shoulders, you do it in the 8th or 11th houses. So if someone often talks or shrugs their shoulders, he probably has planets in these houses, otherwise his shoulders would not be so expressive. With no planets there, the shoulders would not move much.

In the next area 12/7 we find the organs of the upper body. The I/You space is the bodyline that often involves the stomach. Difficult planetary positions may indicate stomach ailments. Below the waistline lies the rest of the abdomen, i.e. the intestinal area 1/6. The fixed houses 2/5 are the pelvis and everything it contains, including the reproductive organs and down in the 3rd and 4th houses the lower limbs, legs and feet.

Other Axes

Let us now look at something else. I have mentioned the head and spine, central nervous system and heart axis, but there are also other axes. All heart functions and issues are visible in the 11th and 5th houses. Popular language is not wrong when it associates the heart with love. We know why the heart is associated with love. The heart suffers if we have a broken heart and our hearts beat more quickly if we are in love, etc. It is a part of human reality that is revealed on the 5/11 axis. Tough, perhaps traumatic experiences in love, even shock experiences, affect the heart. If the heart axis causes problems because it is strongly emphasised, love is automatically involved. This often means that something is wrong in relationships and/or love life, which can lead to physical problems if it is long lasting.

The other fixed axis, 2/8, concerns the digestive tract, from entrance to exit. In the 2nd Taurus house, food enters the body via the mouth, and in the 8th Scorpio house it leaves it. If there is a planetary emphasis here, we should observe the behaviour of the digestive tract, which may include difficulties in swallowing and problems in the oesophagus.

The Horizontal Axes

The two axes 6/12 and 1/7, which both lie directly on the horizon, are associated with the immune system. Here are revealed the body's ability to defend itself against intruders (bacteria, viruses), or if they do enter, to destroy them or render them ineffective. It initially consists of the chemical immune system, which is most strongly and clearly represented by the lymph system. This system of fluids runs throughout the body, transporting agents of the immune system around the body and releasing them into the blood, which then supplies the organs.

Difficulties in our social lives, not in love as above, make us more susceptible to developing an immunodeficiency. The lymph nodes may swell. This is aggravated if interpersonal problems become a permanent condition, especially if these already existed in childhood due to upbringing or traumatic experiences. If interpersonal problems become a permanent condition of isolation and spiritual frustration, these can lead to all types of possible psychosomatic allergies. The 6/12 axis is known for this, and is referred to by many authors as the psychosomatic axis.

The 1/7 axis is associated with coping mechanisms, and therefore the arms with which we defend ourselves and ward off attackers. These are cardinal houses, where one must defend oneself if attacked. The horizontal houses are all about immunity. They are able to close all the body's openings. This activity is expressed in different ways. Bothersome planetary positions may compromise this ability and cause long-lasting infections and repeated toxicities. This weakness is usually expressed by the opening of the 1/7 axis.

So we have now covered all the axes. We now have a really useful astro-medical tool, a basic system.

Question: "What role do the signs play?"

Answer: In the language of the body their role seems to be very subtle. In a medical context, they are very diffuse and have no precisely definable effect. However, it seems that certain genetic information is provided in the sign attribution. What I have already explained is the actual state of the body that one may possess in this life. This is not only influenced by genetics, i.e. the hereditary structure that we are born with, but much more strongly by the treatment that our body receives from the environment during our upbringing. This usually has a very strong influence among other things on posture. The environment has taught us how to treat our bodies and has formed the associated structures that we can ascertain according to this system, i.e. according to the house axes.

Our physical behaviour always has a corresponding mental counterpart, termed the psychosomatic mechanism. The horoscope shows us the nature and location of these mental problems. The psychosomatic mechanism is the same as the body language; it coincides completely with it. They have the same structures and the same apparatus. We can use astrology to work out the language of the body, as well as the symptoms on the same level, there there are no other approaches.

¤ ¤ ¤ ¤ ¤

I am My Own Doctor

How can Astrology help you to be Healthy?

Louise Huber

First published in AstroLog Issue 140-142, June-October 2004

Nowadays we are so surrounded by health information that it is hard to distinguish good advice from bad, most notably in the mass media. Anyone interested in nutritional issues is faced with a labyrinth of suggestions. It is absolutely not my intention to add to these. We know that astrology can be a means of self-help when it is used correctly. I would like to show you how you can use this to benefit your own health.

For example, we know from many astrologers or from our pupils that they feel much better since they took up astrology. It is also a well-known fact that astrologers live to a ripe old age. Why should this be so? Right from the word go, anyone who takes up astrology experiences a noticeable change in their approach to life, which increases the more deeply they penetrate this ancient wisdom of the stars. Their consciousness is expanded, to life-changing effect. The internalising of cosmic laws brings a new dimension to the mind and sensibilities. We suddenly see things in a different light and a different context. Problems, illnesses and conflicts are seen in their rightful proportion to the whole character, thus establishing the distance required to gain greater objectivity and judgement.

We realise that we ourselves can do something to live more freely and harmoniously by identifying the causes of misfortune, illness, problems and wrongdoing and finding new ways to solve problems that we would not have been able to find without a knowledge of astrology. We know that the idea that it is best for people to help themselves in the case of many psychological and health problems is not new. What is new though is the activation of this self-help ability with the aid of astrological knowledge.

So how does this happen? We know from psychosomatics how conflicts and unresolved issues create disturbances in our subconscious that emerge to bother us in the form of illness. We should not therefore be surprised that not only do conflicts and problems have a psychosomatic effect, but also if our subconscious has, or is trained to have, a healthy, positive attitude towards life, then that too must have a psychosomatic effect. That goes without saying. Likewise, as negativity produces conflicts, and unresolved problems have a somatic effect, faith in life, joy, confidence, health, that which within ourselves is sensitive to life and strives for a constant balance, have a healing effect. In many illnesses, this attitude suffices to help to eliminate somatic problems. That is precisely the issue that I would like to formally address.

It has always been my intention in astrology to show this dimension, that we can discover how best to overcome our weaknesses by working on ourselves, by cultivating our talents, be they psychological or physiological. We have been teaching this for years now, also in the context of psychosynthesis. You will remember that Assagioli was the first, at least to my knowledge, to state that psychosynthesis and wholeness can be achieved by consciously accepting and affirming people's positive qualities. This contrasts with the way people were brought up during the past 2000 years, where a negative punishment system prevailed and people were always going on about mistakes, etc. This overemphasis on the negatives actually bred negativity and many types of bad behaviour, which were always brought to our attention because our upbringing made us focus on them. There was so much emphasis on mistakes and shortcomings that people were unable to express their true natures. Thank God that things have now changed. In our times of enlightenment and transformation, the attitude is also changing towards the knowledge that positive thinking can help us to compensate for this outdated attitude.

However, it may seem as though we are now overemphasising the positive. But that is not the case. According to the law of balance, positivity and health are reinforced and spirituality and charisma are activated, so that the negative is automatically pushed back to where it belongs and minimised. On this level, it is not possible to completely get rid of the duality relationship of positive and negative. But we can balance it out with a third pole. I enjoy talking about the three-dimensionality in our physical reality, in our personality, the three-step nature of the developmental process and I would also like to mention it here. It is all too easy to think in terms of a duality or polarisation. It is all too easy to oppose the negative with the positive and to think that good and evil, black and white, guilt and atonement balance each other out. Although we are used to thinking in terms of pairs of opposites, only the third pole enables synthesis to take place, as we shall see below.

A new attitude to life is required, which involves asking the question why. It is liberating to explore the whys and wherefores and ultimately the meaning of life, and not just explaining our destiny by looking at superficial, little things. In my experience, the meaning and "why" questions can only be addressed if one has an understanding of the spiritual side of human evolution. For you to be able to understand synthesis as a factor of the New Age, I must ask you to broaden your minds to embrace the evolutionary process, which involves a dimension that lies behind the polarity of the physical world.

Most of you have surely dealt with such questions. The whole evolutionary process is currently easy to find in the literature. I will therefore limit myself to giving you a brief reminder so that we can understand our current situation and which forces we have at our disposal in the near future to make ourselves whole and complete.

The Evolutionary Process

This permeates the entire natural world. The divine spark incarnates and develops during its passage through the different kingdoms during a long period lasting a few million years in the following order:

1. Mineral kingdom
2. Vegetable kingdom
3. Animal kingdom
4. Human kingdom
5. Spiritual kingdom
6. Deva kingdom
7. Intellectual kingdom

The human soul descends in this form: first it materialises, then develops through the mineral kingdom, the vegetable kingdom, the animal kingdom and the human kingdom, that is the true idea of evolution. What interests us here is the question of what stage we are currently at in the human kingdom. We are all rooted in this level after which there is another, higher level, i.e. the spiritual kingdom.

Now, if you are not yet familiar with this topic, you may think it sounds rather cultish, which is absolutely not the case. This evolutionary theory is not only found in anthroposophy and theosophy, but also in anthropology. The transition to the spiritual kingdom can be made by those who are receptive to it.

At this point, when talking about the transformation of awareness and self healing, I would like to add that it is possible to be your own doctor. This "you" does not mean the small, anxious you who is struggling to survive just like any other person, but the mature individual who tries to be true to their own soul in exercising their spiritual potential. In order to receive guidance or an answer from one's own soul, one must first be aware that the soul and the soul kingdom exist. This dimension is accessible to all. Many forms of meditation are currently available, even religious ones. Various different philosophical, psychological and spiritual movements bring us closer to the knowledge that an eternal spirit lives within us.

Exploring this dimension requires that we regain basic trust, whereby we understand that spiritual forces are at work within us that abide by certain laws and which automatically regulate everything so that life is not endangered and the body always remains balanced to a certain extent. The human soul or our awareness of life plays a key role in this striving for equilibrium, or compensating energies.

This can also be understood from a purely impersonal perspective, when it is called the unconscious or collective unconscious, or the superconscious, but I do not want to go into such topics now. There are various different theories. It is important to understand that neither astrology nor anyone else can help us when our innermost centre of being is concerned, but only we ourselves according to the motto: "I am my own doctor." Self-healing powers are released from our innermost self, and many more things are controlled than we may realise from this core of our being.

In astrological psychology, the circle in the centre of the horoscope is often left empty because we interpret this circle as the centre of being, the soul, the higher self or the divine spark. We leave the circle empty and draw no aspects through it so that when we look at a horoscope we can always see that it is a space that says: "leave me alone!" There is a sphere where astrology ends and the person is connected to their innermost being, to the eternal, to the immortal self. We can become whole by embarking on this path and becoming one with this innermost centre of being. As we become one, we experience the miracle of the activation of the powers within us that have a self-healing function, and have the feeling that we are protected and caught in another dimension.

From this dimension, all suffering and troubles return to their rightful place, where they can no longer bother us. This is already very helpful, especially if suffering, pain or illness is taking over our lives, thereby making it seem more serious than it actually is. Such a concentration on illness often hinders the healing process. That is why one should try to gain some distance from the suffering in order to gradually be able to see it as it is, becoming less afraid of it in the process. There are several stages to this, because any path to any goal has different stages. The path to the self is described in many layers, e.g. with the levels of initiation and the crises that must be gone through at the conversion points.

Using a representation of the five layers, I would now like to show how you yourself can establish the current level of your consciousness. This involves taking into account the individual, their current condition, age, environment and developmental state. These questions should not only be asked in complementary medicine but also in modern medicine and later also in transpersonal psychology. Does the person already have an idea of the path to their innermost being? Is he/she already aware of the concept of evolution? Does he/she know that our development proceeds rhythmically upwards from one level to the next?

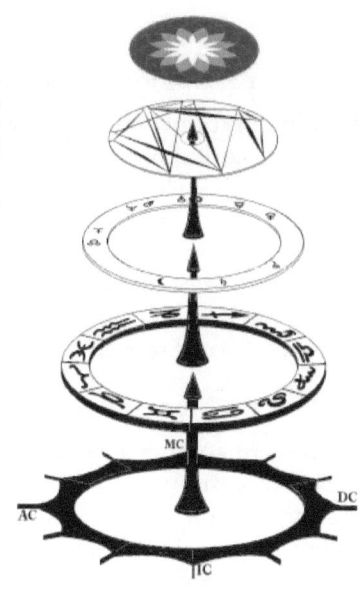

These are all important prerequisites for identifying the person's current needs. Remember that there is no single magic formula that suits everyone. As I said at the beginning, the newspapers today are full of health and nutrition advice. In reality, neither astrology nor medicine nor the complementary therapist has a real formula that could suit everyone. In my experience, each case is different. What is right for one person could be wrong for the next. Each person's constitution is different. We often start by trying to transfer experiences that have helped one person onto another; thinking that what has helped me must also help others. Then we naturally start to pass on our experience, out of love and concern for the other person, completely disregarding the fact that this person has a quite different lymph and cell balance, a completely different psychological and mental constitution and that he does not need our advice at all. On the contrary, it could even harm him.

We would now like to examine the horoscope in its five layers or levels with reference to illness and health.

1st Layer – Material Level: Saturn
Unconscious acceptance of illness, determination
This level corresponds to the house system and Saturn. On this level, the person is largely determined and does what he is told. He is at the mercy of the illness, the doctor and destiny. He takes everything as given and does not know what to do about it. He is dependent on the environment.

2nd Layer – Emotional Level: Moon
Struggling for health, resisting
This level corresponds to the zodiac signs and the Moon, where one protests against illness or suffering. The person starts to wonder, why am I ill? The body's powers of resistance are awakened, one starts to defend oneself and tries to free oneself from suffering. The level of acute inner conflicts, opposing forces and dualities. It is a fruitful learning period that gives us a better knowledge of ourselves, the illness and even life itself.

3rd Layer – Mental Level: Sun
Intelligent countermeasures, search for self help
This level corresponds to the planets and the Sun, and is a period of discovery of the self and of reality. Here the will to self-heal awakens. One rejects any interference from others, listens to oneself and finds ways to help oneself. "I am my own doctor" can be put into practice on this level. One is prone to experimentation, sees the true nature of one's physical make-up by means of self-observation and becomes a researcher.

4th Layer – Motivation Level
Healing by the will and creative actions
This level corresponds to the aspect pattern and the spiritual planets. Change in lifestyle brought about by inner guidance and will energy. Willingness for transformation, meditation, stating one's own needs, finding the right means. One becomes aware of the causes and frees oneself from external influences. The will awakens in positive affirmation: "I want to be well." One sees the unity with the healing powers in nature and in the cosmos that on this level one learns how to use for oneself and for others. Spiritual healing, serving humanity.

5th Layer – Spiritual Level
The centre circle, healing by becoming one with the soul
This level corresponds to the centre circle and the whole horoscope. Becoming aware of one's own soul (centre), the self-healing powers and the creative force by being at one with the centre of being. The person discovers new life sources within himself and sets himself free from illnesses and determinism. He experiences the power of the soul and true love, collaborates on the purification of the atmosphere and makes a creative contribution to evolution by becoming whole, becoming healthy and becoming one.

The First Level
From the perspective of the step-by-step process of the levels of the horoscope, there is a particular type of experience for every state of awareness. In the house system, most people live completely in the environment, they are dependent and other-directed, and wait for others to tell them what to do. You all know that the house system denotes the environment. It reflects all conditioning and behavioural structures that are inculcated into us during our upbringing. It could be said that it is mainly the houses that condition us because the upbringing and societal structures of the culture in which we live leave us barely any leeway to create anything of our own. This state of determinism, if translated into illness, means that the person follows convention; he goes to the doctor and does everything the doctor says. He is submissive to authority and dependent upon the opinions of others. The houses show among other things how dependent we are on authorities in our upbringing, they show how these authorities, the teachers, the priest, the pupils and the parents have influenced us. We are totally unaware that we can actually do something by ourselves, are completely polarised in the outside world and just put up with everything that happens to us.

The inner dimension is usually closed, in any case for as long as the person lacks a concept of individuality or free will. Many people actually reject such thoughts because they are afraid to take responsibility for themselves and therefore find it more comfortable to continue in the same old routine. Many theories can be linked to this idea. As far as illness is concerned, here many people simply accept everything, although they are not inwardly stimulated by it, they are people whose self-awareness is at best limited. Of course, if I may say so and without wanting to attack anyone, belonging to this level are the predictive schools of astrology that allow very little leeway for personal development.

On the outside, with the houses, are the visible symptoms, the physical world. There we see the body as analogy, we also see things as they are and experience what happens in reality. This is where we can see from the outside that something is wrong on the inside. The houses can therefore be seen as the first layer that must be passed through in order to reach the second layer.

The Second Level

This corresponds to the emotional or Moon level. In the context of illness, the theme is the struggle for health. One starts to reflect, it is the stage of revolt against illness, against daily influencing and conditioning. One starts to ask why one is actually ill. Asking this question is the only way to truly awaken the body's powers of resistance. One then tries with all one's might to free oneself from suffering and looks for new solutions and alternative healing methods. That is the next thing we learn on this second conflict level. One learns a lot when confronting something and struggling with the opposites. By entering this conflict of polarities, which is actually not at all enjoyable, one learns to understand and eventually overcome the opposites, thereby learning more about oneself and about life in general. We must pass through this conflict level in every phase of development in life. It is an important experience that is part of every developmental process.

As I have already mentioned, if we are at the mercy of the first level, we are in a way blind and unaware of our power to change things. On the second level, our ego confronts the problem and we ask ourselves: "Do I have to suffer like this?" Then the will is awakened and we decide: "Now I don't want to suffer any more, now I want to do something about it." By deciding to do something, the will is activated and one no longer allows oneself to be determined.

Actually, this approach is very natural and we do this all the time in everyday life. For example, if someone is cold, they immediately get a jacket and put it on in order to free themselves from the pain and protect themselves from the cold. We have many such ways of helping ourselves and doing something without our mothers constantly having to run around after us and give us a jacket when we are cold. In this stage, we all have a certain experience; we know that we can help ourselves. Then comes the third level, which can be identified with the Sun and the planets.

The Third Level

The third level corresponds to the planets. They lie in specific signs and also have a specific character and quality that enable us to function consciously. It is the planets that allow us to act in the twelve houses and their corresponding life areas and slowly dismantle compulsive mechanisms. The planets are organs; depending on which abilities they represent, they allow us to react differently in certain life areas. Depending on sign and house, they enable us to change the world, to do something that corresponds to our inner nature. It is a phase of autonomous development and of searching for intelligent self-help measures.

These ideas can be extended further. The signs are the genetic traits that we have inherited and the houses are the upbringing and the milieu and everything that has influenced us; that is the second level of influence.

These inherited traits give us the opportunity, depending on the sign, to change something in the houses, but only if we are aware of them. As long as we expect the environment to tell us what we have to do, it is impossible for us to find out what we really need, and to what extent we are able to make changes. We need to ask ourselves, "What can we do?" Only when we ask ourselves this question, and this usually happens when we are young, are we able to develop. The new generation between the ages of 16 and 24 no longer wants to be told what to do by its parents, and rebels against them, which anyone who has children knows. Anyone who rebels comes into conflict with convention and has to fight for every little piece of freedom. That is the way to the MC, where one must be prepared to dare to be an individual.

The Fourth Level

The aspect pattern is a deeper layer. We will call it the fourth level, or the period of self-knowledge. In the preceding phases, we have gathered experiences and discovered our limitations. We have tentatively deployed our planets and looked beyond them, have suffered defeats, enjoyed successes and learnt how to deal with these forces. We have already learnt something about ourselves. We become more and more acquainted with the true nature of the structure of our being by observing ourselves.

The further inwards we go, the less we are affected by manipulative power structures. The further inwards we go, the less influential are the laws of the signs, as we now come into the sphere of influence of other laws. You already know that the aspect pattern reveals a deep motivational level that leads us to the core of our being. We cannot just rush into this motivational level and change things straight away.

Most people are unaware of these motivational levels of the aspect pattern, precisely because in order to get there, we need to be still and listen to our inner voice. The intellect, concrete knowledge and external formalities slowly retreat into the background. We reach the inner dimension situated around the core of being, which is influenced directly by the spirit. The planets in the signs and houses are far away. One can correctly see and experience this layer spatially. We must look inwards and listen to our inner voice. This is what we try to do when we take up meditation training, to silence the external so that we can focus on our inner world. We can only do this by looking inward, by producing a kind of vacuum into which the coloured aspect pattern can flow. In this way we experience something intrinsic about other people. Colours stimulate a different sensory perception than that which we know via our intellect as knowledge. Colours awaken our senses and promote intuition. Through intuition, something happens within us, a different life quality awakens and deeper motivations become visible.

Some people may even be shocked to discover there that they actually want to be ill. It is often the case that external causes like unprocessed conflict situations, separations and compensations can make us ill. Others want to be ill in order to receive more love and care. There are many different reasons and each person's reasons are unique. What happens when we make this realisation? In the best case, with this shock comes a spiritual impulse so that we can say with conviction: "Now I want to be healthy!"

Once we decide we really want to be healthy, the energies of the aspect pattern flow into a new, regenerating purifying process that washes away all negativity. "I want to be healthy" is the most important step in the life of an ill person, when he discovers his own power and feels passionately that he wants to live a full life and free himself from false ideas and expectations. As soon as he discovers that only he can change things, then he says with conviction: "I want to be well."

In this act of will he becomes creative. Creative awareness can bring health and happiness to us all. Only by discovering our own creative abilities and knowing that within ourselves on this level we can link our self-healing energies with our soul and avoid being subjected to determining influences. Anyone who actively wants to be well can use their will to change their life and motivation for the better. The same will energy can also help his innermost being to express itself and attract all the positive perceptions and energies that are necessary to become healthy again.

Healing comes not only from our own innermost self; on this level, we come into contact with the universal healing powers of the entire solar system. We approach the core of being and the centre circle means becoming aware of oneself or one's soul and thereby the world soul, which is in harmony with all living things. It awakens the will function as a creative, transforming power. One discovers new sources of life within oneself and creates a healthy world for oneself, becomes freer and freer from the influence of illness and all evil. One experiences the power of the soul and true love.

The Fifth Level

By passing through all four layers, we finally reach our innermost being, our soul, which activates our healing energies. In the different layers we have experienced our own behaviour with regard to our bodies, to illness and to problems. These experiences all come from outside via the zodiac, via the aspect pattern into the centre. In the core, we experience the healing powers of nature and the cosmos, because this centre of being exists in harmony with all living things for eternity. From here we are able to have some awareness of the eternal within ourselves, which brings us back to the stages of the evolutionary process with which we are all connected.

The awareness that within us there is a living soul that is the cause of our existence is not achieved overnight. Reaching this experience of being is a long process. It not only brings us into contact with all the souls in humanity, but also the non-manifested kingdoms. We come into contact with healing powers that come from the so-called deva kingdom, or as it is called in religion, the angel kingdom.

The Deva Kingdom

From the esoteric books of Alice Bailey and other books on the angel kingdom, we know that the deva kingdom is coming nearer to mankind in this New Age and wants to connect with it. We just need to open ourselves up to it and accept its help. Many are now sensitive to this and open their consciousness to new healing powers that flow over all mankind. Almost everyone has heard of esoteric or spiritual healing. Alternative medicine heals with colours, with aromas, with subtle oils like Bach Flowers, etc. Such treatments have been used for some time as the time is right for them, or in other words, because the deva kingdom is approaching the human kingdom. Its aim has always been to reach the human kingdom through the thick walls surrounding it. We must help by being ready to pave the way, or to meet it halfway.

The Spiritual Kingdom

The human kingdom is the connection between spirit and matter. Here the spiritual kingdom meets the so-called animal body. It is the spiritual kingdom that manifests itself for people in order to redeem them and lead them back to the divine source. Roberto Assagioli, friend of Alice Bailey, always emphasised that we now find ourselves at the start of the 5th natural kingdom. The spiritual kingdom therefore offers the hope that all will be well, even though things often look so black in our world. It is not just a blind hope but a visible fact that is often depicted in psychology, religion, meditation and yoga. Everywhere we are experiencing fundamental changes in this New Age. In esoteric terms, the hitherto thick curtain that has hung between these two levels is becoming thinner and more and more people are becoming sensitive to the subtle vibrations of the spiritual kingdom.

The Path to the Self

Holistic and spiritual astrology allows the possibility of taking the path to the self. We can take this path in each individual horoscope from the outside to the inside. The group horoscope meditations that I teach also help us to do this, as they liberate spiritual energies. It is interesting that deep, inner images often enable problems to disappear automatically (naturally not organic shortcomings; it is just that new powers simply flow over us and renew us).

Just as we make our way through the layers of the horoscope to the centre, esoteric constitutional theory can also tell us something about the causes of illness.

The Causes of Illness

Here we make a distinction between the normal causes of illness, i.e. physical, emotional and mental causes, and the deeper more esoteric causes. We use as a basis the human constitution as represented in the esoteric literature (see diagram). An overview of the approach is given in the following.

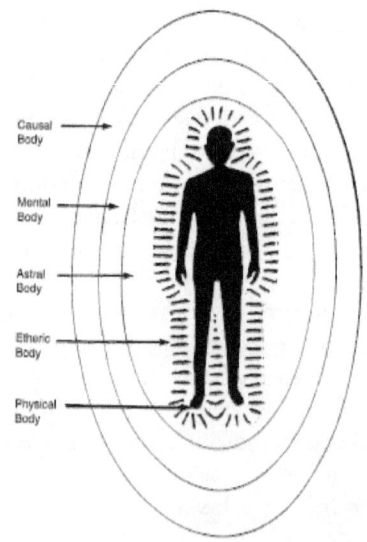

1. General Causes – accidents, bad diet, genetic factors.

2. Causes in the Human Constitution
a) physical body, etheric body – causes are the lack of vitality or excessive stimulation, irritation.
b) astral or emotional body – thwarted or excessively satisfied desires, moods, repressions, frustrations, bitterness, secret longings.
c) mental body – false thinking, errors, heresy, cruelty, harshness, pride
d) causal body – summing up of old behavioural patterns that hold one back and must be dissolved.

3. Karmic Laws of Cause and Effect
Effect of profound causes, usually coming from previous lives. If heavy karma is involved, then healing is impossible. All efforts are in vain. But one should not stop trying because one never knows exactly when the karma will be worked off.

4. Illnesses can also come from the Soul
These almost always serve the process of liberation or development, and require that one ask: what is my soul trying to tell me, what do I have to learn, what am I doing wrong? etc. Illness can also promote further development and overcome blockages and rigidity, freeing new spiritual powers in the process. "Illness as a path."

5. The deepest cause of illness is a lack of harmony between the form (personality) and soul.
This cause is something very fundamental, i.e. the outcome of an inhibited spiritual life. Healing consists of liberating the soul so that its dynamism overcomes blockages and the lack of harmony in the organs and the rest of the body. This is where self-healing comes in. Many people are currently working consciously on this synthesis via astrology, meditation, psychology, religion, education, medicine, etc.

1. General Causes

Accidents, bad diet, genetic factors.
On the physical level, accidents can happen that can be attributed to personal negligence or other people's carelessness. One is also subject to infection from external sources. These often attack people as they go about their daily life, in everyday social contact or due to disease in the environment. General causes also include illnesses caused by bad diet, particularly during childhood. A bad, unbalanced diet makes the body susceptible to illness, reducing its vitality and powers of resistance. There are also certain well-known forms of serious weakness that make a person vulnerable to certain illnesses.

2. Causes in the Human Constitution

The human constitution is very helpful in the investigation of the causes of illness.

a) Physical Body, Etheric Body

As mentioned above, illnesses happen in the purely experienceable sense to the physical body due to accidents or genetic predispositions. The physical body consists predominantly of cells that are animated by the etheric body. When it dies, the physical body no longer exists! The energy escapes via the etheric body and passes on to the planetary, etheric level, with which we are all connected. The etheric body is therefore the root of physical life, which is why our health is largely dependent on the nature of this body. We can animate it by a healthy lifestyle and by being in touch with nature. This perspective shows us the importance of breathing exercises, which connect us with etheric substance or with the prana in the air. This will help us to cope with blockages and atrophy, which are the two main causes of illness on the etheric level and enable us to awaken new sources of life in ourselves.

b) Emotional Body

Next in the human constitution comes the emotional or astral body, which surrounds us like an aura. Here, illness is caused by the under- or over-indulgence of our desires. This includes unresolved conflicts, which often remain stuck for a long time in the astral or emotional body. The repression of secret longings mostly in the unconscious torments us, leading to bitterness, frustration, depression and illness. The emotions should be purified and refined during the course of our development, so that we become receptive to the subtle impulses of the soul. The more we refine this body through the development of our capacity for love and cultivate it through humanitarian behaviour and constructive emotions, the better it assimilates the processes in the inner areas and transfers them to "everyday consciousness". It is therefore largely the purity and integrity of our emotions that determine our health and happiness.

c) Mental Body

In the thinking or mental body, it is usually our minds that determine what is beneficial for our health, according to which belief systems, morality or ethics condition our minds. The causes of mental illness are not well known, but are false teachings, false convictions, harshness, pride, etc., which put a strain on our health. We know that negative thoughts and anxieties are eventually realised and lead to illness. Here too, concentration and meditation can make us more receptive to the more subtle vibrations from the higher levels. There are different movements that focus on targeted mental training, such as certain schools of yoga, the Unity Movement, Alpha training, Huna Magic, Christian Science, etc. They all allow us to become conscious of our mental creativity, so that we can decide for ourselves whether we choose to think positively or negatively. We learn to control our thoughts, to assert our will, to reject negative thoughts and our bond with the healing powers of the cosmos grows.

d) Causal Body

Behind the three human bodies, there lies what is known as the causal body. It is where all earthly emotional and mental experiences are sorted and stored in the form of essences, or life qualities or life motivations. In the horoscope we see these structures in the aspect pattern and it is clear that profound causes for illnesses can also be found here. These usually depend on the karma of the person concerned. As a result of the accumulation of all life experiences from a long chain of incarnations during the course of our development, obstructive or inhibiting structures can appear in geometric shapes that must be disintegrated at a certain point (4th initiation). That happens either through illness or the destruction of the causal body (you can read more about this in Alice Bailey's book *Letters on Occult Meditation*).

3. Karmic Laws of Cause and Effect

In order to better understand the whole context, it is important to say something about the karmic laws of cause and effect. We are all subject to this law of causality, and it plays a more important role in illness than one might think. "As you sow, so shall you reap" is an old saying that describes this law. Since the transit of Pluto in the signs of Scorpio and Sagittarius (1984 – 2008), the bookshops have been full of esoteric literature and there is great interest in karma and reincarnation. Since Pluto entered Sagittarius, this knowledge became widespread and today more and more people want to learn about karma. The ideas of guilt and atonement, punishment and reward, good and evil, black and white, etc. are significant. People ask themselves: "What did I do wrong in a previous life that I have to pay for now?" The law of cause and effect means punishment, retribution, revenge and wars. If one applies this dual approach to reincarnation experiences, many people think if they killed someone in a previous life, they will now be the victim of someone else who will kill them. That is a simplistic structure of karma that obviously does not reflect the whole truth. There is another, three-dimensional approach.

Karma and Dharma

It is also interesting to see a development here. At the beginning I said that there is a third dimension that enables opposites to be synthesised, it is the principle of relativity or rationality that makes us ask for more information or why things happen. In Indian philosophy this principle is called dharma. Put into practice, it becomes what we call "educational karma", which helps us to learn from our mistakes. When we have learnt something, it becomes available to us, and by learning from experience, we can react more intelligently or rationally next time around. If free will is then brought into the equation, we get better and better at making our own choices and with increasing experience are able to live out the subject of this lecture and be our own doctors. This involves avoiding what causes us pain and compensating for the mistakes we have made. Nowadays, many people have already developed a great capacity for this type of thinking and have taken control of their own lives. They live by the motto: "Do unto others as you would have done unto you."

Polarised Thinking

Nevertheless, there are still a great many people who are trapped in polarised thinking. They may be aggressive, strive for revenge, and like to construct images of bogeymen believing that: "we are the goodies and you are the baddies." For many people this is still a normal reaction. However, the latest developments show that more and more people no longer accept this attitude. They have had enough of hostility and war, having learnt through education, religion and development that if they establish real human relationships based on goodwill, if they treat each other with more understanding and tolerance, they feel better and, more importantly, healthier. They can right many wrongs in their environment, because based on their insight, understanding and experience they know that loving and helpful behaviour produces a good reaction from the environment. This is therefore a modern human quality that gives hope for a better world. Actually, many people have already achieved the ability to overcome their karma and to create a new dharma. For us, this is proof that in this New Age we are becoming increasingly aware of the more subtle bodies or higher dimensions and levels.

Incurable Illness

As far as karma is concerned, there is actually also such a thing as heavy karma, which makes its presence felt in the form of incurable illness. We consider the unconscious space in ourselves not only as an accumulation of conflicts arising from our current lives, but also believe that in this space, everything that we have ever done, right or wrong, is stored. That is our unconscious side, what Jung calls the shadow personality, in which everything is neatly logged and the law of cause and effect prevails. When karma emerges from this level and affects us in the form of illness, suffering and separation, we are at its mercy and can do nothing about it, which is why there are some illnesses that cannot be cured. Although we realise this, we should never stop trying to find a cure!

Healing

Nobody really knows when the karma stops working. It is impossible to know this in advance and take it into account. That means even if someone cannot be cured of an illness, they should not stop hoping that one day it will be over and the healing will begin. We should beware of falling prey to determinism or fatalism and simply saying: "It's because of my karma, I can't do anything about it." We then run the risk of falling back to the first level mentioned above, of the astrological houses, where we are simply unaware that we can liberate ourselves from illness. The idea that freedom exists is a principle of inner salvation that activates the self-healing powers and ascends within us like an act of grace. We should never forget this knowledge for it comes from our soul.

The Soul

In the horoscope, the soul is symbolised by the centre circle and links us to the eternal that spans all incarnations and guards our personal lives. It has a profound knowledge of the meaning and purpose of our incarnation. I do not mean that it knows tiny details about our everyday lives, but that its immortality gives it a universal knowledge of evolution and development that extends far into the past and future. This means that the soul knows what is good for us and what we need for our development. Often it is exactly the opposite of what we may think, and taking the esoteric path, or the path to the self, or the path of initiation or whatever you want to call it, may involve a reversal of values. Something that is bad for our exterior life may be good for our interior life.

4. Illnesses that come from the Soul

This shows us that there are also illnesses that come from the soul which promote the processes of liberation and development. That means that these illnesses are necessary in order to gain spiritual awakening and so that inner conflicts may be expressed consciously through the illness. If the illness has this type of origin, we must ask ourselves what our soul wants, why we have this illness, what we must learn and what we are doing wrong. This turns the illness into a learning process that even counteracts physical congestion or hardening, often making it a process of purification or a balancing of misused energies. We are already familiar with this. Sometimes we suffer from an illness because we are too active in our exterior lives and need to calm down and find ourselves again. Illnesses often promote balance, liberation and development.

5. Lack of Harmony between Soul and Form

There is yet another, greater interpretation of the nature of illness, a more esoteric one, which suggests that the most profound cause of illness on our planet is a lack of harmony between soul and form. This concept can only be understood in the context of evolutionary theory, and by accepting that the objective of our lives on this planet is to reconcile the soul and the personality. The goal of all development is to achieve wholeness or integration, integration as a personality, integration with the soul, integration with the evolutionary plan and integration with humanity.

The evolutionary process involves the spirit or the soul becoming incarnate in the human kingdom, the aim of this being the attaining of a relative perfection of man. This will probably only be achieved at the end of evolution, perhaps in 2 million years. This truth could also be expressed in another way, but I believe that this theory is comprehensible and simple. Our concept of time is relative from the perspective of eternity.

Building the Bridge (Antahkarana)

The synchronisation of soul and personality is a process that we can work on consciously, in which we endeavour to become one with the will, the soul and evolution. In the process we can build a bridge to the soul out of the mental or thought content in the consciousness, to facilitate the flow of the soul energies into the personality. This is incidentally the goal of every school of meditation, to connect with the soul, the inner core being. Alice Bailey, for instance, calls this type of meditation work the construction of the antahkarana, sometimes also called the rainbow bridge. This is built during meditation by conscious mental work, which involves using our graphic intellectual capacity to imagine the qualities of the soul. Eventually, this process allows us to create over time a bridge across the abyss that exists in the mental space between the soul and personality.

Freely flowing soul energies

For many people this idea may be new, but it is evident that if an illness is caused by a significant lack of harmony between soul and form, the healing process consists of allowing the soul energies to flow freely. If there is something that we ourselves can do to promote this process, then we should not hesitate to do so. Especially if we realise that the cause of the illness is congested soul energy, we can get this energy flowing by radiating love to our fellow men on a daily basis. We should be encouraged by the knowledge that the soul's only motivation is to love and serve. This is just as much a fundamental drive on the soul level as self-preservation is in the physical world. We actually do not need to do anything except keep our channels clear by meditating daily and opening ourselves up to the soul energies. Nowadays, there are many forms of spiritual stimuli and training, increasingly with a religious element. On the physical level, we can help ourselves by eating a sensible diet, by exercising and conscious breathing or by practising yoga, and on the emotional and mental levels by trying to have good, positive thoughts and by aligning ourselves with the forces of nature and evolution.

These are all ways of helping ourselves and counteracting congestion and energy loss in our three bodies, thus allowing our inner soul life to flow freely and releasing self-healing powers. This is actually the most important way we can be our own doctors. If we are guided by our souls, we will come to no harm and will always do the right thing.

Horoscope Meditations
Astrology uses the method of horoscope meditations in small groups to release soul energies, and I myself have run these from time to time. Those who are familiar with them will notice that they liberate soul energies and trigger healing experiences. We have already had profound experiences with them. The group experience produces a unified consciousness and soul vibrations. These can only be perceived with the heart, by looking, not by the head. However, eventually head and heart must work together and once this relationship is established, healing energies flow through the person concerned, and others say: "His heart is in the right place."

The Moon Node Axes
Behaviour in the case of illness
The position of the rising Moon Node in its house (not in the sign) indicates the path of least resistance for the spiritual ascent of the consciously striving person. From this perspective, it is the starting point for our further development and an opportunity to find permanent solutions for problems. It is therefore of obvious interest in the case of illness. The descending Moon Node lies always opposite it and shows the way backwards, clinging to old habits. It is

not shown in the horoscope, but we always know that it lies opposite the rising Node. The descending Node is also called the Saturn point and the rising Node the Jupiter point. If Saturn happens to lie at the descending Node, old, familiar structures and ways of behaving are present, whose development we must stop, however at the Jupiter point, we find as yet unfinished properties that we still have to perfect. Below is a brief overview of how the ascent of the Moon Node is achieved in each the house. A detailed description of the individual house positions can be found in our book *Moon Node Astrology*.

1st House The ascent is found in personal, autonomous behaviour, once one has stopped hoping for the support of others.

2nd House The ascent is found in the quiet certainty of one's own substance and abilities, after one has overcome doubts about personal resources.

3rd House The ascent is achieved by learning from others, without imposing one's own ideas as the only correct ones.

4th House The ascent is found by taking the family seriously, enjoying family life and overcoming all desires for power and status.

5th House The ascent is found by being willing to take risks and experiment, without being afraid of giving something up or losing face.

6th House The ascent is achieved by personal work and dedication, by serving all kinds of different people, after the demand for solitude and isolation has been abandoned. Quickly and cheerfully doing what has to be done.

7th House The ascent is found in by losing oneself in communal work, marriage and partnership, after renouncing selfishness and putting oneself first.

8th House The ascent is found by breaking free of all chains, bonds and desire for material things, by overcoming the reluctance and fear of loss and change and learning to "Render unto Caesar what is Caesar's."

9th House The ascent is found in one's own thoughts and by being brave enough to make one's own decisions, by travelling and philosophising, after resisting the tendency to follow the crowd.

10th House The ascent is found in the actualisation of one's own goals and becoming a "self-made man", after one has freed oneself from goals set by the family and renounced all home comforts.

11th House The ascent is found in the right choice of friends, in the pursuit of platonic relationships and in the actualisation of ideals, after giving up the lust for adventure and the urge to go it alone in order to satisfy personal wishes.

12th House The ascent is found in solitude, in working on personal improvement and spiritualization, after abandoning the conviction that one's presence is indispensable in the outside world for things to work properly.

House and Sign Position

As far as illness is concerned, the house position should be combined with the sign quality to find out which approach to adopt. From the house position we can discover how one must act practically in order to escape from problems and also from illness. From the sign position we discover the inner abilities that represent another factor that should also be taken into account for a holistic overview.

Example: 6th House with Leo

By way of illustration, let us use the example of the combination of Moon Node in the 6th house with the sign of Leo. The 6th house is, among other things, concerned with survival. One must learn to work and quickly and cheerfully carry out one's duties without hoping for a reward. With this approach to activities in the 6th house, one is able to keep energies flowing. In the case of illness, it is also helpful to take the Leo aspect into account by proactively contributing to self-healing according to the motto: "I am my own doctor!" For Leo, "I am" is the keyword. One must know what is right for oneself.

Although in the 6th house one likes to listen to others and ask them for advice, ultimately one does what one thinks is right. If we combine these two influences, this means on the one hand listening to others, but after internal examination, making one's own decisions. All suffering has so many varied effects that there cannot be one universal formula, but it is up to each person to find their own and this can only be found by combining sign and house.

Polarity

In addition, if we consider things from a wider standpoint, the whole Moon Node axis must be implemented for the personal ascent, and for this we need to deal with the tension field that exists in the polarity of the opposition between the rising and descending Moon Nodes. One side is always stronger than the other and there is frequent conflict, which leads to a state of tension. In other words, the rising Moon Node is the way forward into a future that appears to us a developmental goal, the descending Moon Node is our shadow, which we need to elevate and integrate into our consciousness. From this broad span a third element arises that we call synthesis, which has a healing effect. This process can be linked with the soul energy that flows out of the centre, the core, and which unites the opposites in an individual rhythm.

Moon Node and Axis Polarities

The Moon Node and its axis therefore give us an indication of how we may reach the centre and find healing. This means that the axis should be considered as a whole if we are to find synthesis and healing. If the ascending point is the first step to the solution for psychic, existential problems or relationship problems, the obvious analogical conclusion is that it must also help us to find a way out of illness.

I-You axis 1st and 7th House

With Moon Node in the 1st house, this whole axis is activated, which as we know is connected with I-You problems. As this axis is also the source of the moon node horoscope, in which we can see the shadow personality or the accumulation of life experiences from a series of incarnations, so the causes for I-You problems are usually to be found in former lives. For example, if one has been very dependent on the You, this will be compensated for with a Moon Node in the 1st house, which encourages one to nurture personal expression. Where illness is concerned, somatic processes are involved that originate from an "ancient mistake", such as a persistent competitive attitude or conversely a spiritual belief or dogmatic altruism.

Illness Behaviour on the Encounter Axis 1-7

The old habit with the descending Moon Node in the 7th house, of allowing oneself to be guided by other people, should be overcome. In the 7th house, it indicates an unhealthy dependency on the partner's opinion. The developmental path shown by the rising Moon Node in the 1st house means making one's own choices and decisions. One should pay attention to impulses of one's own physicality and less to the suggestions of other people. If one has the Moon Node or a group of planets on the left side of the horoscope, then one does not like to be helped and wants to do everything oneself. On the right side, one wants to be advised, turns to others and finds a solution in confrontation with the environment or with the partner. There one finds it easier to say: "I cannot help myself, please help me."

Possession Axis 2nd and 8th House
If the rising Moon Node lies in the 2nd house, one must learn to ensure one's own survival, to acquire substance and find joy in gaining one's own fortune. So the person must keep their feet on the ground and recognise that stability is essential. The old ways shown in the descending Moon Node in the 8th house mean overexploiting one's own substance, which is usually sacrificed for an idea. One renounces it in order to acquire a place in heaven. Habitual reservations when it comes to needing to take something can also cause health problems.

Illness Behaviour in the Possession Axis 2 – 8
In the 2nd house, the economic principle prevails and one says: "You scratch my back and I'll scratch yours." In the 8th house, the Scorpio house, the old concept "an eye for an eye, a tooth for a tooth" applies, and is demonstrated among other ways in the "carrot and stick" approach. One only does something if one gets something in return; traditional astrology still calls it the inheritance house. One notices what other people have. "If you help me, you will get something in return," or "You must help me otherwise you won't get anything."

Thinking Axis 3rd and 9th House
This is duality of thought, i.e. both collective and independent thought. One will first question the knowledge of the collective, and then examine one's position *vis-à-vis* the collective, aspire to learn and train, be influenced, learn objectively and dispassionately from all people. One starts to see things in a more non-judgemental way, and learns to accept the relativity of value judgements. The descending Moon Node in the 9th house is usually self-absorbed and arrogant, and thinks that its opinion is the only one that matters. One is incapable of taking in new information, learns nothing new and does not progress. That leads to isolation and therefore also to illness.

Illness Behaviour in the Thinking Axis 3 – 9
In the 3rd house, one says: "I am following doctor's orders," in the 9th house, "What the doctor says is wrong, only I know the truth." That is Sagittarius. So the indicated behaviour when ill is that if you have the rising Moon Node in the 9th house, you should find out for yourself what is right for you. If you have it in the 3rd house, you should follow your doctor's advice.

Individual Axis 4th and 10th House

This axis is usually, along with the Moon Node line, a great challenge for personal growth. In the 4th house, we can imagine the roots of a tree. When the roots are strong and healthy, the tree grows up in to the upper part of the horoscope and there develops a wonderful crown. The fruits of this tree are the achievements of a mature, fully aware person, who can actualise his individuality on this axis. The healthy tree naturally needs strong roots. If they are damaged, the tree will collapse. That is why we should never neglect our families for the sake of our careers.

Illness Behaviour in the Individual Axis 4 – 10

The individual axis contains the opposition of collective and personal goals. In the 4th house the ill person says: "I am nice to you, so that you will help me and be nice to me in return." They need the love and protection of the nest and on no account want to lose the affection or care of the family. They must admit that they need it and should renounce pride.

In the 10th house, the person says: "Nobody can help me, only I can help myself." They prefer to be alone and renounce the protection of a communal life because they do not want to adapt. They prefer to be totally self-sufficient rather than let themselves be helped. Capricorn, the Saturn principle.

Relationship Axis 5th and 11th House

Love and friendship are the themes here. In the 5th house it is all about opening oneself up to and getting involved with the You; in the 11th house one wants to be selective and only connect with those who are like-minded. It is not easy to reconcile these two different attitudes. In every polarity axis, one initially swings back and forth between the two poles. On the one hand, one wants to be loved and bring one's feelings into a relationship, one longs for love and the enjoyment of being a couple. But one is constantly plagued by the fear that one is investing too much energy into it and not getting back what one has put in.

This fixed axis also involves the economic principle in relationships, which inhibits spontaneity or creativity. One sets conditions, in the 5th house one is jealous of everything that could threaten one's enjoyment of life; in the 11th house one is elitist, sets oneself apart and wants to be alone. In many cases, synthesis and the quality of the heart are only developed once one has experienced genuine, true love. Then the healing energies also flow out of the centre into the relationship.

Illness Behaviour on the Relationship Axis 5-11

In every You relationship, it depends on whether the rising Moon Node lies on the right (5th house) or the left (11th). In the 5th house, one says: "I will be healthy if you stay with me." The Leo and 5th house need a partner or a public that gives feedback, so they set conditions. Those with the rising Moon Node in the 11th house (Aquarius principle) only want to be helped by quite specific people, friends or soul mates. With elitist consciousness, they often take refuge in their ivory tower and want to cope by themselves with their illness or problems. They react allergically to social contact and say: "Leave me alone, but don't go too far away." This often hurts those who want to help them, so that they end up with nobody left to help them. This causes a developmental crisis in which priorities must be revised. This involves finding out what is most important for them, love or having things their own way.

Existence Axis 6th and 12th House

This axis is concerned with existence. The 12th house is all about calm self reflection. Here one must be totally honest with oneself and discover where one stands, what one has to offer the world and whether one can cope with one's task in life. The 6th house is where the real struggle for survival takes place. Here one is completely occupied with fulfilling daily duties. The question of existence is a concrete one, and concerns work. One is best able to deal with this if one has the right training and human skills for the job, hence the need for acquiring these skills to be able to ensure survival.

Illness Behaviour on the Existence Axis 6-12

This axis is concerned with self-confidence, if one fails and is unable to satisfactorily fulfil one's tasks, one can easily fall victim to psychosomatic illness.

In the 6th house, one reacts sensitively to failure and defeat in work and in life. One does everything in one's power to eliminate any shortcomings, to educate oneself in order to become better and get a corresponding "better job". Often it is the fear of the You, of the environment and the fear of possible failure, personal defeat and rejection that can make one ill. One then literally takes refuge in the 12th house and hides from others, becoming reserved, shy, suspicious and constructing an illusory world that has lost all connection with reality.

With the Moon Node in the 12th house one also has to struggle with feelings of inferiority. "You must help me, I can't do it by myself." Here one usually feels misunderstood and sorry for oneself. They are furthest removed from the world. "Nobody helps me, everyone is so busy."

Conclusion

These descriptions do not claim to be exhaustive. They can be expanded as desired and are intended to encourage you to make your own interpretations. You can study the horoscope in different houses and signs and from the Moon Node examine your actual behaviour when you are ill. In medical astrology, it is impossible to set universally valid rules. The field is much too complicated and the medical research too complex for a perfect fit with astrological symbols to be possible.

◻ ◻ ◻ ◻ ◻

When the Psyche makes the Body Ill

Agnes Hauser

First published in AstroLog Issue 66, February 1992

Psychosomatic Medicine

The question of what causes physical symptoms can be answered in various different ways:

The scientific explanation is a causal one, unconnected to the patient's actual being; the hermeneutics, who look for sense and meaning, see physical suffering as an indication of the patient's conflict, which has a connection to his character and to his life. The person is a kind of symbol, whose message must be understood.

Psychosomatic medicine combines the two, and involves both psyche and soma in equal measure: it focuses on the state of being ill, and not the illness per se.

Causal conflicts arise when the person's conscious and unconscious forces want different things and these different energies collide. The psychodynamic that plays out between conscious and subconscious causes externally visible symptoms.

These can be expressed and processed in many different ways, for example in therapy, by sublimation into work and career, by degeneration into addiction and perversion, in object relationships in which a certain pattern is constantly repeated on the somatic level.

Here we can distinguish between:

Expressive illnesses, which are easily visible from the outside, such as headaches, asthma and various eating disorders.

Reaction readiness disorders, caused by a long-standing process of deterioration on the vegetative level, such as high blood pressure and ulcers.

Somatisation disorder, which is characterised by frequently changing nervous disorders, otherwise known as vegetative dystonia.

Secondary expressive illnesses, where what matters is the advantage the patient gains from the illness. It is not the medical diagnosis that is important here but the benefit that is derived from the illness.

Thomas

The case of Thomas involves just such a secondary expressive illness. I have known Thomas since he was a friendly, open, eager, deeply sensitive, almost feminine little boy. He is highly gifted and when the illness struck (diarrhoea) he was in year eight of secondary school. It happened towards the end of an Easter holiday spent in Turkey with his parents. The diagnosis was initially traveller's diarrhoea, however it persisted when Thomas returned to school and he had to go to the toilet a few times during lessons. Questioning and teasing from fellow pupils appear to have so mortified him that the diarrhoea got worse in the mornings before he was due to go to school, making it impossible for him to leave the house. Doctors were unable to treat the diarrhoea, and Thomas was constantly off sick, until finally in December 1990 he stopped going to school altogether. After that, the diarrhoea stopped, but now it was the **fear** that it could happen again as soon as he went back to school that literally paralysed him.

Threats, for example by the Youth Welfare Office, were to no avail, no amount of ordering by school and parents, no pleading, no persuasion, not being collected by school friends and not the tragedy that played out every morning between the parents, particularly the father, and the boy. Thomas hid himself away at home, cried a lot, was afraid of being seen and of being questioned about his absence from school and vowed never again to go anywhere without his mother.

Gradually he recovered mentally; the absence from school did him good. He read and learnt a lot, but at his own pace and what and when he wanted.

However, his issues with identity and authority became more and more noticeable.

Separation anxiety and insecurity in social situations alternated with rigorous self-assertion and criticism of the existing rules of interpersonal and family coexistence. The particular target of this power game was the father, who had great expectations and demands for the boy and definitely projected his unfulfilled career aspirations onto him. The relationship with his mother was more relaxed and trusting; the child felt understood and protected by her.

Thomas's opinion of himself varies between high ideals, narcissistic delusions of grandeur and a more sober realism, in which he is aware of his dependency. He wants to know everything and be able to do everything, be a clever boy and says he "lives in his head and seems to be standing next to his body."

His relationship to his body appears to be one of indifference, as though his incipient puberty is of no use to him. The process of growing up, although in a way desirable for him, also seems to cause anxiety.

He longs to travel far away – to America, where he thinks he will find freedom, space and opportunity, far from the pressure to achieve coming from the school and his father.

What kind of **psychodynamic** lies behind Thomas's illness? Diarrhoea involves the anal area and is associated with experiences that the child went through during its anal phase (between 18 months and three years). This is when it first learns to produce something and this is an achievement, the child's first "cultural" achievement. It involves adhering to a certain rhythm as far as place and timing are concerned, which is another achievement in itself, i.e. that of adaptation. In addition, there is an important element of control (the bladder and bowels must be controlled), but also of compulsions and the exercise of power.

Now, if at some point one becomes anxious about not being able to meet the performance demands of the environment or of one's own superego, about failing or being inadequate, one produces diarrhoea instead of the achievement. It is a kind of escape route from anxiety-ridden situations, for others must react to illness and be less demanding.

The fear of failure is therefore Thomas's main problem. The teasing by his fellow pupils was only the trigger for the psychosomatic outcome of a latent, long-standing pressure to perform.

What does his horoscope say about this?

Thomas's horoscope (next page) shows an extreme polarisation:

– a very feminine, emotional, kind and dependent side with the Moon in the twelfth house, the oppositions to Venus and Neptune and the sextile to Saturn.

– the stellium composed of Uranus, Sun, Mercury, Mars and Moon Node in Scorpio, the hard achievement pole in the fifth and sixth houses. This focal area of the horoscope is only aspected in red and green, which in itself indicates very high demands on the self, overloading and energy exploitation.

Thomas's Age Point is currently transiting his Saturn in the third house. Planets in the third house (or in opposition) immediately trigger puberty and indicate on which level it will find its strongest expression. Saturn indicates that it is the body that is now undergoing a pubertal crisis that may be particularly dramatic due to Thomas's physical alienation.

The aspects to the soft planets cause him to adopt a more feminine role. However, now in puberty, he faces the difficult task of finding his sexual identity.

Thomas M.
09.11.1976, 18:45, Erding, Germany

Thomas's physical problems also disturb him intellectually. With Leo in the third house, he wants to shine and stand out. Saturn supports that with a brilliant memory. Two house cusps in Leo also symbolise considerable demands in the third house. However, Thomas is not yet able to cope with them; the pubertal body makes its own demands, which conflict with those of the mind and generate enormous psychological pressure.

Due to the Age Point transit over Saturn, Thomas also experiences an intensive phase of confrontation with the system of constraint and restriction, norms and duties that make him feel anxious. He projects them onto school, which for him is the coercive, conventional, devouring society that threatens to assault him and that he can now avoid thanks to diarrhoea.

The Saturn transit also activates a strong family dynamic: the three ego planets are connected in a Learning triangle and are very interdependent. The square to the Sun is a clear expression of the demand for achievement and success.

The Sun-Moon quincunx symbolises the confrontation with the father and also an Oedipal complex. Although Thomas has long felt superior to him in terms of knowledge and intelligence, he is still afraid of not being able to meet his expectations.

The Moon-Saturn sextile expresses his primary maternal bond and the other aspect to Neptune a great longing for love.

In his current situation, Thomas needs protection and he regresses to the age of a pre-schooler who is unable to go anywhere without his mother. A desperate situation!

The Moon as tension ruler in the twelfth house has little chance of having its needs met.

Extremely sensitive and vulnerable, he has a constant need for solitude in which to process the excitement of the environment and regenerate his psychic strength.

He is also confronted by oppositions to Venus and Neptune, which greatly influence the theme of love.

Neptune has a strong affinity with the Moon, but a very different approach to love. Neptune as a transpersonal planet has a strong idea of what ideal love should be like, completely unburdened by the ego. Situated near the DC, it is aware of the demands of the environment and is always prepared to fulfil them and be kind.

However, the Moon as ego planet has personal aspirations and legitimate demands for love, which conflict with Neptune's goals.

Neptune wants to assert them in the opposition and wants the Moon to make a sacrifice. There is a discrepancy between ideal and reality! The Moon suffers and as love is rarely experienced in the ideal form as required by Neptune, disappointment and hurt almost certainly flow from its opening to the You.

The Moon-Venus opposition is also conflict-ridden. Venus is a subpersonal planet, lying below the ego, which manifests the natural law of survival and harmony. When put under pressure, it needs harmony at any price. The environment sets the benchmark, and the You is particularly pronounced in Thomas's case, as Venus lies almost exactly on the DC.

With Neptune it shares the longing for peace, and need for the You, although on different levels. The Moon's claims and needs are ignored though and it sulks because it has to make sacrifices.

The position of Venus and Neptune in the vicinity of the DC explains Thomas's vulnerability. His loving openness towards his fellow pupils is met with teasing and ridicule because he has diarrhoea. His diarrhoea becomes a source of shame, self-esteem suffers and he is mercilessly exposed. There is also an element of narcissism involved, a particular ego weakness that one would nevertheless not suspect with a Sun-Mars conjunction, and which he can probably not yet even live out.

The Moon is also attached by three quincunxes to the achievement pole of the horoscope. This Gemini-Scorpio axis (corresponding to houses 3-8) is called the Academic axis, also the axis of the "Intellectual Mafia".

Gemini is associated with learning and teaching, and Scorpio with societal structures and their laws and requirements. This axis is responsible for setting academic standards and is the home of doctrines and examination norms. The fixed nature of Scorpio exerts enormous pressure on mutable Gemini. Until the eighth year of school, Thomas was ambitious and dynamic and successfully met the demands of the "mafia". The Moon in the twelfth house can no longer tolerate this pressure though, it suffers, lets everything go and regresses.

The diarrhoea, or the fear of it, lasts for a year. The initial harmless traveller's diarrhoea satisfied the unconscious and found open doors in the psyche. During this period, the Age Point square to Uranus disappears, triggering the psychosomatic process.

Uranus and the whole stellium are situated in Scorpio. According to an esoteric law of nature, a person's strongest place is also their weakest. The strongest point can easily become excessive and overshoot, when it turns into the opposite and becomes the weakest point.

Here is the manifestation level of Thomas's problems: Scorpio wants achievements, but is also associated with elimination (physical and mental) and with the reproductive organs.

Here again, all three levels of the personality are involved: the subpersonal, transpersonal and ego levels.

Mars and Mercury work on the organic, subpersonal level and are the driver for Thomas's motivation, the motor, verbal instrument for action and expression. The Sun as an ego planet bases its self-esteem on them, therefore being completely reliant on the successes of Mars and Mercury. The latter may be particularly painful for a Sun that is almost at the Low Point. It is not only about fulfilling the demands of the environment, but also the very high demands imposed by the self. Scorpio children are often precocious, and are therefore very prone to this.

Along with the conjunction to Mercury, Mars has an opposition to Jupiter. Of the two possibilities, the conjunction is automatically selected, which means the excavating and penetration of the "knowledge clusters" and thereby being filled by Mercury. However, Jupiter in the twelfth house wants to keep its distance as observer in order to activate its own perceptive faculties, thus creating an alternative to the existing way of doing things. Thomas already seems to sense this, as he avoids school and only wants to study by himself.

The activation of Uranus by the Age Point square may also play a role here. As it has already triggered the diarrhoea (an action still below the threshold of consciousness), its combination with the Moon Node indicates a potentially life-determining development.

Uranus forms a conjunction with the Moon Node which, also in Scorpio, is otherwise unaspected. Unaspected role model planets are programmed by the environment, led by others and turn into superegos. Thomas is guided by the ideal concept that he is a clever boy. He has been told this repeatedly and therefore great expectations were made of him. However, the Moon Node requires a development here, to detach itself from the superego and to go its own way – not to blindly follow the pressure of the academic axis but to relate consciously to it. It may be difficult for a fifteen year-old boy, but he already has some experience of rebellion.

Pluto lies shortly before the fifth house cusp. It offers an alternative way of coping with the Moon-Neptune opposition, by hinting at personal development, personal creativity and personal goals. Here he can entertain the idea of going out into the world by himself and wants to disengage step by step from his dependency on love. His dream is to go to America!

Suggested Solutions

Thomas actually did go to America with his parents during the last school holidays!

Things went very well for him there, he felt good about himself and was very motivated to retake the eighth class he missed, to attend school, learn a profession and then emigrate to America.

However, after only four days back at school he had already lost the will to start again.

According to his comments, as soon as he woke up he was stricken by a terrible fear that weighed down on him like a mountain and paralysed all his strength. He cannot see any way out of the dilemmas of school attendance – school refusal, achievement expectations – fear of failure. On the contrary, he is filled with hopelessness, his crisis appears to be more than just temporary and he is starting to suffer from depression.

I think that Thomas should deal with his body for once. Jupiter's powers of observation should allow him to perceive, learn to understand and get to grips with it. That is the theme of his puberty with Saturn in the 3rd house.

The acceptance of his own body is also very important in view of the strong intellectual axis, so that a balance is created between the energies and he does not lose touch with reality.

Thomas should live in the open air, test his strength, climb trees and jump in the water, go hiking in a group and experience any form of creativity.

Perhaps Thomas should also move out of his parent's house for a while and go to boarding school – my suggestion would be a Rudolf Steiner school – in order to live with people of his own age. At home he cannot avoid being confronted with the fear of failure, feelings of guilt and frustration – both his own and his parents'.

However, in any case, Thomas should go to a good therapist who is able to understand the complexity of his problem: the conflicting themes of love and detachment, desire to achieve and aggressive tendencies, his serious problems with identity and authority, his fear and desperation.

At the threshold of adulthood, he needs help that will encourage him to find and go his way, that will catch him in his time of need, that will support his self-affirmation and self-belief and will enable him to be mentally and physically healthy again.

Epilogue

Since mid-October, Thomas has been in a clinic at Starnberger Lake that was especially founded for fourteen to eighteen year olds who have similar problems.

As well as therapy and a lot of sports activities, there is also teaching, first at home and, after sufficient psychological stabilisation, in the neighbouring secondary school. For one year, the health insurance will pay for all costs, after which his progress will be reviewed.

The problem here is Thomas himself, who is fighting with all the means at his disposal, including threats of suicide, to stop himself from being taken to the clinic, or from leaving his "nest".

When the Sweet Things in Life make us Ill

Diabetes in the Horoscope

Birgit Braun

First published in AstroLog Issue 147, September 2005

According to Thorwald Dethlefsen and Rüdiger Dahlke, we can view illness as a lack of harmony that destabilises the previously existing order. This disturbance of harmony initially takes place in the consciousness and is then expressed physically. Dethlefsen and Dahlke see the body as the level on which all the processes and changes that take place in the consciousness are manifested or implemented. This approach corresponds roughly to the psychosomatic model, except that Dethlefsen and Dahlke apply it to all symptoms without exception. (*Krankheit als Weg*, pages 18/19).

We should therefore be able to see every illness as an imbalance in the horoscope, as it, and the aspect pattern in particular, is a symbolic image of the human consciousness. Medical astrology has always followed this approach. Let us take the example of diabetes. Although this is not a psychosomatic illness in the narrow medical sense, I wanted to find out whether psychological similarities could be found in the horoscopes of affected people.

Diabetes is a metabolic disorder characterised by insulin deficiency due to partial or total inhibition of the body's own insulin production in the pancreas. Insulin is a hormone required by our bodies, both to metabolise carbohydrates to give energy and for fat metabolism.

Insulin deficiency leads among other things to reduced sugar absorption by the body cells and increased sugar outside the cells. This means that there is too much sugar in the blood (raised blood sugar level) and too little inside the cells, where it is really needed. The excess sugar is eliminated in the urine via the kidneys. This altered metabolism can lead to:

a) **Early Symptoms**
   Thirst, frequent urination, itching, weight loss, tiredness, impaired vision, frequent infections, slow-healing wounds.

b) **Late Symptoms**
   Circulatory disorders, retinal disorders (eye), kidney damage, coronary sclerosis, heart attack, cerebral sclerosis, nerve damage, muscle cramps (calves).

There are two types of diabetes: types I and II. Type I, characterised by total insulin deficiency, usually appears in childhood or youth. Possible triggers are an inherited tendency, viral illnesses, autoimmune processes and stress caused by pollutants and medication. Before the introduction of insulin therapy in 1922, type I diabetes was nearly always fatal. Sufferers must inject themselves with insulin daily.

Type II diabetes is characterised by a relative insulin deficiency and usually appears with increasing age. It is mainly caused by bad diet (too much fatty and sweet food, too much alcohol) and a lack of exercise. The pancreas is overloaded by increased insulin production due to the excessive and unsuitable diet. However, if these risk factors are avoided by adopting a good diet and taking sufficient exercise, the need for medication can be reduced or eliminated altogether.

Rüdiger Dahlke's description of diabetes in his book *Krankheit als Symbol* illustrates the insulin problem on a psychological level as being *"not receptive to romance (the cells do not open themselves up to glucose); desire to enjoy sweet things (love) and the dolce vita, together with the inability to accept love; not accepting the sweetness of life or allowing it to enter one's innermost being (cells); not allowing oneself to fall in love; unacknowledged desire for fulfilment in love; not trusting oneself to be active in romantic matters."* And in *Krankheit als Weg*: *"Behind the desire of the diabetic to want to enjoy sweet things, and the simultaneous inability to assimilate sugar and absorb it into their own cells, lies the unacknowledged desire for fulfilment in love, coupled with the inability to accept love."*

Dahlke links diabetes to the planetary principle of Venus. Jane Ridder-Patrick also suggests a connection with Venus and Jupiter in her book *A Handbook of Medical Astrology*.

Venus corresponds to the ability to assimilate substances. Using the sense of taste, it selects from the substances available those that are suitable and likely to bring harmony.

Jupiter possesses a sensitivity for right proportion, and the ability to judge, to know what makes us happy and enables us to grow. Biologically, Jupiter has an affinity with the metabolism, for the intake of fats allows the body to grow.

Dahlke's watchword "love", immediately makes us think of the Moon and Neptune, personal and transpersonal love. The Moon experiences self-affirmation through human contact and tender loving care. It is dependent for the satisfaction of its emotional needs on contact with outside objects and other people. The Moon searches for satisfaction by being loved.

Neptune symbolises our most ideal concept of love between living things. With this in mind, it equips us with a refined awareness and allows us to feel an empathetic, loving connection with all creation. Neptune wants to express unconditional love.

Below I present five horoscopes of people who already suffered from type I diabetes in childhood or youth. Their bodies produce no insulin. The data come from Lois Rodden's Astrodatabank. The position of the minor planet Chiron can also be considered, as it is often involved in the appearance of illness, but it is not included in the aspect pattern, which would distort the Huber-researched interpretation of the aspect pattern. Verena Bachmann writes about Chiron as follows: *"Chiron aspects in the horoscope may indicate specific physical illnesses as well as mental injuries. Chronic processes and irreversible physical injuries are associated with Chiron. It encourages us to accept and learn to live with physical suffering instead of fighting against it."*

Example 1

This woman was diagnosed with Type I diabetes in 1954 at age 7. At age 24 (July 1971), she went blind, a dreaded side effect of this illness.

There is an opposition between Venus and Jupiter at the Low Point of the Encounter axis in an Irritation triangle with Uranus. Moon lies square Neptune in different quadrilaterals. The Moon in particular has a number of aspects to process. In addition, Chiron is near the AC, where it could indicate a fundamental, constitutional weakness, where imbalances in consciousness could easily be expressed on the physical level.

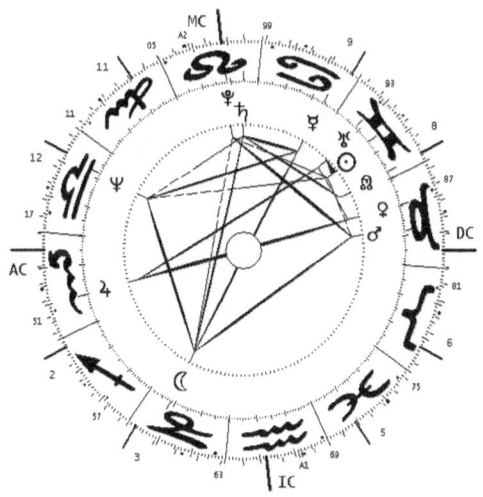

Example 1 Woman
05.06.1947, 16:31, Salt Lake City, Utah, USA

At age 7, the AP was around 8° Sagittarius in the 2nd House, sextile Neptune and semi-sextile Moon. At 24, the AP was situated at around 9° Pisces, sextile Moon and quincunx Neptune.

Venus/Jupiter directly indicate a "pleasure problem", a lack of harmony between the love of life and the love of pleasure, which would primarily be expressed in social situations. This can indicate frustration in social situations, e.g. she may feel overlooked or that her femininity is not really appreciated. Uranus is connected only via one-way conjunction with Sun with the rest of the aspect pattern; otherwise the Irritation figure is detached. This triangle is prone to exaggeration, restlessness and excited activity, which is hard to coordinate via the LP, or is initially not perceived by those responsible for her upbringing. The energy stored in the opposition looks to Uranus in the green aspect for a way to resolve the state of mutual pressure and blockage (opposition) and the rigid behaviour this causes. Uranus urgently longs to be released from this tension. This figure contains a tendency to outbursts of anger (Mars is also at the DC), which however due to the LP position tend to be diffused by the environment or not taken seriously, which could increase the frustration. They could also make romantic relationships difficult or even impossible (Mars at the DC square Pluto).

There is a square between Moon and Neptune in an Achievement triangle with Mercury as part of two quadrilateral figures with Saturn, the Sun and Mars. This partial aspect is likewise an indication of disappointment in love, as her possibly excessive demands for love are not met. The predominantly red-green aspect colour indicates great pressure; no solution and harmonisation seem achievable, which is a source of constant frustration and irritation for the sensitive theme. A disappointment in love or rejection in childhood could have been the trigger for the illness, as at the time of diagnosis Moon and Neptune were activated by the AP.

Example 2

This woman's type I diabetes was diagnosed at the end of December 1983.

There is a close conjunction between Venus and Sun, which means that her self-confidence is closely identified with the Venus theme, indicating a great need for harmony. Both are in opposition to Pluto and Moon Node, which could indicate reflex and exaggerated behavioural

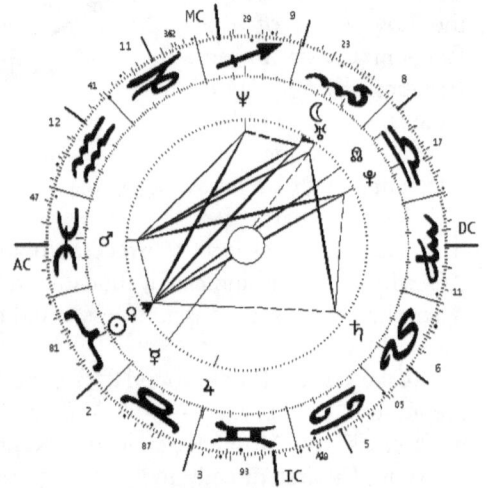

Example 2 Woman
06.04.1977, 04:24, Ottawa, Canada

mechanisms related to the need for harmony. Shortly after the 1st house LP, in the shadow of the 2nd house cusp, a self-esteem problem is indicated, as is the refusal to let go of the "sweet and tasty things" of the Sun/Venus conjunction. Mars at the AC on the other hand shows an aggressive feisty approach, although its presence in Pisces and square Neptune may subdue this somewhat.

Jupiter is unaspected at the sign border between Taurus and Gemini and therefore, at least in the first half of life, may not be particularly helpful in gaining a balanced perspective on circumstances.

Sun and Venus are also in a figure with Moon and Neptune. They form an [incomplete] Trampoline with Mars at the AC, which reveals great sensitivity and the need to continually adjust to new situations. This flexibility may be compromised by the retrograde Venus in the shadow of the 2nd house cusp and in opposition to Pluto and Moon Node.

The location of the "love" planets, Moon and Neptune, at the LP could indicate "frustration experiences", as in Example 1, rejection or being passed over. Keeping healthy is of fundamental importance for Saturn on the 6th house cusp. Saturn in this position could indicate an inherent disposition to illness, hence the need for the body to be treated with the greatest care and attention. Illness can shake Saturn's self-confidence, especially as here it may be sensitive to challenge from the square from Uranus in the 'death and rebirth' 8th house.

The diagnosis was made exactly at the time the AP transited Chiron and was semi-sextile to Jupiter.

Example 3

Type I diabetes was diagnosed at age 9. At age 24 in 1968, gradual blindness set in as an additional complication.

Here Venus is strongly aspected by Neptune and Moon, as well as Mars/Uranus and Pluto/Moon Node. The Moon lies at the MC quincunx to Neptune. Jupiter is at the AC sextile Saturn and is otherwise unconnected to the rest of the aspect pattern. The illness was noticed at the AP transit of Neptune in the 2nd house (self-esteem!). A life theme was probably also triggered

Example 3 Woman
31.01.1944, 19:00, Vancouver, Ottawa, Canada

here. The incipient blindness is denoted by an AP trine to Jupiter at the AC. The previous year, it was opposite the weakly connected Saturn (possible indication of a weak physical constitution).

The Trawler figure formed by Venus, Moon, Mars/Uranus and Neptune, shows a certain laziness, a rather acquisitive attitude with the desire not to let go of the things one has collected. The Oscillo figure between Venus, Moon, Mars/Uranus and Pluto/Moon Node makes her react very sensitively to various kinds of vibrations and environmental stimuli.

The Moon is at the focal point of an Achievement triangle formed with Sun and Pluto/Moon Node. This denotes a theme of achievement: love and affection must be worked for. At the MC, all eyes rest on this Moon, it could feel under great pressure to always be loved and well received. Mars/Uranus forms a compensative pole to the opposition. This again makes it obvious that there is an achievement mentality (achievement brings harmony and balance). Also the whole quadrilateral Animated figure is concerned with achievement and the acquisition of substance.

These three examples show an astonishingly high degree of consistency with Rudiger Dahlke's theories and their transfer into the symbolism of astrological psychology. It is true that all three patients are female and therefore naturally more closely in touch with the Venus theme than men. For this reason I have also examined the horoscopes of two men.

Example 4

The diagnosis was made almost exactly on this man's 21st birthday.

Venus is in a linear figure with Uranus, detached from the rest of the aspect pattern. The Moon depends on a wide conjunction with Sun/Mercury. These two factors are not very strongly connected and therefore may not be that accessible to the horoscope owner However, there is a conjunction between

Example 4 Man
17.04.1958, 21:54, Washington D.C., USA

Jupiter and the rising Moon Node and Neptune, both of which have an expansive effect (the North Node is usually associated with Jupiter-like qualities), and could indicate an excess of Jupiter. They are grouped around the 11th house LP and again denote rather introverted forces, which were hardly, if at all, stimulated by his environment during his youth. They are also in opposition to the subjective intellect, or desire to analyse of Sun/Mercury in house 5. The contradiction between expansive good faith and healthy rationality, perhaps even profound thought (Mercury is retrograde and aspected to Pluto and Saturn), is however repressed by the inclusion of a large blue pentagon. In general, the red-blue pentagon can lead to an 'either-or', or 'all or nothing' attitude, which is the very antithesis of unconditional love.

At the time of diagnosis, the AP was quincunx Neptune, which again could indicate that the love theme was the disease trigger. Neptune is also connected with the libido planet Mars, which is in close conjunction with Chiron.

Example 5

This boy came down with Type I diabetes at age 7.

At that time AP was sextile Venus, approaching opposition to the Uranus/Neptune conjunction in the 8th house. Venus is in conjunction to the Sun just before the 12th house cusp with a one-way trine to Uranus/Neptune and a one-way square to Saturn, making a retrograde Learning triangle. Moon and Jupiter are both in the 4th house, although not directly connected to Venus or Neptune. Mars, the libido planet, is aspected to Jupiter and Moon.

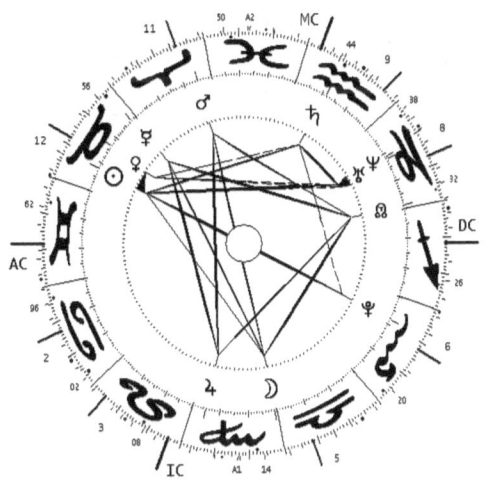

Example 5 Boy
12.05.1992, 07:42, Richmond, VA/USA

The aspect pattern is at first sight confusing, and it is not easy to clearly make out the lines. Moon is connected with Mars and the descending Moon Node in an Achievement triangle, which as a whole, were we to also to draw in the rising Moon Node, produces a large quadrilateral with a karmic character which makes it difficult to change the way one does things. The Moon-Mars opposition (compulsive love, defiance) probably means that unreflective behaviour rooted deep in the consciousness is constantly repeated. The expansion principle of Jupiter creates the possibility for the release of tension via the quincunx to Mars and via the trine to the rising Moon Node. As well as the Learning triangle, Venus is also weakly attached to the Achievement triangle between Sun, Saturn and Pluto, which could show a rigid achievement orientation that would tend to preclude sensitivity and the love of pleasure. These factors could all together also indicate a problem with pleasure or even with love, however this is not so clearly indicated here as in the other examples.

It is striking that in all five horoscopes the Venus principle is connected to the Neptune principle, either by direct aspects or by sign/house position (Venus in Pisces or 12th house, Neptune in Libra or 2nd/7th house).

We see that Dahlke and Dethlefsen's diabetes theories are satisfactorily borne out by the example horoscopes, even though five is naturally not enough to constitute a thorough statistical sample.

¤ ¤ ¤ ¤ ¤

The Tarot and Astrological Psychology

Similarities between the Trump Cards as an Analogy of the Zodiac

Ruth Schmidhauser

First published in AstroLog Issue 111, August 1999

There are 78 tarot cards in total, 22 of which form the major arcana or trump cards. The major arcana depict man's developmental stages in striking illustrations.

The 56 cards of the minor arcana are grouped into 4 suits, each of which corresponds to an element:

      Pentacles: earth
      Cups: water
      Wands: fire
      Swords: air

The minor arcana therefore reveal how the different developmental stages are experienced in the different elements.

The following cards belong to each suit:
      2-10
      trumps: Jack
                 Cavalier/Knight
                 Queen
                 King
      Ace

Correspondence with Astrological Psychology

Cards 2-10: The Houses
They describe external situations and events. Growth through the experiences that life brings.

Trump cards: The Zodiac
They describe inner insights, experiences and abilities. Growth though self-observation, bodily signals, etc.

Ace:
The developmental peak of the element concerned. Acceptance of one's own constitution. Energetic flow of elements with associated wellbeing.

Trump cards:

Page: Mutable cross.
His posture and gestures correspond to the mutable cross.

Queen: Fixed cross.
The queen represents the feminine quality of the element. She is devoted and receptive.

King: Cardinal cross
The king represents the masculine quality of the element. He is a dynamic leader, with sceptre in hand. He is a goal-setter.

Knight:
Unlike the other trump cards, all cavaliers sit on a horse and pull on the reins with their left hand to bring their mount to a halt.

The horse symbolises the inner drives. The cavaliers process old emotional patterns (e.g. fears), for which more time is required. They are not associated with any cross; they 'ride' back and forth between the other trump cards that represent the element in its respective cross.

Cavaliers show the moment of weakness or the eruption of unconscious, still unresolved experiences. In playing card decks, there are no cavaliers; there are Jacks (below), Queens (above) and Kings.

The King of Wands: Aries

Aries can suffer from excessive energy, impatience or impulsiveness. Its task is to tame this Martian impatience in order to be able to think before acting.

KÖNIG der STÄBE

Mercury, its esoteric ruler, gives it the ability to think before acting, which could enable it to act as a spiritual pioneer.

The tamed impatience of Aries can be seen in the King of Wands. Thanks to his maturity, he is able to control himself and his strong will allows him to be the master of his own life. The King of Wands is the image of the mature Aries who channels his strength in order to accomplish his desired goals, and is aware of his responsibility.

The Queen of Pentacles: Taurus

Taurus may be inflexible, stubborn and excessively acquisitive and likes to keep everything under control. Its task is to get in touch with nature, to experience itself as part of nature in order to get in touch with its elemental power.

KÖNIGIN der MÜNZEN

Its esoteric ruler is Vulcan, a subtle planet whose properties are similar to those of the volcanoes we see here on earth. An active volcano reveals the elemental power of the Earth's interior. This is also what should happen to Taurus: it must discover the power of nature, of mother Earth, within itself in order to gain complete confidence.

The Queen of Pentacles is an image of devotion and of harmony with flourishing nature, and therefore with confidence. The great throne and the roses decorating it symbolise her power, as do her red clothes. The Queen of Pentacles represents the mature Taurus, who is at one with nature and who no longer needs to cling on to her resources.

The Page of Swords: Gemini

Gemini is prone to absent-mindedness, a lack of focus or the inability to form an opinion. His task is to unite the two souls within his single body in order to find lasting truths, so that he no longer embraces new ideas every day like a weathervane.

BUBE der SCHWERTER

His esoteric ruler is Venus, which wants to make him more discriminating so that he can find an inner harmony based on a permanent value system against which new information can be checked. This would give him inner security and allow him to pass on his knowledge.

The Page of Swords enthusiastically and easily separates what is important from what is not, until the clouds in the sky become more and more distant. The Page of Swords is the image of the mature Gemini, who has his feet on the ground and finds it easy to take decisions and pass on what he knows.

The King of Cups: Cancer

Cancer can suffer from moodiness, hypersensitivity and emotional dependency. His task is to overcome his sensitivity and neediness in order to have a big heart for the people around him.

The esoteric ruler is Neptune, who wants to guide him to the trusting, unbiased love that can grow out of self-love. This will enable Cancer to feel loved, accepted and valued and be able to respect and love others non-judgementally, thereby activating his self healing powers.

The King of Cups gives the impression of strength and stability. He has tamed his own desires, taken the sceptre in his hand and now offers his cup. We can still see in his face how hard his task is. The King of Cups represents the mature Cancer who no longer gets bogged down in his feelings and who is now able to offer true love.

The Queen of Wands: Leo

Leo is prone to pomposity, vanity and the need for approval. Its task is to be generous instead of pompous, warm-hearted instead of vain.

Its esoteric ruler, the Sun, wants to teach it how to be radiant and charismatic. Life on our planet is only possible thanks to the sun's warmth. It wants to give Leo a warm, non-judgemental charisma that is a product of joy and gratitude.

The Queen of Wands is powerful and telepathic and, with the sunflower, places herself at the service of life, which means that she no longer expects everything to revolve around her.

She offers warmth and protection for those who seek it. The Queen of Wands represents the open heart and stability of the mature Leo.

The Page of Pentacles: Virgo

Virgo is prone to excessive tidiness, perfectionism or anxiety. His task is to overcome anxiety and a tendency to be critical in order to develop his special healing abilities.

His esoteric ruler is the Moon, who can provide him with emotional fulfilment once he finds a meaningful task in which his ability to heal (make whole) can be brought to bear.

The Page of Pentacles offers up his coin (abilities) with great love and devotion. He is in harmony with himself and the environment. This is the mature Virgo, who is emotionally fulfilled and is not afraid to offer and put his resources at the disposal of others.

The King of Swords: Libra

Libra is prone to indecisiveness, aestheticism and excessive diplomacy. Its task is to find a balance between the internal and external in order to avoid getting bogged down in superficial matters and to allow its aesthetic sensibilities to bring joy to itself and to others.

Its esoteric ruler is Uranus, which wants to show that intuition can lead it to the security of knowing the truth, thus enabling it to exercise the judgement of Solomon. This inner security would allow it to make room for beauty, as it would not have to waste its energy in superficial matters.

The King of Swords sits up straight, with complete dignity and clarity. His sword points slightly to the right. His decision-making ability allows him to be a man of action. The ring on his left hand is his connection with all that is beautiful. The King of Swords corresponds to the refined Libra, whose inner security enables him to adopt this upright posture.

The Queen of Cups: Scorpio

Scorpio is prone to pessimism, pedantry and jealousy. His task is to become so changed in a process of death and rebirth that he can accept water (emotions) and let it flow, and stop following stale ideas and being so controlled.

His esoteric ruler is Mars, the warrior, who enables Scorpio to win the war against his fears by facing life's challenges and not trying to avoid them by being controlling. This eventually allows him to rise like a phoenix from the ashes of his old habits and belief systems.

The Queen of Cups gazes lovingly at the cup that she has created. She is the very embodiment of flow and harmony. The Queen of Cups represents the mature Scorpio, who is able to fully exploit the healing power of water for the purposes of creativity and healing.

The Page of Wands: Sagittarius

Sagittarius may have an excessive desire for independence, which can give him problems with authority; he may also have the impression that he knows better than others. His task is to seek the truth, to find it, to put it into practice in life and to keep on looking until he gains wisdom.

His esoteric ruler is the Earth, which can give him the ability to discriminate, if his truth is organic and may also be transferable. It enables him to seek the truth not only in the outside world but also within himself.

The Page of Wands is very enterprising, yet stands with both feet on the ground and grasps his wand with both hands. He is ready for the search, for adventure and therefore able to maintain contact with the Earth. The Page of Wands represents the mature Sagittarius, who no longer allows himself to be carried away by his enthusiasm and has recognised the three-dimensional nature of truth.

The King of Pentacles: Capricorn

Capricorn can suffer from isolation if he follows his goals too tenaciously, making him appear cold and unapproachable to others. His task is to draw strength from nature and as he accomplishes his goals to become softer and softer until he is finally able to offer support to other people.

His esoteric ruler is Saturn, which enables him to be as firm as a rock and yet still be maternally protective. His individuality and stability will enable him to lead others and show them the way.

The King of Pentacles sits surrounded by carefully pruned greenery, his facial expression is soft and caring, if somewhat distant. Nature flourishes around him, as his care is borne of respect. The King of Pentacles represents the mature Capricorn, who turns towards other living things with love, respect and great responsibility.

The Queen of Swords: Aquarius

Aquarius can suffer from arrogance, aloofness and pure mental genius. His task is to develop his intuition and the power of his heart as well as his mind. His esoteric ruler is Jupiter, who wants to guide him towards sensory alertness, which will eventually enable him to think with his heart and his head, thus making all dimensions accessible to him.

The Queen of Swords has freed herself from the chains of the intellect; her head is above the clouds and her thoughts can flutter like butterflies. The Queen of Swords represents the mature Aquarius, who has overcome her excessive intellectuality in favour of the lightness of an open heart.

The Page of Cups: Pisces

Pisces is prone to excessive adaptability, sensitivity or willingness to make sacrifices. His task is not to sacrifice himself for others but to serve as a channel between heaven and Earth. He is the only zodiac sign to have a connection between the two cups, which represent the earthly and the celestial levels. His esoteric ruler is none other than Pluto, which explains the enormous potency of Pisces. Pluto can enable Pisces to receive messages from the forces of light and make them accessible to other people, thus also making a special dimension of healing possible.

The Page of Cups appears strong and self-assured; he has confidence in the heavenly levels that have equipped him with special perception so that he can communicate with the fish in the cup, which he does with great curiosity and love. The Page of Cups shows the mature Pisces who is guided by his feelings and in touch with the divine level, enabling him to radiate strength and security and to understand the language of the universe.

◻ ◻ ◻ ◻ ◻

Images of Man

The Seven Bach Flower Groups and the Twelve Astrological Houses

Christian U. Vogel

First published in AstroLog Issues 148-151, November 2005 - May 2006

Basis and Objective of this Article

Bach Flower Therapy is based on a system of 38 basic mental states developed by the English doctor and herbalist Dr. Edward Bach (1886-1936), to which correspond the essences of spring water and 37 flowers, grasses, bushes and trees. They form an open system of 38 energies that can be combined with each other as desired. There are no essences that must be used together and none that are mutually exclusive; no limit as to how long they may be taken, etc. Their prescription in therapy is a highly subjective process, requiring great attentiveness and accuracy and the deepest possible understanding of the individual flowers, their spheres of influence and their different levels. Bach divided the 38 essences into seven thematic groups.

Astrology is also a system whose elements (aspects, planets, signs, houses) are admittedly subject to certain rules, but there are an infinite number of complex combinations within the scope of these rules. Interpreting these combinations and working with the subjects of the horoscopes is also a process of the highest subjectivity and requires attentiveness and accuracy and the greatest possible understanding of stars and people. Astrology is based on the number 12; there are 12 signs and 12 houses.

The mental states described by Edward Bach form the emotional and mental building blocks that make up our conscious and unconscious minds. They are archetypal models common to all people – and to a greater or lesser extent also to all other living creatures. States that are very similar to the themes of the Bach Flower remedies are frequently found in horoscopes, in all areas from aspect pattern to houses and from the first to the last stage of the developmental path.

Working with both systems involves a combination of both science and art – the art of healing.

Juxtaposing these two systems – which is the objective of this paper – combining them in a set way, should never lead to any formulae such as "if x, then take y." This would mean forcing them into a Procrustean Bed, which as we know meant death for those involved. Instead we should try to sense something of the energy that is generated when two living systems come so close together that sparks of awareness start to fly and energy starts to flow between them. I used my intuition in choosing how to link the seven flower groups with the twelve houses. Whether this attribution is "correct" must be demonstrated to the reader by the affinity between the flower principles and house themes and by the power of the images produced by these connections.

Edward Bach and Astrology

In his published writings, Edward Bach makes a few references to astrology. He is on the one hand convinced of the potential of astrology to be an important aid in his work with flower remedies, and that his flower therapy will act as "a contribution to the purification and understanding of astrology" (1). Here he is of course talking about the state of astrology in the 1930s, which to modern astrologers resembles the darkest middle ages, and one in which astrology was most definitely in need of "purifying".

On the other hand though, Bach considered the existing knowledge of the connections between flowers and stars to be too tenuous to be made public. The sophisticated approach to the human psyche via the horoscope afforded by astrological psychology now allows us to consolidate and expand this knowledge.

Bach also feared that a wall of theories might be erected between healer and patient, rather than a simple, direct identification and understanding of the patient's state of mind. A familiar feeling for any therapist who has experienced how easy it is for the mind to wander and start thinking about the right flowers or the appropriate constellation in the horoscope rather than focusing on the patient.

Connecting Principles: Intuition, Analogy, Synchronicity

Astrology and Bach Flower Therapy are systems that seek insight and healing for the soul and by the soul. Both do this in ways that run counter to modern science, at least insofar as it is applied today. Both involve an ultimately magical concept that is based less on logical causal chains than on analogies and contexts, on associations and synchronicities, in line with Hermes Trismegistus' famous "as above, so below", not the theory of the law of the excluded third. It is an extremely open concept of "both...and", and not "either ... or".

In his search for the right flowers for his "new medicine", Bach allowed himself to be guided not by his vast knowledge of agents and traditional applications but by his inner eye, by the echo that a plant evoked in his soul. Their habitat, their colour and shape, the way they flowered and decayed were not studied with his analytical intellect but with the more profound objectivity of his sentient soul, with which he also identified the connections between these plants and the mental and physical suffering of the people he was trying to cure.

Only in a second stage does this "magic" medicine become a form of alternative medicine, in that its effect on patients is observed as holistically as possible. This means there is not simply an expectation of a specific, precisely defined effect, but rather an observation of any effect at all that could be viewed as a step along the path to recovery, be it on the physical or the mental level. From this process of inner contemplation and external observation emerged a typology of 38 "archetypal" states of mind or types of reaction, allowing every possible mental state to be both described and appropriately treated.

Astrology has also since its inception involved a combination of two different processes. Firstly the intuitive understanding of what cannot be grasped intellectually, since the only way it can be depicted is in symbols (the signs of the zodiac). Secondly, the accurate observation of heavenly bodies and their measurable paths and of people and their ways that can only be recounted.

Although it is possible to measure the position of the planets in houses and signs and their angle to each other with great accuracy and describe them in mathematical and geometrical language, the way in which the individual experiences "his star of destiny" cannot be calculated, it can only be recounted and its true profundity can only be grasped in the language of symbols. It is the act of becoming aware, of naming, which triggers a process of healing.

In practice, it is quite rare for me to rely only on my intellect or intuition in composing essences. In most cases, I allow the client to spontaneously and blindly pull between one and three bottles out of a basket containing all 38 essences. This highly unscientific and almost indecently simple method of spontaneous selection has proved to be extremely reliable and accurate in the 15 years I have been working on an almost daily basis with Bach Flowers. It also enables me to concentrate totally on the conversation with the person sitting in front of me, on their story and on helping them to understand what these particular flowers have to say to them at this particular moment.

In collaboration with the founder of modern quantum physics, Wolfgang Pauli, C.G. Jung developed the term 'synchronicity' or – as Pauli wanted to call it – meaningful coincidence (2). The Exclusion Principle formulated by Pauli states that subatomic particles with asymmetrical movement patterns are kept separate from the energy field of particles with symmetrical patterns. Without this principle, the cosmos would collapse into a particle soup. Neither is it caused by some kind of mutual influencing of subatomic particles, but on an acausal, abstract pattern whose effects cannot be explained by a causal 'cause and effect' mechanism. In parallel to Pauli's work on theoretical physics, Jung developed the idea of "acausal ordering" in a single field, in which world and psyche, inside and outside, I and You are no longer separate but are acausally correlated. According to Jung, substituting the causality principle with that of synchronicity is the only way to provide an adequate description of the world and the psyche.

For Jung, astrology was therefore a synchronistic phenomenon and his writings on the thousand year-old Chinese oracle the I-Ching can also be applied to the process of spontaneous selection in the case of the Bach Flowers, in which case the blindly chosen essences represent the hexagrams of the I Ching stalks, and the qualities attributed to the essences represent the interpretations attributed to the hexagrams. Jung says on this subject:

> *"But it is not up to me to objectively establish the validity of the I Ching statements... (I) therefore deal simply with the amazing fact that the qualitas occulta of the time-moment became legible by means of the hexagram of the I Ching. One is dealing with a relationship between events that is not only analogous to astrology but even essentially related to it. The moment of birth corresponds to the thrown stalks, the constellation to the hexagram and the interpretation of the constellation to the text allocated to the hexagram." (3).*

Bach Flower Therapy and Astrological Psychology

We will never know exactly why Bach divided his 38 flower essences into seven groups, and why he attributed certain flowers to certain groups. However, we can say that the flowers in each of the seven groups are all very closely connected to each other. Together they describe a certain way of reacting to the world, more comprehensively and profoundly than the individual flowers could by themselves. A single Bach Flower describes a detail, while the group shows all the different facets and possible manifestations of the problem, thus enabling a deeper understanding of the personality structures involved.

The same levels and the same trouble spots are addressed by both the astrological houses and the Bach Flower groups: we live in a set environment that makes demands of us, has expectations of us and threatens or persuades us and it is up to us to decide how to react to it.

We initially confront these external impulses not as conscious wholes but as 'split personalities'. We are split into an external person referred to by Bach as the "personality" and by C.G. Jung as the "persona", and an inner person (Bach's 'soul'), i.e. our profound structures and basic motivations that are so hard for us to understand. Astrologically, the persona corresponds to the person who is more or less trapped in their unconscious (especially represented in the house horoscope). What we call the soul in the context of this article is represented by the aspect structure of the horoscope, which represents our basic motivations. The self, the 'centre of the consciousness field' (Jung) lies between these two apparently separate parts of the personality, predominantly represented in the horoscope by the position in the signs of the zodiac of the three personality planets.

We use this self, which esotericists could call the "ego", to try to gain mastery over the inner and the outer. It deals with the external impulses (i.e. coming from the houses) and tries to gain a clear understanding of its own wishes and needs. These are strongly influenced by the mostly unconscious and therefore unconsidered impulses of the four tool planets and the three equally unconscious and unconsidered spiritual planets trapped in their superego roles. But the ego itself is just a single, discrete and well-defined part of the whole horoscope and the whole person, which therefore limits the scope both of its understanding and of its possible prevalence.

To truly become whole, we must connect with every part of our horoscope. This initially means finding out the position of the planets in the signs, then becoming aware of our aspect structure, which involves learning to integrate the empty, infinite, blank circle in the centre. For this circle represents everything in us that we cannot know or be conscious of and that is only discernable in ideas, symbols and projections. Only this circle is powerful enough to allow us to transcend the limitations of our restricted ego consciousness, leading to what Jung called the process of individuation. This means liberating ourselves both from the illusory masks of the persona and from the suction effect of unidentified unconscious images. Astrologically, this means that if we exist purely on the level of the houses (or allow ourselves to be ruled by our tool planets), we will never know how completely healthy we could be by integrating all levels of ourselves. Or, as Bach said:

> *"We must absolutely and definitely become free so that all our actions, no, even all of our thoughts, come from ourselves, thus enabling us to live and give spontaneously and only spontaneously." (4)*

Common Goal

Astrological psychology and Bach Flower therapy have very similar approaches to the description and analysis of human suffering. They also share the conviction that self-knowledge and self-realisation allow us to become healed and whole. The path within starts outside us in the astrological house system and in the infinite number of tiny reactions with which, in adapting to our environment, we also become alienated from ourselves. Bach's flower essences were intended to help us become aware of these and break them down.

This path within would not be accessible if the inside and the outside were really as different as they may at first appear. But the heavens are reflected in the smallest puddle and what is above is also below, so that which we see outside is always a reflection of what is inside. Our apparently most external reactions to our environment therefore reveal what is hidden most deeply within us. But we only see ourselves, and are only seen by others, in the distorted mirror of the projections we send onto the projection surfaces around us. The world that we see around us is therefore our own innermost self, but we do not recognise it as such.

Astrological psychology and Bach Flower therapy should lead the person on his path step by step by helping him to recognise his projections for what they are and to understand his actions as the true expression of his own being. The person is the creator and the centre of his world. By bringing the centre of his understanding of himself and the world into the middle from the periphery, which is standardised, fixated and obstructed by all manner of images, prejudices and ghosts, he redeems both himself and the world. In the empty, untouched centre of the horoscope, the little self flows into the great Self, from where it reflects an undistorted image of the true self into a new world.

The Seven Flower Groups in the Twelve Houses
In Houses 1 and 2, Flower Group 1:
For those who are afraid.
In the first two houses, the basics of the individual essence are laid down: being and having. The person takes his place in this world in the 1st house. He occupies this space by virtue of his existence; it is his first possession without which his existence would be impossible. And as a being cannot occupy a space without possessing certain qualities, the first house is the house of appearance. It attests to the nature and reality of this one individual in this world.

By manifesting itself, a being delimits itself from the rest of the cosmos. It separates itself from the infinite and defines itself and its space as separate from the You, sets boundaries and must henceforth defend its independence and space. *"Only I am myself, everything else is the other, the different, the outsider, the ultimately threatening."* This is how fear arises. By discovering that they were different individuals, Adam and Eve lost their innocence; fear, shame and guilt were awakened within them, the paradise of oneness was lost, even before God banished them from it.

With the loss of innocence, the individual is awakened and can become the creator of his own world: the first projection appears. For instead of Eve finding the origin of her actions in herself, the snake becomes the personification of evil, which she blames by her insinuations. And God joins in by cursing the snake and placing antagonism between it and man. The first enemy is born and the fear of the snake still obsesses man to the present day. But the unity between Adam and Eve is also destroyed, for he denies his guilt and tries to blame Eve. The first betrayal sows the first mistrust between people and since then, man has been a wolf to man and – as we know from Elias Canetti – can only find peace as the last survivor.

This explains why the first house is ruled by Mars, the God of War. The person is born armed to fight. Man creates weapons and armaments not as an expression of courage and vital energy, but because of his fear of others. No person, no tribe, no nation arms itself in order to attack, but instead is driven by fear and the belief in the need for self-defence. Even though appearances may lead us to think otherwise, deep down inside, every aggressor, no matter how powerful, feels attacked or at least threatened, which is the only way his behaviour can be understood. Man is born with a deep fear that unconsciously affects the way he thinks, feels, perceives and behaves.

That is why the cardinal signs are so well armed: the horns of Aries and Capricorn, the shell and pincers of Cancer and Libra's subtle manoeuvres and intrigues. In the cardinal signs the memory of the first conquest, the first occupation lives on, the memory of the fact that attack is the best form of defence, and the knowledge that a being that stops expanding is doomed to stagnation and eventual death.

In the 2nd house, this fear receives a first, apparently rational justification: the person becomes a possessor. Possessions must be fought for and defended, for they evoke envy and jealousy. Under the influence of the fear of the first house, the person cannot imagine another way of relating to his possessions. The idea of possessing and fighting for what one owns is therefore an intrinsic part of the person, with the emphasis on possession and fighting.

In contrast to the cardinal principle, the fixed principle is not concerned with expansion. It has already found its space. Taurus no longer approaches us as a warrior, rather as a bodybuilder who is interested in mass not action. The important thing now is consolidation and reproduction with the established boundaries. The bull gathers its cows around itself, always ready to defend them and its territory against possible intruders, and he reproduces. But this Venusian, lustful act gives rise to a threat on his own territory coming from his male offspring. The enjoyment of possessions creates new unrest and forces him to fight again.

Possessions are always under threat. That is why it was so important for Francis of Assisi to distance himself and his brothers from all worldly possessions. He knew that possessions have to be defended and that this defence causes fear and that it is fear that separates man from man and sets all living things against each other.

Rock Rose and Mimulus describe external fears, tangible, concrete fears that can be confronted and overcome with the courage of Aries.

Rock Rose stands for shock, for terror and panic; for states from which the person suffers without realising that as long as they last they can somehow be put into perspective. There is only fight or flight, complete akinesis, blind flight or berserk battle courage, controlled by the autonomic nervous system as it fights for survival. Mimulus, on the other hand, corresponds to the greater or lesser everyday fears of nameable things, people, situations; fears that the person hides from himself and his environment as much as possible, as they do not correspond to the image of strength and security that he would like to portray in these houses.

Cherry Plum and Aspen stand for fears that come from inside instead of being triggered by concrete, external events and correspond more to the character of Taurus.

Cherry Plum stands for Taurus' fear of the anger or desire he feels growing within himself. From the outside he still appears calm and relaxed, but something has irritated him and continues to irritate him, and he fears the moment when his self-control is no longer able to hold back the energy inside him and it will break wildly free. Aspen is the (at first still quite gentle) warning of a still unknown danger, a threat to the apparent peace, the apparently safe possessions. Taurus knows that anyone with possessions is threatened, so that the nervous system is therefore hyper vigilant under its "thick skin" and is sometimes barely able to distinguish between real and imaginary threats.

Red Chestnut helps Taurus to free itself from its emotional connections to people and things. It is the flower that helps to raise our consciousness and strength above the restricting limitations of our fears, desires, cravings and greed (Venus) into the free, consciously acting level of the heart (Vulcan). We are then no longer guided by the heaviness of our emotions that oppress others and ourselves, but by the constructive deployment of our all-warming fire.

In Houses 3 and 4, Flower Group 3

For those who show insufficient interest in present circumstances.

Once we have passed through the first two houses and found our appearance and space, our personalities are moulded by the collective in the next two houses. Once the highly egocentric energy of Aries and Taurus has enabled us to be incarnated in the world and to find our place as an independent, separate being, we now consciously encounter the world that we have previously only experienced as "the other". The You should now emerge from the unfamiliar and threatening non-self.

In the Gemini house, the unicellular organism splits into two and the I encounters the You. The I still remains cautiously on his own side of the IC/MC axis, but at least starts to perceive the You from a distance, to observe, imitate and exchange information. This is his first experience with society and its rules and demands and he finds out how different it is for the first time. He is no longer a law unto himself. The sphere in which he is his own lord and master has been reduced.

The experience of irritation and frustration is now added to the fear and readiness to fight of the first two houses. The I discovers that the world is occupied by people and opinions, by groups and their ideas that while opening up new forms of self-perception, always require adaptation in return, and he was not taught how to adapt by Aries and Taurus.

Yet more adaptation is required in the 4th house if we want to be accepted into the circle of the family, tradition and the emerging faith. Here the self must cross the dividing line to definitively enter the hemisphere of the horoscope ruled by the You. While in the 3rd house, the self can still decide relatively autonomously whether or not it wants to join a group, the family removes this choice. It must belong to the family whether it likes it or not.

The way in which the I relates to the You from now on is determined in the bosom of the family. (This process is depicted by the Family Model in astrological psychology.) Its physicality and emotionality are integrated; its need for closeness and protection is kindled and simultaneously the old need for space and independence is reawakened. From now on, we must learn to live with this conflict – the conflict of the 4/10 house axis.

Even more strongly than airy Gemini in the 3rd house, Cancer swings between intimacy and clinginess on the one hand and withdrawal, protection and defence on the other. Whereas the mutable principle finally says a non-committal "yes" to the You, the cardinal principle remains armoured and wary in all searches for closeness and is extremely cautious and selective about whom he allows near him, only admitting those who do not threaten him but give him strength, thus allowing the I to become we.

The flowers of the third Bach group tell of the different forms of intimacy and independence. The 'insufficient interest' in the present is the hesitancy of the wild bull at the door of the stable, out of which wafts the tempting smell of hay and cows.

Clematis is the flower of the dreamer who wanders between worlds but is at home nowhere. Clematis fluctuates between different ways of life: between freedom and independence or the intimacy and warmth of the stable. Like Gemini, Clematis looks simultaneously at this world and the other, but ultimately fails, because it does not manage, as Gustav Meyrink said: "to be a whole person on both sides." The flower essence helps the dreamer to be fully present in the world without losing touch with his dreams and imaginings. This is why Bach lets the Clematis say: *"Decorate the places where you live and strive to make them beautiful, just as I try to decorate the hedges so that I have been called 'Traveller's Joy'"* (1).

Clematis also belongs to the 4th house though, where we connect with the individual

clematis

and collective unconsciouses (Jung) and our roots grow "down to the mothers", into the deep current which only reveals itself in the form of dreams, fairy tales and visions. This current is the water of life without which, on our path to the 10th house, our humanity would wither and fade away. However it also harbours the temptation of the sirens and mermaids, and if we are not careful we can succumb to the fascination of the unconscious and lose ourselves in it.

Honeysuckle pertains completely to the 4th house and our roots. This is a state of over-indulgence in the past, where one is absorbed in memories of the past and dreams of earlier, better times, of deceased loved ones, of everything that has been lost and is no more. One collects, keeps and guards with passion all that one can: old school reports, first love letters, the first nappy, family photos and films... But old slights, demands and wounds are also to be found in this well-protected safe of memories. Wherever possible, one tries to cheat time and to halt its inexorable march or just to slow it down.

It is true that in its own way, Cancer does protect a genuine treasure of traditions and inherited knowledge, but only the essence of the honeysuckle helps him to make the treasure useful in the here and now. It keeps what is passed down free from the mould and old cobwebs of clinging emotions so that what is worth keeping can shine and be distinguished from what is merely kept for its own sake.

White Chestnut – the white or horse chestnut is a typical Gemini flower, as it stands for unfettered thinking. This flower is the purest representation of mutable air. In the White Chestnut state, thoughts chase each other, one idea supplants another and memories jostle for position. It is a stream of undigested, unfiltered information of all kinds, constantly going round in circles or reappearing, that flows through and swamps our brain.

horse chestnut

White Chestnut is addicted to information, to assimilating it and passing it on. To this end, this person goes onto the "piazza" of the 3rd house (e.g. internet) to meet and communicate with other addicts there, totally addicted to the flow of thoughts, but unable to distinguish what is important from what is not. And in this state of supposed up-to-date-ness, of purely mental informedness, he loses touch with the ground and with reality. Personal sensory experience is replaced by what is said, thought, heard and read. In this supposed state of connectedness, he loses touch with his own reality. The purposeful, meaningful and tangible progress in the world required of Gemini by Sagittarius opposite is replaced by a virtual everywhere and nowhereness that is ultimately static.

Related to the White Chestnut and originating from the same tree is the **Chestnut Bud** essence. This person is also carried away by the horses pulling the sun chariot of his thoughts faster than he can cope with. If he were not forced to do so, he would never follow any of his projects through. There is always something new to distract him before he has finished with existing issues. Time and again he falls into the same traps, as he has not taken the time to examine more closely the reasons why he fell into them.

Once his attention is drawn to the repeated pattern of failures, energy wasted in all the half-finished projects and the ultimately unsatisfying repetition, he makes a sudden, complete change from Gemini into Cancer, stops talking, is hurt and offended and withdraws into his 4th house to sulk.

Wild Rose is also at home in both houses. This plant has an affinity with Venus due to its charisma and its characteristics. Venus and Neptune, the two planets of love, are the esoteric rulers of Gemini and Cancer. They symbolise in Gemini the step from unfruitful rationalism to Venusian wisdom

wild rose

borne from a love of life and in Cancer from clinging and selfish emotionalism to Neptunian unconditional love.

Wild Rose is the escape from demands of the world, of life, of the inner compulsion for action and experience that are all perceived to be too tough and too much to cope with, into a soft cloud of unobtrusive resignation. This turning away from the world is not perceived as such. Enveloped in an often subtle aura of Cancerian huffiness, every call to arms and action is fended off with pseudo-rational arguments from the 3rd house. Jung would probably say that this person is trying to deny his anima's call for destiny. It is "not that bad after all" and "something that just has to be lived with." Thus did Sleeping Beauty lay sleeping behind her Wild Rose hedge until she was kissed awake by a love of the world and of life that knows that roses also have thorns.

Olive and Mustard are two flowers of exhaustion. They are used when a person has become too involved with the demands of the house, losing touch with his inner sources of strength in the process. Mustard moods are just as fickle, changeable and varied as the Moon. They are the result of an insufficiently conscious and controlled balancing act between the rational pressures to adapt and practical constraints of the 3rd house in which Gemini wants to defer to external demands, and the imperturbable voice of the unconscious that emanates from the depths of the water, from cardinal Cancer in the 4th house. In the powerlessness and enforced cutbacks of a Mustard state, which may be expressed as inexplicable, mild unhappiness, migraine or even full-blown depression, the person's batteries are recharged and he is given a new opportunity to get the balance right.

The essence from the flowers of the olive tree is characterised by two images, firstly the olive tree itself, which is a symbol of limitless vitality. It has been tirelessly and inexhaustibly growing, blossoming and bearing fruit for hundreds, if not thousands of years, deeply rooted in the earth that supports and nourishes it, drawing strength from its roots that reach down into water currents deep below the earth that has been dried out by the Sun of man's will and the wind of restless thoughts. Secondly it is the image of the dove returning to the ark with an olive branch in its beak bringing the news that the destructive emotional floods have retreated to their subterranean river systems and that the earth is walkable once more. An olive state therefore compels the person to make peace with himself and the world and to reconnect with nourishing Mother Earth underneath his feet right down at the IC, so that he is once more able to grow and strive upwards.

In Houses 5 and 8, Flower Group 6:

For those who suffer from despondency and despair.

As we traverse houses three and four, we are influenced and coloured by the collective and its images and dreams, concepts and opinions. We now carry within us the egocentric desire for self-assertion of Aries and Taurus and the need to adapt to and be rooted in the collective of Gemini and Cancer. We must learn to reconcile all of these desires in a way that is right for us. That is why the next step takes place in two fixed houses.

It is through confrontation with the outside world that we find ourselves. Through friction both with one significant other and the multitude of others we meet socially, we are able to experience ourselves after the converging and merging of the IC. We now find ourselves to be both newly separate and yet still related and connected. In the 5th house, we experience the external pressures of competitors, rivals, a loved one's resistance to being conquered and the expectations of the public. And yet it is our own volition that compels us to accept the challenge, the cardinal fire of Aries, which must find its own form of self-expression in the Leo of the 5th house.

External pressures are also experienced in the 8th house, exerted by society and its strict rules. The rules of conduct that hold back the impatiently forward-thrusting Aries, the boundaries between mine and yours that frustrate Taurus, who would prefer to acquire everything he can see and touch. But we can also see the rewards that are there for those who play by the rules: rank, status and respect in society, the security of personal possessions and access to community resources.

Once more we find ourselves in a complex and demanding tension field. We are constantly torn between the inertia of Leo, the striving for security of Scorpio and the fire of the Sun that burns in Leo's heart, the Martian fighting spirit that allows Scorpio no peace. This also explains the ambivalent nature of the animals that symbolise these two houses.

The lion is the king of the animals and ancient symbol of the Sun. It is the heraldic animal of choice of all rulers from the times of the Pharaohs to the present day, and, in the Christian context as *sol invictus*, is even linked to Christ. At the same time though, it is also the great, death-bringing corrupter, from which no-one and nothing is safe. According to the Bible, Satan too goes around "like a roaring lion, seeking whom he may devour."

The dual sign of Scorpio/Eagle appears equally divided. On the one hand, the "King of the Skies" is also a ruler, a symbol of the self and of the divine of the highest rank and yet also the enemy that in an unguarded moment steals the lamb right out of the herd. On the other, Scorpio, a symbol of the fear of our own unconscious lurking in the shadows that is capable of killing itself with its own poison and simultaneously transforming itself into the Phoenix, who sets fire to its own nest in order to rise again from the flames.

Together the two signs form one half of the fixed quartet of the four Christian evangelists: Matthew, Mark the Lion, John the Eagle/Scorpion, and Luke Taurus the bull. In ancient Egypt they also represented the four Suns of Horus, of which three had animal faces and the fourth had a human face – Matthew the late angel, or Aquarius in astrology. Just as the four Sons of Horus bear the canopy of heaven, the four evangelists surround the throne of the Lamb of Christ and connect heaven and earth.

Life and death, procreating and dying, fighting and surrender are therefore so present in the signs that these two houses rule, more closely connected than anywhere else in the zodiac. The individual who has gained awareness in the first four houses here has the opportunity to transcend his own limitations and achieve sexual union with the You and personal creativity in the 5th house and union with society in the 8th. But just as sexual reproduction and the death of the individual are connected on the bottommost rung of the ladder of the animal kingdom, among unicellular organisms, so the entrance fee required by society is the sacrifice of old, purely individualistic forms in favour of new social ones. It seems obvious that even the lion and the eagle may find such a difficult task discouraging, which is why the flowers intended to treat despondency and despair are attributed to these two houses.

Among all the plants Dr. Bach chose for his apothecary, two are considerably more ancient than the rest in terms of the history of the earth: **Larch** and **Pine**. The dinosaurs brushed against them millions of years before the first prehistoric man trampled across the first flower meadow. These two plants therefore stand for two influences that deep down in the foundations of each one of us constitute the basis for all ensuing personality distortions: the feeling of guilt and the feeling of inadequacy, which in astrology are always connected with Saturn, the ruler of all fixed things.

In the 5th house, the I wants to prove itself to be greater, stronger, cleverer and more beautiful than all its competitors. It wants to conquer, to be admired and to feel that it is powerful and invincible. To this end it fights with all the resources that it has acquired during its earlier path of growth. But at least two are needed for a fight, and sometimes the You is stronger than the I. The I has its first taste of defeat and the pride of the lion is hurt. It starts to doubt its own greatness and strength, its Sun shines a little less brightly and is less confident of victory. The excessive reinforcement of this experience, e.g. in an upbringing where too much pressure is placed on the child, results in a loss of self-confidence. The child withdraws and entrenches himself behind all manner of internal and external walls. He forms an artificial concept of strength from random status symbols and finds himself in a world of his own making where he is the victorious (or even the suffering) hero, or he becomes addicted to alcohol and other drugs that make him feel strong again. Larch is the essence that allows Leo to find himself again and restore his self-confidence.

In the 8th house, Scorpio makes tentative efforts to fit into society with its abstruse rules. He inevitably makes mistakes and society punishes him with its contempt. He is accused and feels guilty. He often does not even know what he did wrong; he senses that something was not right, that something is wrong with him and he feels guilty. Even nowadays, something similar can happen when a girl is born instead of a wished-for boy. She does not know what she has done wrong, but senses the unspoken disapproval and feels guilty. Later this person will voluntarily be a scapegoat for anything and everything; she will never be satisfied with her own performances and will always feel that she could have done better. Very often, she also finds partner who knows how to exploit this weakness. Pine is the remedy that helps the wounded Scorpio to accept herself and lift herself out of this hellfire of guilt and self reproach as a reborn phoenix.

Oak belongs to the 8th house. Here the person has become too involved with the demands of society and plays the role of someone for whom no job is too big, who can do everything, to whom any responsibility can be entrusted without hesitation and who never tires or weakens. They are conscientious, reliable and indispensable. Scorpio's good sense of smell is used to immediately sense when something is not completely in order, or something that cannot be completely controlled. Oak essence helps him to extricate himself from the role of the other-directed slave of his duties and enjoy the freedom of being himself. The lesson here is to allow one's own character and freedom to develop while respecting the status quo and existing laws, rights and duties.

Willow is an oak that instead of taking this path to freedom has remained a victim and has become resentful and bitter. It judges purely on externals and sees itself surrounded only by people who are apparently better off. Its achievements are not appreciated, its efforts not rewarded, and in true Scorpio fashion, this resentment is not openly expressed. Instead, under an often deceptively quiet surface, the poison simmers away, only making its presence felt by occasionally letting off fumes that gently but effectively poison the atmosphere.

Crab Apple is also intended for those who are completely fixated on externals. The rules of society of the 8th house are completely internalised and the slightest deviation from them make this person anxious. A small spot on a white blouse, a small contravention of any rule of decorum, spelling or hygiene can induce these perfectionists to totally lose perspective. They become obsessed with this small discordant note and the relationship to the living, breathing whole is lost. Naturally, in this state, the person's own body with all its expressions and needs also becomes a problem. This flower is also connected with the theme of morality of the 5th house. For only a maiden clad in spotless white who sits under a white-blossomed crab apple tree lays the equally white unicorn his head in her lap; but Adam and Eve discovered they were man and woman when they ate from the apple and were ashamed of their nakedness.

Elm is the flower for the temporarily overextended Leo. He has taken on too much, he wanted to win too many battles at the same time and now finds himself surrounded on all sides by hostile armies and by mountains of work that overwhelm him. But excessive mental burdens can also diminish his fighting strength. This can become too much even for a Leo heart to bear; in the worst case a heart attack can be the result. Elm does not make the mountains disappear but it changes the way we see them. An unconquerable rock face is replaced by a more manageable sequence of steps.

Star of Bethlehem is the flower of the wounded Leo. This essence heals old and new wounds be they physical or mental. As long as a wound is open, the soldier is handicapped. He retreats and stays under cover as much as possible. Nobody likes having salt rubbed into an open wound. However the 5th house requires the courage to take risks, it requires direct, close contact with the You. But how can we love again when we cannot get over the pain of a lost love? Star of Bethlehem gives the wounded fighter new courage and vitality and takes him out of his corner back into the ring.

In the state for which the **Sweet Chestnut** is intended, the fighting Leo has been wounded too often or too seriously. He feels that he has received the killer blow and can no longer pull himself together. He is incapable of seeing a way out of his situation and feels out of his depth. Sweet Chestnut stands for the theme of death and rebirth, which means that it can help Leo to let go of his former self image to become free to live a different kind of life. It is not he himself who has reached the end; there is just no longer a place or a future for his old, fixed role. This is a moment of total fear and desperation, all he knows is that he must abandon the old but he does not know which new he is getting into. There is no way of avoiding the terror, the death of the self; only if he is willing to go through this dark gate can he reach the shining new light that awaits beyond the threshold.

This moment arrives for Scorpio just as it did for Leo in the 8th house, for the theme of death and rebirth belongs here at the low point of the whole horoscope. This moment is ultimately the *raison d'être* of the Pluto-driven Scorpio. He was born to consciously step through this gate of transformation in order to rise again beyond it as an eagle.

In House 6, Flower Group 5:

For those who are oversensitive to influences and ideas.

After coming into the world and becoming rooted in it in the first two houses, being shaped by the collective in the next two houses and reaching a first maturity by confronting the You and society in houses

5 and 8, society now wants to benefit from the individual. Until now, he has been developing, having experiences and trying to find his own, unique self. Now society asks for something in return: the individual must give of himself and his abilities in the form of work, service and devotion. The issue is no longer acquiring independence but the willingness to contribute to a greater whole, to put personal interests aside and put the demands of the You first.

But the 6th house is also all about the first and most important of all tasks, being true to oneself. This is the only way we can make our own special contribution. Excessive adaptation and over-involvement in our duties causes us to lose touch with our unique, irreproducible potential.

Our contribution to society would then just be a poor imitation of a misunderstood original. The fire of enthusiasm would be missing, thus rendering our work worthless. Only if we can find ourselves in the task and in the way that we perform it will we be able to implement the energy from our core (fundamentally influenced by our aspect pattern) in a way that is meaningful for the collective.

We need to see a meaning in our work that transcends the material reward received for doing it. An inner meaning that makes us creators in our own right and of our own choosing instead of slaves dependent on the mercy of the Lord. If we are not able to exercise this right and volition, our repressed individuality will seek alternative forms of expression. These may be in mental or physical illness, inner resignation or destructive behaviour in the workplace, in the abuse of power inside or outside the family, or in other kinds of meaningless activities that are damaging to society as a whole.

It is not work in itself that makes people ill, as the old name for the 6th house: "work and illness" may lead us to believe. Instead it is other-directed, alienating work with all the repression that this entails, repression that awakens Pisces in the 12th house. The unconscious makes its presence felt and sends unhappiness and illness as messages that the conscious wants to reconnect with the depths below.

Virgo lives in this house and is particularly susceptible to its temptations. For the Catholic interpretation of Mary as one who only serves and suffers has suppressed the vitality of the young woman who was once a symbol of liveliness and *joie de vivre*, which men also found unsettling. The Moon is the esoteric ruler of Virgo. Its light and dark sides remind us of Virgo as the Queen of Heaven, and the Moon goddess, the "Queen of the Night". Pisces, rising out of the dark, unconscious depths, is integrated into an aware, autonomous personality with these archetypal images of powerful women that symbolise wholeness.

Virgo has lately been even further diminished because excessive individualism has caused us to lose touch with what serving can also be. Self assertion or self loss are now the only options we have and Virgo has therefore almost lost its power to heal and make whole. There are very few people left who know the strength, joy and deep satisfaction of voluntary service.

The 6th house is the house of mutable earth. Its basic motivation is therefore devotion and attention to the You. But this devotion should be down-to-earth, conscious and mindful of its own roots. It should be a devotion that has hands and feet and where head and heart are in harmony. The earthly sensitivity and commitment must be complemented via the Virgo-influencing Mercury in the form of intellectual penetration, rationality and logic. For Mercury is the Messenger of the Gods, who brings light and consciousness to the darkness of the Earth.

Mercury is the god of commerce, who balances interests and brokers and arbitrates where there is a conflict of interests. The 6th house is primarily concerned with balancing the interests of the individual with those of society as one negotiates the terms of a contract. Many people remain stuck on this level of awareness. The process is actually the development of awareness. We should not try to get the highest possible remuneration for the least possible work or vice versa. The important question is: What do I have that is truly mine and truly unique, that I can give in my work, my commitments and my service to the world? What is my talent, my gift of the gods that my Mercury can help me contribute to the human family? How can I express my individuality as fully as possible in my work?

The four Bach flowers of this group should help the individual to dissociate himself and avoid losing himself and his path in all the demands of the outside world. They are also therefore important aids for all therapists and counsellors who want to help at all costs and risk over-identification with clients. At the same time, they can help them to better understand and identify many defence and resistance mechanisms.

The truest expression of this house is actually found in **Centaury**. In this state the individual is totally outward facing, anxiously waiting for any sign of a wish, a need of the other, and completely out of touch with his own wishes and needs. Always ready to read any wish in the other's eyes, focusing their whole perception totally on it, seeking to pre-empt every possible demand by meeting it, this person is very open, very sensitive and easily hurt. However, their readiness to help does not come from an inner strength that can give without losing of itself, but from an inability to say no, from the inability to set adequate boundaries, out of feelings of guilt. He is therefore a natural victim who never has to wait long for someone to show up and turn him (or also very often her) into a victim.

This essence can help us find our self-esteem, thus eliminating our dependency on the You. Then we can start to take responsibility for our own lives, get back in touch with own strength which we can use in our authentic, personal tasks.

Walnut is a kind of special case of Centaury, involving transitions and making a fresh start. The person has made a decision to start something new, be it on a large or small scale. In their head, everything is clear; it is just not so easy to put it into practice. They are prevented from taking the first step by external and internal resistance. Objections that may be expressed, unexpressed or only feared on the part of all those who would somehow be affected, whose personal claims on this person could be jeopardised. The energy of the walnut forms a firm shell around the still vulnerable mental form of the decision and protects it from the bleak wind of the external and internal worlds that are determined to cling to convention and continuity.

Agrimony is the flower that can treat the inner agitation caused by the feeling that one cannot cope adequately with a particular demand from the environment. When confrontation and disagreements are in the air, and he wants to do all he can to restore peace and harmony. When he is willing to give way and to deny himself to make other people happy again. When he refuses even to acknowledge his worries and problems, and uses his energy mainly to preserve or restore as quickly as possible the impression that he can cope. In this state, the pull of the 12th house can also be very strong: the temptation to shut himself off, to repress or even better to drown his sorrows in alcohol and other means of distraction or papering over the cracks rather than face the problems.

Holly stands for the shadow side of Virgo, where she is no longer kind and friendly and ready to help, but full of anger, rage, frustration, envy and suspicion. These feelings are expressed more in little, everyday spiteful remarks and unfriendliness, or even just in thoughts, than in big outbursts. For this reason they may even be found in those who are considered by themselves and by others to be above such nastiness. They are the reactions of those who feel belittled, inferior and exploited in the house of work and they are the aggressive energies that they must fight in this house in order to progress. They are the energies whose opposites, i.e. unconditional serving and healing and universal love, are represented both by Virgo and the opposing 12th house.

In House 7, Flower Group 7:

For those who care too much about the wellbeing of others.

In the 7th house, like the 6th, there is also the danger of self loss. But here the danger is not that the individual allows himself to be ruled by the You. Instead, the I actively and deliberately oversteps the You's boundaries. In this cardinal house, the ego wants to exert its influence. Like Virgo, Libra also wants to help and heal, but it is not open to influence and willing to be led by the person seeking help. It knows what it wants for and from the You and it knows how to get it.

Libran will is exclusively directed towards the You. It does not want something for itself, but the You is the object towards which its energy is directed, hence its position in the 7th house, at the You point, because here it has direct access to the You. It is far away from the ascendant, the point of ego-relatedness. The first moment of entering the world, the first occupation, is now a distant memory. It is no longer the ego itself that matters, just its effect on the You. With every thought, with every action, it touches or crosses the boundary between the ego and the You.

After all the fighting and learning steps that have gone before, Libra's existence seems to be so safe and so taken for granted that it is hard for it to still be interested in ensuring its own survival and further development. The You side of the Libran scales is weighed down by the gravity of the whole world, while the scale of the self springs up into the air, filled with nothing but this one small self whose every sense and aspiration is directed towards the You.

This is the house where relationships are cultivated. Not for professional purposes or to capitalise on them, not for some low material benefit. Relationships here are conducted for their own sake, and in order to reflect the self. A whole network of relationships is constructed to reflect this self as diversely, lastingly and intensively as possible, and every relationship is woven into the network with many fine threads.

Thoughts, ideas and impulses are sent out into the world from this house in order to produce an echo, to achieve an effect. But there is no great vision, no established worldview behind it. It is the house of cardinal, not fixed, air. It wants movement, not fixed form. Uranus, the lord of the thousand ideas sends its energies into this house, bringing fickleness and unpredictability where the exoteric ruler, Venus is more concerned with beauty, harmony and the balance of interests.

Between the selective and yet still adaptable Venus and the iconoclastic Uranus, between its own longing for the You and the impetuous self-assertiveness of Aries in its shadow, Libra searches for its way. That is the difference between the 6th and 7th houses, between

Virgo and Libra. The silvery, loving and devoted Moon is the esoteric ruler behind the attentiveness to the You of Virgo, and its counterpart Pisces in the 12th house is sensual and searching for meaning at the place of the "return to the father's house". However, behind Libra's interest in the You lie the powerful and reckless energies of Uranus and Aries.

Libra tries to find its way between the force lines of Venus and Mars, devotion and conquest, or on the esoteric level, Uranus, who seeks wisdom beyond all boundaries and Mercury, the mental pioneer, who as Prometheus rebels against the gods and their laws in order to bring fire and the light of awareness to mankind.

The five essences that Bach attributed to this group show different forms of the excessive influence of the You, which, typically for the 7th house, of course only means well and the acting ego does not even realise that there is a problem.

Chicory is the flower of emotional possessiveness, manipulation and self-pity. It is the mother/father who is willing to do everything for their child on condition that the child does what they want and remains a child, even if it grew up long ago. Just like Venus, it always manages to find something to correct and improve and is profoundly offended if this kind of interest is not welcomed unreservedly. If this happens, it is capable of using all imaginable means of power, from charm and seduction to intrigue and extortion (e.g. a well-timed migraine). It is only happy when the loved ones are either physically present or can be contacted, controlled and cared for, by phone (or text) at any time.

It is usually very difficult to make such a person aware that they are in this state, as the defence mechanisms react so quickly and any question, no matter how subtle, is immediately interpreted and responded to as an attack.

Vine stands for the most direct, blunt attack by the I on the You. In the vine state, the I knows quite simply what it has to do, what needs to be done right now, and what is best for the You. The cardinal air is not diplomatic and charming here, but unequivocal, direct and bossy. In critical situations, that can be a very helpful quality, but as a habit in everyday social interaction it is thoughtless and hurtful. The problem in dealings with power and authority that this essence is intended to treat can admittedly also take on a completely opposite form. In this case, the person rejects any kind of hierarchy and opposes any authority. The urge to influence the You that is present in all of us is forced to creep in through the back door. These different forms of imbalance are always rooted in an unperceived or repressed conflict with the parents, the first You that the child encounters.

In the state for which **Vervain** is intended, the person wants use the 7th house as a base for proselytising and conversion. They have one idea with which they want to change the world, even though this unfortunately means starting with their own family. As long as they are in this state, they are immune to criticism, and not even tiredness and exhaustion can stop them, as they have completely lost any objectivity with regard to their own actions. A barely controlled willingness to always be completely committed, irrespective of how appropriate or meaningful this great commitment really is, seems to be a determining part of the personality. "Inflation" is the name Jung gave to this state of being overpowered by an idea, self-found task or role. This behaviour is most likely here in the 7th house at the opposite pole of the house of self-perception and self-expression.

In **Rock Water**, the water from a freely flowing, ancient mineral spring, we find Venusian selectivity in the form of the implacable "Guardian of the Threshold" and behind it, Uranus as a hard, technocratic superego. Personal wishes, needs and dreams are repressed in order to confront the You with absolutely irreproachable behaviour. This guardian of the threshold is only visited by those who can demonstrate an equally highly moral exemplary inner and outer attitude. Anything soft, playful and spontaneous is filtered out and replaced by calm and order, anything else is taken in the pincers and put back where it came from. In order to soften this stone-hard attitude Bach chose the water of an ancient, long-forgotten mineral spring; the gentle, highly adaptive water that finally wears down hard stone, that springs in the form of a life-giving source from the hard rock. Rock water restores the life and fertility of Venus and the prophetic knowledge and wisdom of Uranus.

In **Beech**, Uranus and Venus criticise, judge and condemn people, things and situations, either out loud or just mentally. The friction between the I and the You engenders an appropriately allergic reaction. The person may not be able to see or even acknowledge his own mistakes. He is completely trapped in negative projections and can only see the You as bad and bad in the You.

This attitude towards the You brings the person to a state which goes completely against the demands of the 7th house: he isolates himself and ends up completely alone. Even those who initially agree and support him in his censoriousness increasingly turn away from him. This external isolation is a mirror of the inner split of conscious and unconscious, in which an overcritical Venus offloads everything it does not like and projects it onto the You. This "princess and the pea" will make life hell on earth for her prince and her mother-in-law, if a mature Uranus does not help her to break through the egg shells of her self-centredness and embrace life with openness and love as befits the spirit of the 7th house.

In Houses 9 and 10, Flower Group 2:
For those who suffer from insecurity.

The astrological houses do not stand for abilities and talents or for weaknesses and strengths, they stand for the demands that the individual places on himself via the environment, demands to which he must react, whether he wants to or not. Destiny will bring the demands to the person in various forms, and he will have to confront them. The course of his life is determined by the way he reacts to these demands and whether or not he is able to cope with them.

While the above-mentioned eight houses concern the personal growth of the individual and the concrete demands of society on him, the individual in houses 9 and 10 must now reap what he has sown. Here he must show how much he has grown.

This is where his own mind and essence should want to develop independently, freely and without protection. The artist stands at the top of the circus dome, the safety net has been taken away. Now he must let go of his last firm grip on inherited, acquired ways of thinking and behaving in order to let himself fall into empty space.

Two signs depicting ascent rule these two houses: in the 9th Sagittarius, firing its arrow to the highest goal, and in the 10th Capricorn, unwaveringly striving for the highest peak. Two signs that aim right for the top and yet still have their feet on the ground.

The old symbol for Sagittarius is the Centaur with the bow and arrow. The Centaur, which in itself symbolises the unity of two levels, the conscious and unconscious, the human and the animal, the light and dark sides of human nature. From this mythical creature, one figure in particular has remained: Chiron, the famous doctor and teacher of the almost divine Achilles. By being able to create from two worlds and connect the light of the conscious with the fathomless powers of the depths of the unconscious, Chiron was able to dispense healing and wisdom to those who came to him.

What even he could not offer though was transcendence and immortality. Even his most famous pupil could not escape the fate of all mortals. He remained attached to the Earth and descended on his death into the bleak shadow kingdom of the dead, which bore the shadowy memories of the things he did and did not do. That is why the Centaur was given the bow and arrow. It is the weapon of the god of light, of Apollo, with which he hunts down Achilles who is blind with rage and at the mercy of his urges. It is the arrow of human longing, with which he wants to transcend his imprisonment in matter and enter the unknown and the infinite.

The arrow is the third human dimension, that of the spirit that transcends body and mind. The centaur is firmly grounded on his four hooves, and the earth's power flows through him, manifesting in his reflexes, his instincts, in his dark origins. The developing consciousness of the human ego is expressed in his upright upper body, which has skin and hands and feels, thinks and acts in this, his world, his community. And the arrow leads him beyond, beyond the limits, influences and demands of society. The arrow represents the demand of the 9th house: to be led by inner wisdom to something higher and deeper, led by discovered beliefs, led by intuition to find the way from the ego to the greater self.

While in the 9th house, appropriately for the mutable fire of Sagittarius, it is above all thoughts, ideas, visions and intuition that expand man's mind, the 10th house is all about real actions. This is the domain of the cardinal earth of Capricorn. At the gateway stands scrutinising Saturn, who only lets through those who have a head for heights and are sure-footed, who are not frightened if the narrow path twists and turns through cracks and crevasses, who are ready to stick with their 9th house vision in the rough terrain of the 10th house. The final step to the summit is only taken by those who no longer only act in their own interests but climb out of devotion, in service of their neighbour, at which point Saturn changes and returns to the people of the valley transformed into a wise, knowing individual.

Just as in the case of Sagittarius above, the old symbol for Capricorn was also a dual being: that of a goatfish, an extremely strange beast whose head and upper body resemble that of a goat and whose lower body resembles that of a fish. Even more clearly than the goat, the goatfish symbolises the ascent out of the watery depths of the 4th house into the solitary heights of the 10th, while at the same time reminding us that in order to reach the heights we must experience both sides of our being: the hard and the soft, the thinking and the feeling, the active and the dreaming. It reminds us here at the highest point of the horoscope of the beginning in the house of Aries and the end in the house of Pisces. Here, where the person attains the culmination of his development as an individual, is where the beginning and end of life, of origin and decay in the very basis of all existence come together.

The five flowers in this group relate to this difficult process of becoming self-aware, liberation and ascent from the roots into the collective space, then onto the developmental process in the crown of the tree of life in the houses of the individual space.

Wild Oat stands for the mental state that initially causes the person to look for new paths: an inner unrest and restlessness, a searching that does not know what it is searching for. From the outside, everything seems to be fine, the person seems to have everything he could want, but is still restless and dissatisfied. Perhaps he already senses the freedom up at the MC after the restrictiveness of the collective down below. So he is looking for something quite unique, something quite special that did not exist before, which could give meaning to this freedom. But he is looking in the wrong place. He is looking in the outside, instead of deep within himself. This is why he jumps from partner to partner, from job to job, from course to course, from hope to hope and never finds peace.

Wild oat guides the gaze and the search inwards, to the authenticity of the true self. The path goes inwards and straight up, to the only place where one can truly find peace. "Our heart is restless until it rests in You," as Saint Augustine said.

What the person learns in the 3rd house is first and foremost to rely on the knowledge, views and opinions of others, which must be unlearnt in the opposing 9th house. **Cerato** helps him to do this. Wherever he is in danger of losing himself in the endless and contradictory chatter of other people's information and opinions versus his own voice of reason, Cerato restores the connection to his inner wisdom. Cerato is the flower of intuition that is attributed to the fire element, the ability to sense inner order and reality in the apparent chaos of cast lead. This essence therefore helps the person to find his own path and its inner voice warns him when he is in danger of losing himself, of going astray, of running the risk of being seduced by an ideology or losing touch with reality in order to have "perspective", his inner voice, now reinforced by Cerato calls him back to himself.

Scleranthus is the flower for those who are indecisive and erratic, who although no longer influenced by the opinions and actions of the crowd of the 3rd house, are still at war with themselves. Those who cannot manage to reconcile two souls in one body, who are torn back and forth, who are always discovering new facets of the problem, who struggle for balance and want to do the right thing by all parties and therefore miss the decisive moment where it would be right to send the arrow purposefully towards its goal. Scleranthus helps to reconcile above and below, inside and outside, light and dark together in the higher third party that unites them.

Hornbeam helps those Sagittarians who are tired and weary of the treadmill of living an unconscious life to bring a spirit of freshness. It stimulates the person's Jupiter, his spirit and his senses and makes him willing and able to climb out of the same old rut and to discover a new world, where he is no longer surrounded by the tedious monotony of everyday life, but by an exciting, challenging world of the unknown and the enticing. This is not done with some artificial stimulant, or forced external change, but with alert senses and a completely open, receptive spirit opening himself up to the reality around him by changing his consciousness and transforming from the IC to the MC.

Gentian is the flower for the Saturnine Capricorn, who on his ascent to the summit only sees himself surrounded by obstacles, resistance and opponents and thinks the only way to salvage the situation is by better and better controls, more accurate forward planning, more precise thinking through of the situation. He then fails just before the goal because some small detail does not work exactly as he had envisaged. If he goes through this too often, he will abandon his objective and withdraw into an extremely bleak solitude, where the water of the emotions, both happy and sad, is lacking and from which he repels any intruder, no matter how well-meaning. Gentian brings back the openness, the courage and risk-taking, the joy in real human encounter and the reminder that Saturn too is just a small, meaningful part of a transcendent whole, which it serves and that supports it, just as the 10th house does not represent the end of human development. Only when he can let himself fall again, when his ultimate trust is no longer in himself but in the depths of the 4th house out of which he has climbed, will he have reached his goal.

Even in its external appearance, **Gorse** seems defensive and unapproachable, and even this spirit has surrendered to the apparent superiority of a malevolent destiny. It has solidified in resignation because things are not going as it had planned. Although it may occasionally be persuaded to make a new start, its mind is made up, its sentence has been passed and it is just waiting for it to be reconfirmed. It shuns the abundance and diversity of life that refuses to obey its rules. Gorse therefore opens the door to life. It reconnects the prickly Saturn of the horned goat head with the wise, knowing Saturn of the fish, thus restoring the goatfish to wholeness.

However, according to legend, Gorse is also the plant from which the Roman legions wove Christ's crown of thorns, so that in this plant, the crown, the symbol of the utmost grandeur, temptation and egotism at once becomes the symbol of deepest humiliation, self conquest and humility, yet again closing the circle of triumph and devotion of the individual in the 10th house.

In Houses 11 and 12, Flower Group 4:

For those who are lonely.

Libra in the 7th house ushers in a new stage in our life journey, illustrated by the image of the two ceaselessly interacting opposing scales, each trying to outweigh the other but only able to do their job by working together as one. The 7th house brings maturity as we move from the unawakened-unconscious space into the responsible-conscious space. From now on, we can and must decide; we have renounced paradise in favour of free will. The image of the interdependent opposites now accompanies us in the form of different symbols through the houses until the 11th. In the 8th house, we find the tension between Scorpio and the eagle, in the 9th the centaur that belongs to two worlds, in the 10th the dual nature of the goatfish and in the 11th that of the water bearer. We do not become whole again until the house of Pisces, a greater, conscious wholeness that can only be acquired at the expense of our dearly bought individuality.

We encounter the image of the 'half fish' for the second time in Aquarius. While in the Capricorn goatfish it evokes fighting, hardship and advancement, in Aquarius it suggests ideas and awareness: a human head and upper body. The visions of the mutable 9th house can therefore be put into practice in the cardinal 10th and now in the fixed 11th house, experience gained from visions and actions can be consolidated into cognitions, guidelines for behaviour and ideals. For this to really work instead of causing new hardship and struggles, we must reconcile air and water, i.e. thinking and feeling, not by dissolving or merging them but by becoming aware of the two levels. The old dirty water of the unconscious, egotistical emotions – psychologically speaking the contents of the shadow – are poured out, so that the vessel can be filled with the clear water of spirit for the benefit of all mankind.

The water bearer holds in his hand the trident of Neptune/Poseidon, the old god of the sea. He used this trident to shake up the earth, stir up the water and open and shut the gates of the tempests. The trident is therefore a symbol of dominion over the destructive power of the elements. That is why the divinities and masters of tantric Buddhism bear a three-skulled trident, to show that they have overcome the lower, selfish impulses. The three prongs of the spear also symbolise the three refined energies of empathy, knowledge and power, the three bodies through which the completely enlightened individual manifests his true, primordial nature. So here too, awareness replaces unawareness and freedom replaces inhibitedness, not by the natural powers of Leo being obliterated from the opposing 5th house, but by becoming aware of them and integrating them into the greater self. The image of man is added to the three animal fixed sign symbols thus making four.

If we manage to gain self-mastery and are no longer guided by our impulses but by our consciousness, we have achieved the objective of the 11th house. We have become mature enough for the highest form of relationship between two people, that of friendship. Instead of treating the You as a rival or someone to be exploited, we now encounter him as a conscient being, and it is in this encounter between individuals that we attain the highest level of emotional and mental personhood. Emotionally and mentally, we have forsaken egocentricity and are completely devoted to the You. Saturn and Uranus – the exoteric rulers – have realised their limitations, they have unified their potentials and have found meaning and synthesis in Jupiter – the esoteric ruler.

In the 12th house, in the sign of Pisces, we find love. As before, we start off with Jupiter and the former ruler of Pisces, Venus, as prisoners of our senses and sensuality. But we gradually become aware of their transience and the emptiness of their promises, which causes Jupiter, guided by his co-ruler Neptune, to seek a deeper meaning of life. We swim to freedom, exposing ourselves to loneliness in the process and begin to search the depths of the ocean. We dive down into the depths of the soul, of our unconscious where we find all the beauty and horror of our own, unknown worlds. We encounter the persona, the external appearance and realise it is just a reflection of the surface of our ocean, a tool and vehicle for our earthly journey. We meet our shadow, the receptacle in which we have collected everything that we are but do not want to be and in which we discover the roots of love and hate, of fear and desire. We pierce through layer after layer, from the personal to the collective unconscious, at which point we realise that we are inextricably linked to the rest of humanity. Even deeper down we go, to the most ancient drives and instincts, where the human soul meets the animal soul, or 'nature', and finds their common root.

If the person delves down deeper and deeper, until *"pleasure and pain, freedom and captivity at the deepest point of all... run together into one,"* then *"one finds water there and the water is called compassion and nectar."* Nectar is the tantric food of the Gods, which dissolves *"convictions founded on faith in the self."* The drink, which is fatal for the little self, is drunk from a skull cup and therefore guides us over into the kingdom of Pluto, the esoteric ruler of Pisces and the 12th house, the prince of the underworld.

However, as we have learnt in the 8th house, Pluto is not only the planet of death, but also of rebirth. And anyone who at the deepest point of all has drunk of the water of compassion and devotion will find the way back to the light, to the world of man. Anyone who – like Jesus in the Christian tradition – has trod this path into the depths out of love cannot be retained by the underworld. He comes back a changed person though, and is from now on, as the Bible says: *"in the world but not of the world."* He will be lonely among men, but yet connected to them by love and compassion. He will move among men like a fish in water and the water in which he moves, which is now his element and which carries, nourishes and protects him, is love.

Pride, aloofness and arrogance are the key concepts for **water violet**, and they also describe the temptations of the last two houses. Whether by birth, personal achievements or just high ideals that one feels obliged to live up to, in the 11th house one always stands a little above others. Even if they are ideals of serving, helping one's neighbour or spiritual visions, there is a distinct temptation to feel a little bit better than other people. In the 12th house, it is the desire to withdraw from this loud, rough and vulgar world, which leads us not to find peace in ourselves, but to the coldness of isolation. By turning away from the world in order to avoid being tainted by it and so that our nobility and purity are not troubled, then it is pride and arrogance that lead us on our supposedly enlightened path into our own depths. They will lead us to a place that corresponds to our nature and from which we will find it hard to escape, as we will then also refuse the help that this essence could bring us.

When Edward Bach was still at the developmental stage of his flower therapy, and he thought that with seven flowers he had already found all the essences needed for all people and situations, he prescribed **Impatiens** for the type of the inquisitor: hard, irritable, impatient and judging people according to self-set criteria. Even some of the negative images of this flower have been transferred to others, it is still characterised by impatience, irritability and the expectation that others are just as quick, versatile and enthusiastic, and this flower image should also continue. It is a state that is strongly influenced by thought, as only ideas are able to move quickly enough and this person constantly suffers from the slowness of circumstances and of people around him. If at first sight he seems very lively, open and interested, it quickly becomes apparent that this openness has very clear limits and that his belief in progress lacks human warmth. Impatiens here acts as a 'decelerant', so that Jupiter as the esoteric ruler has the chance to give the revolutionary Aquarians Robespierre and Saint-Just something of the corruptible joviality and sensuality of

Danton, before they despatch him via the guillotine from their 11th house of idealism into the 12th house.

If a person in the Impatiens state is insufficiently attentive to those around him, he is in a **Heather** state. He will do anything to draw attention to himself in order to escape the loneliness that he so fears. He uses the most obscure pretext or the slightest opportunity to make others interested in him. Of course, he achieves exactly the opposite of what he intended. He loses sympathy and interest; anyone who can runs away when he appears in search of an audience. Nobody has an inkling of this person's loneliness and desperate longing for love behind the intrusive and annoying façade. Behind this inability to see and address this real personal lack there is usually an endless history of being unseen, ignored and unaccepted, a lifelong banishment into the 12th house. Heather helps these people to disengage from their obsession with their own needs and not to expect help but to devote themselves to their neighbour and to see their needs instead. For by giving, the person immerses himself in love and by seeing others with the eyes of the heart, he frees himself from loneliness.

Bibliography

Edward Bach, *Die Nachgelassenen Originalschriften*
C.G. Jung/Wolfgang Pauli, *The Interpretation of Nature and the Psyche*
Richard Wilhelm/C.G. Jung, *The Secret of the Golden Flower*
Edward Bach, *Blumen die durch die Seele heilen*
Chögyam Tryungpa, *Heart of the Buddha*
Bruno und Louise Huber, *The Astrological Houses*
Bruno Huber, *Astro-Glossarium*
Louise Huber, *Reflections and Meditations on the Signs of the Zodiac*
M. Scheffer/W. Storl, *Die Seelenpflanzen des Edward Bach*
Vom Geist der Blüten, *Botschaften über Bach-Blüten, Spiritualität und inneres Wachstum*

◻ ◻ ◻ ◻ ◻

Contacts and Resources

The Astrological Psychology Institute (UK)

A MODERN APPROACH to SELF-AWARENESS and PERSONAL GROWTH

Astrology has become recognised as a valuable tool for the development of self awareness and human potential. Bruno and Louise Huber researched and developed this approach over many years, combining selective astrology with Roberto Assagioli's psychosynthesis. Our courses are based on their results and inspiration.

PERSONAL GROWTH Most of our Diploma students not only learn astrology, chart interpretation and astrological counselling skills, but find that the course helps develop their own self understanding and personal and spiritual growth.

COURSES We offer Foundation Modules to those new to astrology or to the Huber Method. Our Modular Diploma Course teaches the Hubers' psychological approach to chart interpretation for working with clients. Details are in our prospectus.

EVENTS Our programme of seminars, workshops and conferences includes annual workshops that are an integral part of the Diploma in Astrological Counselling.

CONJUNCTION Our magazine *Conjunction* contains articles, news and supplementary teaching materials.

API (UK) Enquiries and Membership
P.O. Box 29, Upton, Wirral CH49 3BG, England
Tel: 00 44 (0)151 605 0039; Email: api.enquiries@btopenworld.com
Website: www.api-uk.org

API(UK) Bookshop
Books and API(UK) publications related to the Huber Method.
Linda Tinsley, API(UK) Bookshop
70 Kensington Road, Southport PR9 0RY, UK
Tel: 00 44 (0)1704 544652, Email: lucindatinsley@tiscali.co.uk

API Chart Data Service
Provides colour-printed Huber-style charts and chart data.
Richard Llewellyn, API Chart Data Service
PO Box 29, Upton, Wirral CH49 3BG, UK
Tel: 00 44 (0)151 606 8351, Email: r.llewellyn@btinternet.com

Software for Huber-style Charts
AstroCora, MegaStar, Regulus, Regulus Light Special Huber Edition.
On CD: Elly Gibbs Tel: 00 44 (0)151-605-0039
Email: software.api@btinternet.com
Download: Cathar Software Website: www.catharsoftware.com

Publications on Astrological Psychology

THE COSMIC EGG TIMER
by Joyce Hopewell & Richard Llewellyn

Introduces astrological psychology. Use your own birth chart alongside this book and gain insights into the kind of person you are, what makes you tick, and which areas of life offer you the greatest potential.

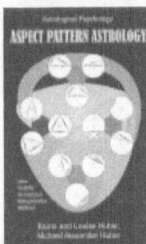

ASPECT PATTERN ASTROLOGY

Understanding motivation through aspect patterns. Essential reference work. The aspect pattern reveals the structure and basic motivations of our consciousness. Over 45 distinct aspect figures are identified, each with its own meaning.

The Planets and their Psychological Meaning

Shows how the positions of the planets are fundamental to horoscope interpretation. They represent basic archetypal qualities present in everyone, giving clues to psychological abilities and characteristics, growth and spiritual development.

ASTROLOGICAL PSYCHOSYNTHESIS

Astrology as a Pathway to Growth. Bruno Huber's introduction to this holistic approach to astrology and Assagioli's psychosynthesis, following the premise that the soul is at the root of all developmental processes. Focus on intelligence, integration, relationships.

MOON NODE ASTROLOGY

Combines psychological understanding with the concept of reincarnation, bringing a new astrological focus on the shadow personality and the individual's evolutionary process. Includes the psychological approach used with the Moon's Nodes and the Node Chart.

Books by Bruno & Louise Huber except where authors otherwise indicated.

A Modern Approach to Self Awareness and Personal Growth

LifeClock

The horoscope is seen as a clock for the person's lifetime, with the Age Point indicating their age as the 'time' on the clock. Those trying it invariably find significant correspondences between indications in their birth chart and meaningful events in their lives.

TRANSFORMATION

Astrology as a Spiritual Path. Describes processes of transformation and personal/spiritual growth as natural stages in human development, related to astrological indicators in the birth chart. New material on Dynamic Houses, Stress Planets, House Chart, Integration Chart.

AstroLog I: Life and Meaning

There is now a substantial body of experience in the 'Huber Method' documented in the German-language magazine *AstroLog*. First selection of articles translated into English, on astrological psychology and its relevance to life and its meaning. Various authors.

The Living Birth Chart
by Joyce Hopewell

Aims to provide insight into the full power of the Huber Method and give a feel for its practical use, with numerous examples and exercises enabling the reader to experience the approach for themselves.

ASTROLOGY AND THE SEVEN RAYS

Linking astrology with the seven rays of the ageless wisdom enables people to recognise their own deepest qualities. The Hubers introduce the psychological application of the rays and how they can be determined in the horoscope. A new approach to esoteric astrology.

Published by HopeWell, PO Box 118, Knutsford, Cheshire WA16 8TG, UK

www.ingramcontent.com/pod-product-compliance
Lightning Source LLC
Chambersburg PA
CBHW022051160426
43198CB00008B/195